The Offshore Money Book

The Offshore Money Book

New Edition

How to Move Assets Offshore for Privacy, Protection, and Tax Advantage

Arnold L. Cornez, J.D.

CB

CONTEMPORARY BOOKS

Library of Congress Cataloging-in-Publication Data

Cornez, Arnold.
  The offshore money book : how to move assets offshore for privacy, protection, and tax advantage / Arnold Cornez.—2nd ed.
      p.   cm.
    Includes index.
    ISBN 0-8092-2517-4
    1. Tax planning—United States.   2. Estate planning—United States.
3. International business enterprises—Law and legislation—United
States.   4. Tax havens.   5. Foreign trusts.   I. Title.
KF6297.5.C67   2000
343.7304—dc21
                                                                    99-36082
                                                                    CIP

This publication is intended to be an accurate, academic, entertaining, and educational presentation on the very complex subjects of international financial matters, ideas, operating styles, theories, and related global topics. It is sold with the understanding that the author and publisher are not engaged in rendering legal, accounting, or any other form of professional services. If ideas presented herein are to be used by the reader, legal advice and/or other expert assistance is required; the services of a competent professional person should be sought.

Caveat: Offshore finance is an extremely complex topic and a likely trap for the unwary or unsophisticated—avoid the school of hard knocks! Some of the content may be considered controversial or too aggressive by some persons. By being presented, it is not in any way being endorsed.

The author, editor, publisher, and/or their agents and employees shall not be held responsible for any damages as a consequence of any party utilizing the materials contained herein.

Cover and interior design by Rattray Design

Published by Contemporary Books
A division of NTC/Contemporary Publishing Group, Inc.
4255 West Touhy Avenue, Lincolnwood (Chicago), Illinois 60712 U.S.A.

Printed in the United States of America
International Standard Book Number: 0-8092-2517-4
      05 MV 15 14 13 12 11 10 9 8 7 6

To Judie, my wife.
My thanks for your support
during the solitary process of
writing this book.

CONTENTS

ACKNOWLEDGMENTS

I WAS THE "coach," and this book is my "team's" effort, though most of the people involved didn't even know they were players on my team. They were my mentors and skeptics; they flattered me in discussions, but were the very advocates of the devil. And indeed, the credit for this revised book should go to the hundreds of people who have most graciously shared their priceless knowledge and secrets with me over the last fourteen years. I was an insatiable dry sponge, and this book is the essence of the efforts of those years, my "give back" to those who have helped me along the way. From simple grape juice comes VSOP cognac; from the lowly potato comes Absolut; and from sifting through my daily journals and lifetime experiences for grains of knowledge comes the update to *The Offshore Money Book*.

During the final, formative months, the following persons onshore and offshore directly contributed to this work, and my acknowledgments are in order.

Vernon K. Jacobs: CPA, CLU; editor, *Offshore Tax*; from Prairie Village, Kansas. My unending thanks for your major contribution on the complex issue of taxes in Chapter 11.

David S. Lesperance; barrister and solicitor, Dundas, Ontario, Canada. My thanks for a major rewrite of Chapter 10, on the subject of second passports and citizenships.

My thanks also to the following for materials used in this book:

- Jay D. Adkisson, Esq., Irvine, California
- E. L. Bendelow, Basel Trust Corporation, St. Helier, Jersey
- Terry Coxon, Petaluma, California
- J. Richard Duke, Esq., Birmingham, Alabama
- Barry S. Engel, Esq., Engelwood, Colorado
- L. Burke Files, Tempe, Arizona

And last, but certainly not least, my thanks to my loving wife of nearly thirty-five years, Judie, who served as editor in chief (with due apologies to Danielle Egan-Miller, my editor at NTC/Contemporary Publishing Group, without whom this revised edition could never have been finalized). Judie was my unabashed critic and distant comfort during the periods of necessary solitude for the research and drafting of this revision—everything I needed my best friend to be.

Introduction to the Revised Edition

SO MUCH HAS transpired in the offshore world since the first edition of this book . . . an entirely new industry, the offshore financial services business, has grown at a hyperbolic rate. I am not exaggerating; you will see for yourself.

Daily we are faced with business, financial, and personal decisions that must now factor in instant worldwide news, events, and needs, both good and bad. Even your vacation plans can include a diversion—exploration of offshore business sites, locales for offshore wealth preservation and privacy, or perhaps even foreign retirement as a future expatriate. How would you like your retirement and Social Security checks going to your bank in Nassau while you're bone fishing in Andros?

Airline magazine ads attempt to seduce you with slick color advertisements of allegedly tax-free (don't you believe it!) tropical paradises, while the *Wall Street Journal* carries advertisements in its Thursday classifieds encouraging you to buy or form your own private offshore bank in some unpronounceable or unlocatable South Pacific jurisdiction. What is one to do?

Advertisements I have read make such claims as:

- "Making a tax-free fortune"
- "How to earn tax-free investment returns of 30 to 250 percent per year, year after year"
- "How to earn tax-free income offshore for the next twenty years"

You be the judge of the veracity of these claims.

The insidious growth of worldwide taxation of the "haves" drives people to seek out estate planning tools for tax reduction and wealth transference, including sophisticated offshore structuring. Not to do so is financially irresponsible to one's surviving spouse and progeny.

Offshore asset protection, privacy, and international financial planning seminars abound. Unfortunately, they are mostly presented by those service providers with a not-too-hidden agenda, wanting you as a client. Which ones are good, and which skirt on tax evasion? While some, such as SHOREX (a must-attend show), are a great learning experience, your mere attendance at others offshore may result in an invitation to an IRS audit party. Would you walk around with your name and city on a badge in Cancún at a seminar? Absurd, but some people do it. How do you avoid being drawn into the shady side of the offshore world? Questionable structures and the wrong service providers can cast an everlasting shadow on you and yours.

As ambitious as it may appear to you (and even to me), this revised edition of this bestselling offshore money book will address these and other issues. I've tried to make the revised edition even more functional than the first. I have made an effort to be as neutral as possible and not show any unwarranted geographic biases. But I don't like Panama as a jurisdiction, so there—I've voiced my first bias. You'll ultimately need to retain a consultant who will tell you the whys for some tax havens, but your reading this book will make the consultant's job easier. After reading the book three times, I am told, you'll know the right questions to ask.

Some readers have likened the previous edition to a fireside chat; I've attempted to continue in that vein. This book is intended for the newcomer to the field, as well as the intermediate. If you need more in-depth information on any topic, you will probably need to seek out the more advanced publications intended for the legal and accounting community, as well as the numerous newsletters available on the Internet or by mail. But be careful not to read yourself into an advanced case of confusion! Too many offshore books are merely sales and marketing tools. Eventually you will hire a professional offshore service provider to sort out your questions and custom-design a structure for your unique situation. You don't have to be clever to go offshore, you only have to hire people who are.

The extraordinary growth of the offshore financial industry has spawned an exciting enterprise for attorneys, CPAs, and financial planners—those willing to make the investment of time and energy. When a pair of Denver, Colorado, attorneys, Barry S. Engel and Ronald L. Rudman, presented their premier seminar on the offshore asset protection trust concept in 1987, they could not have envisioned the offshore financial industry that flourishes today, benefiting U.S. professionals and clients and the offshore financial community. For convenience and out of legal and administrative necessity, Engel and Rudman reinvented the obscure South Pacific jurisdiction of the Cook Islands and brought the phrase *asset protection* into the everyday lexicon. Their timing could not have been more fortuitous: the birth of the Internet as a major communication tool and information-gathering medium, combined with daily news reports of the U.S. litigation explosion, marked the unfolding of the information age. The litigation explosion caused people to seek out asset protection—the product that Engel and Rudman marketed. Copycat professionals sought out offshore affiliates and the Internet opened the door to acquiring the needed "electronic associates."

In one of my favorite books, *The Sovereign Individual: How to Survive and Thrive During the Collapse of the Welfare State*, authors James Dale Davidson and William Rees-Mogg discuss the current transition from a computer age (forget the past industrial age—it's gone!) to the information-based society. This must-read book helped me define and understand my mind-set and throw off my mental limits and adjust to the transition of the U.S. to a datacentric society. The traditional geographic barriers to commerce that previously required government consent, tripping over bureaucratic obstacles, or diplomatic efforts are being transgressed by electronic commerce.

New working (and personal) relationships are being created daily on the Internet. More and more offshore financial planning and asset protection newsletters are being published. Some are free; one costs $595 per year and is well worth it. I have acquired clients worldwide over the Internet, not personally meeting them until later in the relationship.

It's easy to feel overwhelmed when first researching offshore finances. Books and so-called informational websites abound on the Net. It's difficult to distinguish between the good and the bad, the tax compliant and the tax evader, the professional and the scammer. The fierce competition among the tax haven jurisdictions has them badmouthing each other for the business. Offshore money is a profit center for many struggling countries, and in many cases the income generated equals or approaches revenue from tourism. In Bermuda, income from the insurance business exceeded tourism starting in mid-1995, and in 1998 international business expenditures were $758 billion, compared with visitor expenditures of only $472 million. New jobs in banking and financial services pay much more than service and maintenance jobs. International business is a proven boon to these economies, increasing per capita income and consumption.

The old adage remains true: If it sounds too good to be true, it probably is. Offers of tax-free income offshore are suspect, as are multilevel marketing schemes selling offshore trusts coupled with Visa cards providing "tax-free" money. Promises of returns of 25 percent a week should make you run to the nearest exit, but greed seduces people every day. Don't enter the shady side of the offshore world: once you've entered, reformation and tax compliance may be difficult or impossible.

I feel compelled to crusade against the fringe offshore community—those who intentionally practice overly tax-aggressive methodology or out-and-out tax evasion, those who use concealment and secrecy as their primary tools, and those who scam the uninformed consumer with overpriced and misrepresented products. The misrepresentation principally occurs with false promises of U.S. tax avoidance.

Writing on the sensitive topic of offshore finances necessitates a defensive posture because of our extremely litigious society. I have the luxury of being able to express opinions as an author, as opposed to the stringent requirements of writing as a reporter. Regardless, I have my concerns about lawsuits for defamation, so I can't name names of individuals or companies. But I certainly can tell you which concepts I don't like and why, and you then can be your own judge and jury. I suggest you create your own safety checklist as you read this book. If you want actual names and all the gory details of who's doing what to whom in the offshore world, subscribe to David Marchant's well-respected *Offshore Alert* newsletter. He is the white knight of the offshore world, taking on the evil empire, fighting it, and defending litigation as well. (See Appendix B, page 283 for further details on this publication.) The Internet is rife with dubious offers and claims. Study before you invest offshore.

This book is intended to save you countless hours and dollars and to ease your initiation into the offshore world. Once you've ventured offshore, even in the smallest manner, you will be drawn into the exciting stream, learning to think and act globally. It is a new and exciting way of life—a new beginning—offshore!

A Note from the Author

*You cannot discover new oceans unless you have the
courage to lose sight of the binding shore.*

ANONYMOUS

IT IS REGRETTABLE that a public misperception that "sunny climes
are for shady people"—that offshore is for wheeler-dealers—per-
sists to this day. In this book, I attempt to counter it. Misconception
breeds fear, and fear begets reluctance. Hence, I originally titled this
book *The Offshore Money Book: A Comprehensive Guide for Reluctant Americans.* If that has a familiar ring to it, you are dating yourself. In 1958, authors Bill Lederer and Eugene Burdick penned the
bestseller *The Ugly American.* It described a stereotype of the newly
affluent—rude, arrogant, demanding, unskilled middle-class Americans—creating a negative image of the U.S. worldwide. With apologies to those authors, that first title for this book still appears
particularly apropos, as the stereotype of the American going offshore is a person who is timid and misinformed, yet still demanding.
Unfortunately, the offshore professional must patiently educate the
inexperienced, reluctant American before they can work together.
This book serves that professional's need as well, and I hope it continues to be favorably received in the offshore professional commu-

nity and is provided to clients without being thought of as a competitive threat.

While the typical European child is multilingual and might see a parent traipsing off to another country for business just for a day trip, Americans by contrast are culturally and linguistically limited. Americans are seen from offshore as provincial and isolationist.

Foreign nationals, unlike the reluctant American (RA[1]) or perhaps the reluctant Canadian as well, are more inclined toward and comfortable with investing worldwide. The RA continues to be self-restricting, at least geographically, by keeping his or her money at home in the United States. French and German business owners avoid what they perceive to be confiscatory income taxation by their respective countries by using offshore companies (conduits) to earn and retain a significant portion of the profits on each transaction (earnings stripping) through "upstreaming."

Blame it on the negative press, the sensationalism of articles in the media, and intimidation (perceived or real) by the IRS. Blame it on being uncomfortable with the concept of an offshore bank or brokerage firm. Blame it on not knowing the strange new vocabulary: *nominees, beneficial owner, trust protector, company, members, control of assets, remote vesting, choice of law, family protective trusts, international business company* (IBC), *asset protection trust* (APT), and so on. Or blame it on all of the above. That defines the mission of this book. Folks, we're going to work on your reluctance and make a behavioral change in you—if you *want* to change. The best predictor of your likelihood to adopt some of the ideas in this book is your past flexibility.

You need to psychologically adapt to thinking globally, as the remainder of the offshore world presently does. Let's catch up! I can probably help those of you who are ready for a progressive solution. I can't help you if you are a control freak!

I have concluded that the mystery of the offshore financial world to the RA is primarily cultural and environmental, but that's rapidly changing. Negative press that perpetuates the attitude that going offshore is an illegal activity practiced only by tax cheats, criminals, money launderers, terrorists, and drug lords certainly doesn't help. Negative portrayals of tax havens, such as in John Grisham's novel

The Firm, tarnish the image of the tax shelter too. Yet there are thousands of honest hardworking professionals managing unknown trillions of U.S. dollars in global funds in the world's international financial centers (IFCs) on a daily basis. Notice that I use the word *managing*, since the actual money is probably parked in London, Tokyo, or New York. Banking, asset and portfolio management, trustee and company management income derived from these services has far surpassed the income from tourism in many countries that were formerly just vacation destinations and near destitute. Tax havens are racing to elevate their stature in the world financial community, to be characterized as international banking and financial centers, to attract clean money, and to not be just another lower-tier, third-world tax haven in some obscure, exotic locale.

Among the many questions asked of me in the period during which the prospective client and I evaluate each other (yes, it's a two-way street), are "How can I trust those people offshore? Are they going to run off with my money?" or such blunt variations as "I trust you Arnie, but you're no kid—what happens if something happens to you?"

I vet clients quite thoroughly since I don't want to be drawn into any unsavory or illegal scheme or a fraud on a creditor—I don't wish to be anyone's unwitting pawn. Is there an undisclosed smoking gun in the client's past or future? Does he or she have a hidden agenda? Life is too short to play tax evasion, frustrate-the-creditor games or to turn a blind eye to suspicious conduct; I don't want to get involved and end up wearing a striped suit in the federal country club.

Trouble often comes where you least expect it. I was contacted by Sante Kimes, who needed help moving her assets offshore. Mrs. Kimes sounded like a sweet little old lady, and her adult son lived with her. She called me twice at my home, sweet-talking at great length and encouraging me to travel to Las Vegas to meet with her and her son for a free dinner. Her son was apparently too busy golfing in major tournaments to visit me at my office. It didn't pass my smell test, so I declined twice—and I never heard from her again. Later, I discovered that she used the first edition of *The Offshore Money Book* as one uses the yellow pages to locate the offshore people she needed. As it turned out, this "sweet little old lady" and her son were charged in an 82-

year-old millionaire's disappearance and slaying, as well as the disappearance of the millionaire's assets. It's likely that the money went offshore. A New York detective got my phone number from Mrs. Kimes's telephone bill, among many others with offshore area codes.

So you can see, offshore asset protection is risky business for the settlor and the professionals who set up asset protection structures. To avoid trouble for both parties, it's important that everyone involved take certain precautions. For example, the service provider should require from the settlor recent (less than three months old) letters of reference from the settlor's attorney, banker, and CPA (see Figures 1.1–1.3).

All this legalese aside, nothing can make a point as well on the issue of confidence in the offshore professionals, or get so deeply into your own heart, as when your daughter tells you the same thing: "Dad, I feel comfortable about the concept of what you are doing, except what is going to happen when you're not around any longer?" You must have the backup team and plan identified for your client. Yet somewhere around $5 trillion dollars (including countless billions from Americans) are professionally entrusted to offshore asset and portfolio managers, trustees, bankers, nominees, asset protectors, and so on. Who really knows how much flight capital is out there? These numbers are generally estimates from others that are perpetuated. I know of no agency that has an accurate means of keeping count.

The Cayman Islands are the fifth largest financial center in the world. John Mathewson was an American owner of a Cayman Island bank. He was sentenced for money laundering and commented that around 90 percent of the depositors in the Cayman Islands were Americans. The level of flight capital from U.S. persons (and any country in trouble) increases because of warfare, as a lack of confidence in government grows, as government grows without bounds, as the cost of government grows out of control, and as the federal deficit grows without limit. Flight is further precipitated by concerns over the gradual erosion of personal privacy, as more and more powerful computers begin linking databases never before accessible. Where will it end? Give me your driver's license number and I can determine more about you than I'll ever want to know.

Figure 1.1: Sample Letter

Date

Name
Business
Address

To Whom It May Concern:

I am an active member in good standing of the state bar of _____, and a member of the federal bar in _____. I am entitled to practice in all state courts in _____, as well as some federal courts in _____.

[Name] has requested that I write this letter for his confidential use. I have known [name] for ___ years, since 19___. Our relationship has been [select one: *exclusively professional* or *professional and social*].

I have found [name] to be of very high character and fair in his business dealings. I am not aware of any unconscionable conduct on his part. I have the highest regard for [name] and his talents. [Add further complimentary comment here, if possible.]

I would be pleased to provide further references or responses upon request through [name] to maintain the privacy of this communication.

It is a pleasure to assist [name] by providing this private letter of reference.

Sincerely yours,

[signature]

Figure 1.2: Sample Letter

Date

Name
Business
Address

To Whom It May Concern:

I am the senior vice president of [bank name], in good standing with all licensing and regulatory agencies.

[Name] has requested that I write this letter for his confidential use. I have known [name] for about ___ years. Our relationship has been [select one: *exclusively professional* or *professional and social*].

I have found [name] to be of high character and fair in his business dealings. I am not aware of any unconscionable conduct on his part. In spite of some of the difficulties he has experienced, he has conducted himself in an honorable fashion.

Kindly contact me for any further information.

Yours truly,

[signature]

Figure 1.3: Sample Letter

Date

Name
Business
Address

To Whom It May Concern:

I am an active certified public accountant in [name of state] in the United States, in good standing with all licensing and regulatory agencies.

[Name] has requested that I write this letter for her confidential use. I have known [name] for ___ years, since 19__. Our relationship has been [select one: *exclusively professional* or *professional and social*].

I have found [name] to be of very high character and fair in her business dealings, and I am not aware of any unconscionable conduct on her part. [Add further complimentary comments here, if possible.]

I would be pleased to provide any further references upon request through [name] to maintain the privacy of this communication.

It is a pleasure to be able to assist [name] by providing this private letter of reference.

Sincerely yours,

[signature]

Rampant litigation, outrageous jury awards that amount to social wealth reallocations, and threats of confiscatory direct and indirect taxes on you continue. Some call it "jackpot justice." I am not a historian, but I recall some gems of interest.

The concept of *in trust*, which may have all started with the Egyptian pharaohs, was refined in the early Greek and Roman periods and further developed under Islamic law and in fifteenth-century England, when the English Crown attempted to nationalize (read: "confiscate for taxes") land belonging to their wealthy citizens. Citizens cleverly responded by conveying their property to the Church and leasing it back for life at the reasonable rate of a peppercorn a year. Even the Crusaders did their "estate planning" (with trusts) before they left on their mission for the Church (or was it really the Crown?).

In modern times, overly aggressive tax collection (Venezuela and Russia collect pots, pans, or anything else that can be carried off as a tax payment), political instability, and war exacerbate flight capital. Stronger currencies encourage the flight to quality currency. Switzerland briefly had a flight capital problem in the 1970s, but it was not what you might think. The concern was what to do with all the flight money coming *into* their country. To discourage the reception of further flight capital, they introduced the concept of *negative interest rates* to stem the tide. It didn't do much good, as the interest penalty was acceptable to those needing a safe harbor for their wealth.

They say that flight capital from the U.S. is accelerating at a surprising rate (not surprising to me). Currently, the capital flow to the offshore tax havens increases—and the phenomenal growth continues. American CPAs and tax lawyers have attempted to stay legal (tax compliant), protect their clients' assets (and derrieres), and stay one step ahead of Congress and the tax collectors. The outflow of cash from the U.S. to offshore entities (for example, Swiss annuities and business investments) is growing exponentially. The reasons are numerous, and this book addresses them.

But this book is primarily an attempt to demystify the offshore world and offshore finance for you, the RA—to give you the self-confidence you need by expanding your working knowledge of creative international estate planning and mechanisms and the new offshore vocabulary for family wealth conservation. As a business-person, you need to react to global opportunities, or perish at the hands of your competition. As you go international, you will face a unique set of problems not encountered by onshore companies.

A new vocabulary has evolved in the global business community, as well. The following terms will become part of this new lexicon: *transfer pricing*, *advanced pricing agreements*, *branch profits*, *anti-conduit financing rules*, *upstreaming*, and *earnings stripping*.

This book does not present the offshore bank as a panacea for all your offshore needs, because that simplistic solution doesn't work for most RAS. Nor are the offshore bank, the family limited partnership, or the family protective trust totally bulletproof solutions. Each of you has a different agenda. There is no such thing as one size fits all, a mass-production solution, or a kit. Beware of those people offering a package deal that is intended to substitute for professional advice. If you accept that statement as a major premise, you have mastered Step One. I discourage you from utilizing a consultant who forces the square peg into the round hole. For example, an offshore bank is not the answer for everyone. Don't allow yourself to be hurried. I have seen clients take longer to proceed offshore than the gestation period for a pregnant elephant.

Step Two is the realization and acceptance that going offshore may *not* be the solution for you. What are you trying to achieve by going offshore? A Nassau company formation acquaintance disclosed to me that about one-half of the Bahamian companies formed are not around for a second year. If it is not possible, not practical, not economically feasible, why go? If all your wealth is tied up as equity in U.S. real estate, your options are very limited. (See the concept of *equity stripping* in Chapter 10 [page 144], or exchanging highly appreciated real property for an offshore private annuity [Chapter 9, page 126].)

During the course of drafting this book, I reaffirmed that the steps for going offshore are not necessarily purely objective. Consequently, it could drive the objective side of your brain crazy. It's not simply a matter of taxes or fears of being a potential litigation target. Look at the cost of asset protection as you look at the cost of life insurance. You pay it, but don't ever want to collect.

Accept that there is more than one correct personal plan for going offshore. Exactly how you ultimately structure your offshore vehicle may vary from advisor to advisor. Recognizing this element of subjectivity, my first disclaimer would be in order: Yes, there are several ways of proceeding; many probably will work, but one may be better for you. Let's hope this book helps you identify the best way—or, at least, that after reading this book you will be able to ask the right questions. The only dumb questions are those you don't ask. This book will help you formulate questions to ask your OS professionals.

Also, this book is *not* a detailed list and description of tax havens, offshore banks and professionals, sources for offshore credit cards, tax-avoidance techniques, and so on. However, I have alternatively identified many tax havens and provided a key point analysis for you as an educational exercise in Chapter 15. A comprehensive look at the world's major tax havens would take a book in itself, and other authors—Hoyt Barber, Anthony Ginsberg, and Adam Starchild, to name only three—have previously done a fine job on the topic of tax havens. Although presently somewhat dated, theirs remain fine reference books. (See Appendix B for a list of more current books.)

Halfway through the writing of this book, I had misgivings of pretension. I must confess that I don't know everything about going offshore. However, my personal resolution was, since I probably knew more than you and had brilliant associates to guide me, I could teach you or at least guide you, if you let me.

This book comes with due apologies to other pundits in the field, just in case I may have misstated something. Please send me a note, and I'll remedy the problem in time for future revisions—this project is intended to be an evolving, ongoing process.

Communication to me by E-mail would be preferred, to: off shore@bahamas.net.bs, via mail to P.O. Box SS-19461, Nassau, Bahamas SS19461, or by fax to (242) 356-2095. Thanks.

To further assist those of you who are computer literate (or want to be) and can surf the Internet, I've included some relevant World Wide Web (WWW) sites. I also refer you to Appendixes B and C for a more comprehensive listing of Internet sites. A caution is in order: Although the websites were confirmed at the time of drafting this book, they seem to change often. If the address is no longer current, you should do a search. The world is going high-tech, and if you still think that Java is only coffee, you'd best get on-line!

For you "hands-on" paralegals who want to know everything, I have taken some of the legal terms and tax issues unique or applicable to the offshore lexicon and attempted to define them in everyday English for you.

Occasionally, attributes that I believe are favorable are identified with a plus sign (+). Conversely, negative characteristics are marked with a minus sign (−), or where really bad with the triple whammie of (− − −). For example: long statute of limitations (−). Complex issues such as double taxation under multinational tax treaties, although accepted as a reality of life, must be ignored in this book because of their complexities as well as limitations of space and personal knowledge. The subject of the formation of an offshore mutual or hedge fund is also beyond the scope of this book.

I may have been overly ambitious in this book. For the first time, to my knowledge, an author has attempted to integrate the trilogy of international estate planning, financial planning, and asset protection into one book and as one subject, *offshore economics*, as it should be. Most other authors have treated each of these three subjects in a partial vacuum. I trust I have not disappointed you in this effort.

Simpler issues, such as how to legally outmaneuver the tax authorities (euphemistically called *loopholes*), are addressed. All tax issues are indeed very important, but since they would require a more in-depth tax analysis and explanation than is appropriate in this primer, I deem their complexity beyond its scope. After all, I'm the author and I have license to say so. Perhaps that will be the topic for my next book. . . .

Endnotes

1 In some other tax literature you will encounter the abbreviation RA being used in reference to a resident alien.

An Introduction to the Reluctant American

Terminology

LET US DISCUSS terminology at the onset. If at any time you see a word you don't recognize, go to Appendix A for assistance. I use the terms *foreign, offshore, transnational, worldwide, global, cross-border, international, transworld,* and *multinational,* in this book, but I'm not yet ready for the term *global village.* My preference is the modern term *offshore* (OS), a word being used by most of the global community. Os is an international term meaning not only out of your country (*jurisdiction*), but possibly out of the tax reach of your country of residence, domicile, or citizenship. The term *foreign* carries confusion, and I avoid it—except in Chapter 11, where it is appropriate in the context of U.S. taxation and IRS reporting. For example, a Delaware corporation operating in California is characterized by the State of California as a *foreign corporation* doing business in California. The Internal Revenue Service uses a number of tests to label a trust as a *foreign trust.* Some of the tests are:

1. Under 1996 tax laws, a domestic (onshore) trust is one which is subject to the jurisdiction of a U.S. court.

2. It is a domestic trust where the primary supervision and control is by one or more U.S. persons who have authority to control all substantial decisions of the trust.

3. Every other trust is a foreign (offshore) trust. Elsewhere in the book I refer to a foreign trust as an *asset protection trust* (APT).

All the IRS forms for reporting transfers offshore, parties to an offshore trust, or offshore ownership of corporations are couched in terms of foreign trusts. The terminology is inconsistent: the meanings of some words differ depending on with whom you are speaking and the subject at hand. I will use the word *foreign* when referring to IRS tax forms and U.S. taxes for consistency with the Internal Revenue Code (IRC).

Further compounding the terminology problem is the U.S. mutual fund industry's use of the terms *global fund* and *international fund*. A global fund is defined as a fund that invests in the U.S. and offshore, while an *international fund* invests only offshore.

Offshore doesn't necessarily refer to some tropical island jurisdiction. Austria, Liechtenstein,[1] Ireland,[2] Monaco, the U.S., Switzerland, Luxembourg, the Netherlands, Gibraltar, and Andorra, to name a few, are considered to be offshore and, by some, to be tax havens. It depends on who you are; your citizenship, residency, and domicile; your source of income; your objectives; and favorable tax treatment under double-tax treaties.

The IRS has labeled numerous jurisdictions as being used primarily to reduce tax liabilities and restructure income. In addition to the more commonly known or high-profile tax havens, the IRS includes Bahrain, Grenada, Nauru, the Turks and Caicos Islands (TCI), and Vanuatu.

Are *You* a Reluctant American?

You are a reluctant American if one or more of the following items applies to you:

1. You believe that only tax cheats and criminals need to place some of their estate offshore for privacy and financial peace of mind. (The word *estate* as used here encompasses all of your assets—that is, your wealth. You don't have to be very wealthy—or dead—to have an estate.)

2. You have used the same domestic (U.S., or onshore) attorney and certified public accountant (CPA) for twenty years and you won't go to the bathroom without calling him or her first. This book encourages regaining (reclaiming) your financial privacy. You need to practice what I have defined as "professional diversity"—your onshore and your offshore team of professionals. This book also encourages another new concept for achieving privacy, which I have labeled "geographic diversity." Now is the time to diversify offshore. It's very likely that your existing professionals are very competent in what they have done for you to date, but most are fearful of sending you offshore and are probably not honest enough to tell you so. They most likely know little of dealing with business matters on an international scale. They too are worried about malpractice lawsuits, and their philosophy is to discourage what they don't fully understand to avoid potential liability rather than to encourage exploration and open themselves up to the risks of personal litigation. They may be very comfortable professionally and not wish to take on a new and very complex topic, namely asset protection using offshore vehicles.

   The initial personal planning, strategizing, structuring, integration with estate and financial planning, and creative methodology are at the heart of asset protection and the most difficult phase by far. The easy part is putting the structure in place.

   Presently, there is no professional obligation upon an estate planner or other professional to encourage the esoteric area of offshore asset protection strategies. I predict that will change! However, the more "modern" attorney, offshore consultant, service provider, and CPA are thinking offshore as a further integrated estate planning and asset protection (AP) tool and not as an independent technique in a vacuum. They have added the terms APT and IBC (international business company) to their everyday vocabulary (more on these terms below). Financial greed may also preclude your current professional from sending you offshore where they will lose control over some of your financial matters and perhaps eventually lose you as a client.

3. You can't trust anyone offshore with your money. How many U.S. banks appear on the list of the largest twenty banks in the world? Few. Some offshore banks have higher reserve requirements than U.S. banks. Very professional, proud, and honest people are working in the offshore community, and they are at your service. How do they get into your circle of confidence?

4. You need to have your every asset in your own name and be the king of the mountain; you are a control freak.

5. You can't enjoy the use of a French chalet or a Lexus without actually being on the title and owning it.

6. You think you're going to take it all with you when you die.

7. You don't think we live in a litigious society in which numerous groundless suits are filed, or you don't believe that you are at some risk of litigation (what I term the "ostrich syndrome") and of an unpredictable judgment for damages against you. You don't believe that the complexity of our legal system (overwhelming regulations and litigation) and taxing structure hold you hostage to the legal profession, CPAs, and the IRS.

You are no longer a reluctant American when:

1. You can practice low-profile living. You don't need to brag about your assets at cocktail parties. You can discreetly and legally conceal part of your wealth offshore, away

from prying eyes, potential litigants, and computer databases. (You can't conceal it *all*, since that would constitute a fraud against your future creditors or claimants.)

2. You are comfortable with professional and geographic diversity for your wealth conservation and management. You accept that law-abiding people go offshore with some (not all) of their wealth.

3. You accept that there are other stock exchanges offshore providing excellent investment opportunities not afforded to U.S. persons. The word "person" as used in this book refers to an individual (including a third party or "straw man"), business, company, partnership, corporation, IBC, LLC (limited liability company), or any other entity with legal standing recognized in the jurisdiction of its creation.

4. You fantasize about spending some of your retirement time in a Caribbean condo or in Monaco and having your grandchildren visit you there.

5. You're tired of the slow erosion of your personal privacy and you want to do something about it.

6. You recognize that it is not only the other person who gets sued, that litigation is rampant, and that it is not going to get better under the present U.S. legal system. (Pressure placed upon Congress against tort reform by those who benefit from the present system makes substantial changes unlikely.) With a surplus of imaginative attorneys creating new theories of liability, you must plan ahead for that contingency. This is especially important if you are in a high-risk profession and have the potential problem of being uninsured or underinsured against a runaway jury verdict.

7. You accept the *new trilogy*: you consider international estate planning, international financial planning, and asset protection. And don't overlook two other factors— taxation and insurance.

8. You can intelligently discuss the subjects of offshore incorporation, use of nominees, departure tax or expatriation planning, global estate planning, asset protection trusts, wealth preservation and conservation, and asset and portfolio management services.

9. You find the income tax system unfair and incomprehensible and believe that the IRS is out of control. You are aware of the differences among the terms *tax avoidance*, *tax evasion*, and the cute term betwixt the two *tax "avaison."* You know that the IRS has a tax haven department and monitors tax haven activities, but you are in compliance and can sleep at night. You know where the fuzzy line is between tax avoidance and tax evasion and tread carefully. (I suspect that the IRS purchases all the books on going offshore, too! I got a call one day from an IRS purchasing agent to buy my books, and she even wanted to put the purchase on the IRS's credit card.)

10. You are not a control freak and do not need to make every decision personally. If you are, no one can help you!

11. You recognize that through knowledge you acquire power. What you learn from this book by keeping an open mind may change your life forever!

12. You feel insecure about the massive U.S. national debt, and this domestic monetary crisis makes you hedge your personal finances.

13. You are willing to become more computer literate to harness the vast offshore resources available on the Internet. Just sample some of the sites identified in this book, and you certainly will concur that it was well worth the time and financial investment to get on-line.

Endnotes

1 On a per capita basis, Liechtenstein is one of the world's richest countries.

2 Ireland is unique in that it is the only European Community (EC) country that, as an incentive for tax haven business, offers tax-free benefits to nonresident companies.

2

Getting Started: Recognizing and Overcoming Your Concerns

THERE IS MORE to going offshore than the act of opening up a private and personal offshore bank account or forming an offshore corporation. That's no big deal! Open a copy of *The Economist* and read all the advertisements from offshore banks wanting your money, as well as company formation firms offering to create an instant international business company (IBC) or exempt company for you. Such activities should be part of a bigger personal plan, a total structure that won't be obsolete in a few years and can accommodate potential changes in your personal life (divorce, marriage of children, birth of grandchildren, and so on) and your global business needs.

Chinese philosopher Lao-tzu once said, "A journey of a thousand miles must begin with a single step." The first step is to identify your concerns.

- What do you do? You can more easily find out what to do than how to do it. (A qualified professional will show you the hows.)

- Whom do you use for the different roles—the trustee, the nominee, the asset manager, the trust protector?
- How much do you trust them? How do you protect yourself from unsavory offshore people and companies?
- Where do you go? What's the difference between a tax haven and an international banking center?
- How much does it cost to set up and sustain offshore accounts?
- Who will provide the international formation and annual services?
- What type of banking services are required (for example, public versus private banking)?
- What type of flexibility is needed when establishing and administering the trust?

If you've started and are already offshore, ask yourself the following questions:

- Why did you go offshore?
- Are your offshore arrangements legal and tax compliant?
- Why did you select the structure?
- Is your current structure the best for you, both now and in the future?
- What do you do now? How can you improve your current structure?

The Structures

I use my own planning terminology in this book. I might state that the final *operating structure* is composed of individual *entities* or *boxes*. For example, the first entity (box one) is owned by box two, and box two flows into box three—that is a *three-box* or *three-entity structure*.

Every entity has its place. The structure could flow from onshore to offshore and back again using boxes or entities that can be one or more of the following:

- The international business company (IBC) or an exempt company, a company incorporated within a tax haven but not authorized to do business within the country of incorporation; the IBC or exempt company is intended for global operations
- The asset protection trust (APT) or the foreign asset protection trust (FAPT)
- The family protective trust (same as the APT)
- The family settlement trust (same as the APT)
- The private investment bank (PIB), a bank not for general public banking
- Annuities
- The private family or charitable foundation
- The captive insurance company
- The limited-duration or life company
- The company limited by guaranty, the guaranty/hybrid company
- The real estate family limited partnership (FLP), a variation of the limited partnership (LP) for providing asset protection for the "crown jewel"[1] real property asset
- The offshore mutual or hedge fund
- The limited liability company (LLC)
- The Nevada corporation with bearer shares
- Timeshare resorts

And these inadvisable structures:

- The unincorporated business organization (UBO or BO), a company treated as a trust for tax purposes
- The business trust organization (BTO), the pure trust, or the so-called Massachusetts trust
- The common law or pure trust as a tax avoidance strategy

The Participants

The role of the *offshore trustee* remains the same as that of his or her traditional onshore counterpart. However, the use of *nominees* is not a traditional U.S. mechanism. The OS trust usually uses an IBC. Offshore nominees are utilized as shareholders and/or directors and/or officers of the IBC for the ultimate in privacy. (Caveat: If nominees own and control an IBC, the assets of the trust are no longer yours. Only the tax reporting obligation and duty remain with the grantor. The control of the assets and ownership are in the nominees.)

The role of *trust protector* is unfamiliar to most Americans. In simple terms, the protector is the watchdog of the trustee and the trust assets. The duties or powers of the protector generally include:

- Co-signing on bank or brokerage accounts with the trustee
- Joining the trustee in selecting the trust's asset managers or advisors
- Replacing the trustee or relocating the trust to another situs

The protector could be a company, committee, or individual. The risk of using an individual in this function is that upon the disability or death of that individual, the trust is without a protector. I would strongly suggest that you not create an APT or an FAPT without including a trust protector. Depending upon the *trust deed* (the trust agreement), various powers are given to the protector. The protector may legally be given the power to discharge the trustee, replace the trustee, and veto the proposed actions of the trustee, where these powers are provided for in the trust deed.

When in doubt, the trustee seeks the consent of the protector. When an action that is not in the normal course of trust business is required of the trustee, the trustee will seek the concurrence of the protector. A very powerful role indeed! The protector should not be given enough power that he or she may be considered as a cotrustee, and may even be a U.S. person. Some believe that using a U.S. person as a protector is dangerous because the U.S. courts can exert much greater influence over a U.S. person. Even more problematic is where the grantor is his or her own protector. Grantors who do this are usually too controlling, and are perhaps not good candidates for offshore APTs.

The *asset,* or *portfolio, manager* has a traditional role. He or she is appointed by a written contract with the IBC or the APT. It can be a fully discretionary account, or limitations can be imposed by the contract under the terms of the APT or by the officers of the IBC. Fees to the asset manager can be based on performance achieved or on a percentage of the valuation of the estate under his or her management. However, asset management can be obtained from quality offshore brokerage houses, which only charge the traditional brokerage fees and perhaps a small percentage of the portfolio as a discretionary management fee.

The OS trustee is usually an individual or small trust company licensed and regulated by the tax haven. This is directly contrary to the domestic U.S. concept of using a commercial trust company, such as the trust department of a bank. There is no difficulty in securing a high-quality, professional individual to act as the trustee for the OS trust, but this person will not assume the liability for U.S. IRC compliance and will hire an expert familiar with U.S. tax filing requirements.

The Question of Trust

Mistrust is probably the biggest deal killer for most RAs. If you can't trust your offshore professionals, nothing can help you! I am not a salesman trying to talk you into going offshore. My agenda is to raise your comfort level with the concept of going offshore so that you at least reach a point where you will allow yourself to trust offshore professionals, to heed their counsel and follow their advice.

Your trust and confidence can be raised by a combination of the following factors:

1. Selecting offshore professionals is not a matter of picking out a name in the Isle of Man yellow pages as you customarily select onshore services, but the phone book does provide some guidance. I usually "borrow" one phone book from each country I visit.

2. You may initially rely on a referral from a U.S. consultant, but comfort comes with time. Take small steps and gradually build upon them as your acceptance level increases.

3. Act on your gut instinct after listening to a speaker at a seminar who impresses you.

4. Traditional standards of due diligence still exist. Don't expect to be given references by the clients who have gone offshore—obviously. But, inquire and expect professional references from attorneys, CPAs, and others. And do follow up on these references.

5. Go to the offshore consultant who is an established expert or writes a newsletter for advice. If the consultant is not concerned about putting his or her advice in writing for the whole world (and the IRS) to see, it should be credible.

6. Stay away from the promoter who offers a flat price for running you off to an island in the South Pacific regardless of your unique needs. One size never did and never will fit all.

7. Avoid those who promise exorbitant OS returns on your money. Don't lose sight of the fact that high returns come from higher financial risks, or even scams. You don't have time to earn it back again! There is no magic about going OS that will earn you the highest rate of return with low risk. It has been said that the safest place to double your money is to fold it over once and keep it in your pocket! Retain your prudent guidelines and conservatism.

8. Don't abandon those traditional safeguards and high standards you've developed for selecting your domestic professionals. You need to trust and listen to your acquired wisdom and instincts. Don't compromise. If you don't like people, don't use them, no matter what you may have been told by others. Prepare for a long-term relationship. Prepare too for the possibility of your second

generation working with a second generation of offshore consultants. Consider what happens if you become disabled or when you are deceased. Could your spouse or significant other work well with the offshore consultant? I encourage, as an absolute minimum, the dinner meeting with the reluctant spouse who doesn't care to get involved in financial matters so that there is at least a modicum of communication, a social relationship, and some agreement with respect to the final offshore decisions.

9. Service providers generally fit into one of two categories: those who have cookie-cutter approaches for everyone, and those who design customized solutions for you. Obviously, you'll feel greater confidence in a professional who caters to your unique needs.

In many cases, spouses are unaware of what is happening financially in a family partnership. This leaves the tremendous burden of educating the survivor to the OS consultant—clearly, not a role we relish. If your spouse truly doesn't have an aptitude for investment management, then at least share your personal plans with a financially astute child. Doing so will give you the comfort of knowing that the financial dynasty will continue in the event of disability or death.

The Costs

I see OS APTs for sale from Belize for only $200. Here, like anywhere else, you really can't get more than you pay for. A no-frills Bahamian IBC can cost as little as $875. But what do you have after you purchase it? Be honest with yourself. You very likely have no basis of reference to evaluate the quality of the product being offered to you. You can't just buy OS products in a vacuum. I repeatedly tell my clients that they should never buy OS products at "sale" prices.

For a trade-off study and a fully up-and-running, turnkey structure consisting of an APT and IBCs, with all the bells and whistles, all nominees in place, bank account, brokerage account, and so on, you will pay between $10,000 and $15,000. If your gut reaction to the above numbers is alarm, then going offshore may not be economically feasible for the size of your estate, or you have a false sense of the value-added phenomena and the costs of going OS the correct way. You are purchasing the expertise that goes into creating a legal, tax-compliant, functional offshore structure. Besides, the U.S. dollar is still way down in value worldwide with respect to most major world currencies and doesn't buy as much as it used to. Have you traveled to Europe lately? I use the "Snickers test," and surprisingly, it works. When a candy bar sells for 50 cents at full price in the U.S. and for 69 cents in a supermarket in Basseterre, St. Kitts and Neris, the "RA cost of living index" tells me that food is 38 percent more expensive on St. Kitts. Easy to do. U.S. candy bars are popular and for sale worldwide, even in Moscow.

The OS structure could be done in phases. It may not be necessary to put it all in place the first year. This would defer some of your setup costs, but may subject you to some unnecessary risks. Staging is not generally recommended unless absolutely necessary as a planned strategy, never because of implementation costs.

Also, get a handle on the second-year costs, or subsequent years' costs. Your OS consultant should be able to give you an estimate of these future costs within 10 percent.

International Services and Setup

The U.S. is the most litigious society in the world, and it has spawned an entirely new defensive industry—the so-called "asset protection" specialty.

Numerous professionals and companies, onshore and offshore, are competing to set up your structures. Offshore operations are a source of both initial revenue and continuing revenue from ongoing annual fees. A word of caution is in order: Once company nominees are put in place, it is extremely difficult, when compared to the U.S. legal system, to replace them. Registered agents and nominees won't readily relinquish their roles and future income—but if you persevere, they will eventually do so.

Don't confuse the substitution of nominees in the IBC with the absolute right in a trust indenture to discharge the trustee, even without cause. I recently saw a Bahamian trust deed drafted by a Los Angeles attorney that provided that the trustee could only be discharged for cause, but it didn't define what constituted cause. He was one of the cotrustees: you use your own imagination here. You need to clearly distinguish between the attributes of the exempt company (IBC) and the trust (APT).

Endnotes

1 A crown jewel is generally an office building, shopping center, or apartment house with highly appreciated value. It generally doesn't include the family residence because it is not business oriented.

3

Why Go Offshore?

The dog with a bone is always in danger.

OLD AFRICAN PROVERB

The nail that sticks up gets driven down.

OLD JAPANESE PROVERB

WE ALL HAVE different agendas, we think. Yet if you speak confidentially with others who are similarly situated, you will find much commonality in the considerations for going OS and the concerns that precipitate such thinking. Simply speaking, it is more difficult for a creditor to access offshore assets. In an offshore court of a tax haven, the judges generally grant less (or no) punitive damages than is the case in the U.S. Let's initially discuss why you *don't* want to go offshore.

Reasons to Stay Onshore

- The U.S. government insures your funds on deposit with onshore banks. There is no equivalent of America's FDIC or FSLIC banking protection[1] anywhere else in the world, except for Canada and the Isle of Man. Canadian banks provide some protection through the Canadian Deposit Insurance Corporation (CDIC), while the Isle of Man provides very limited protection for 75 percent of the account but with a limit of around $30,000. In June 1999, Mexico created a bank bailout agency—the Bank Savings Protection Institute. The new Institute has the power to take over insolvent Mexican banks and make them whole again. If an offshore bank account is represented by the bank as being "insured," it is with a private insurer. Offshore banks do fail! In 1999, there was a scandal involving a bank "insurer" called International Deposit Indemnity Corporation (IDIC) in Nevis. With IDIC suing the government of Nevis for reinstatement, the outcome was unknown at the time of drafting this book. Your protection is only as good as the financial reserves of the insurer. On the positive side, consider that in many international financial centers (IFCs), banking regulators require higher bank reserves than are required in the U.S. This makes for a "safe" haven as well as a tax haven. Many banks in the major havens maintain one dollar in reserves for each dollar on deposit!

- U.S. stock brokerage accounts are insured by the Securities Industry Protection Corporation (SIPC), an agency of the federal government, against losses (for example, your broker running off with your money). Many brokerage houses supplement this with private insurance.
- Many offshore people consider the U.S. (Nevada, Delaware, Wyoming, Utah) to be their tax havens.
- The U.S. is the most politically stable country in the world, with only two major political parties, regular elections, and a safe and currently financially sound and insured banking system.

- The maximum income tax rate in the U.S. is lower than in many other industrialized countries.
- The rate of inflation in the U.S. is relatively low.
- Your estate and financial planning needs can often be met by onshore planning. There is a surplus of onshore planners.
- There are no express exchange controls in the U.S., though many indirect controls and disclosure requirements are imposed. You may wire transfer any amount of funds offshore. (The privacy of such wire transactions is an issue addressed elsewhere in this book.)
- U.S. currency remains strong and freely convertible to other world currencies, and the "Ben Franklin" is the unofficial currency for most of the world.[2] More $100 bills circulate outside the U.S. than inside, by a ratio of about two to one.

Reasons to Go Offshore

At this point you might ask, "If the U.S. is so good, why go off-shore?" There is a myth perpetuated by the press and the IRS that people only go offshore for illegal purposes or to hide something. Wrong! To try to identify all of the reasons why you would want to go offshore with some of your assets would be almost impossible. However, we can identify some of the major factors. Some may appear redundant, but this list was created in an attempt to encompass as many common concerns as possible.

- A quest and hunger for renewed personal privacy and confidentiality. With faster, more powerful computers tying together more and more databases, there might ultimately be no financial (or personal) privacy left in the U.S.
- Concerns for financial security for you and your family for your lifetimes, and perhaps for your financial dynasty.

- Fear of the future. Is the Environmental Protection Agency going to charge you for removing contaminated soil on that parcel you sold in 1990 at a clean-up cost of $1,000,000?
- Rampant litigation, vexatious litigants, predator plaintiffs and attorneys, and rogue juries giving runaway awards in the United States. Appeals on such verdicts are prohibitively expensive and rarely successful. Will you be the next victim?
- Concerns with the U.S. government. Is the United States going bankrupt? Is it there already? There is no real surplus until the national debt is paid off! What will be the long-term effects upon you (such as increased taxes) to balance the budget in seven to ten years and "eventually" clear up our children's and grandchildren's deficit?
- Fears with respect to the integrity and quality of the U.S. banking system as bank after bank is swallowed up in megamergers.
- Hidden and confiscatory taxes; crippling, oppressive, and costly governmental thickets of regulations; and red tape from mediocre bureaucrats. Through regulations, the government controls your business, your wealth, and you—not the other way around, as our founders intended.
- The possibility of divorce and related problems, or the expenses of a prolonged separation; protection from the conduct of an imprudent spouse or an aggrieved significant other; alternatives to a prenuptial agreement.
- Potential business failure, insolvency, or bankruptcy.
- Anticipation of debilitating illness and its financial drain.
- Provisions for your retirement.
- Providing for your spouse and progeny during your lifetime and after your death.
- Providing after your death for a disabled spouse or child, an insolvent adult child with poor money management skills, a relative, or a friend.

- Protection of a lump-sum disability award (such as personal injury, worker's compensation, no-fault settlement) against future claims by creditors.

Certain government and business interests don't want to see your assets go offshore:

- Your friendly banker and, in general, the American banking system. As the level of flight capital grows, there are fewer dollars in the U.S. banking system. A staggering two-thirds of the $100 bills in commerce circulate offshore! Banks make money on the arbitrage between what they pay you for the use of your money and what they charge others to rent money. They also make money by providing banking and financial services and transactions. As money flows offshore, the U.S. banks make less money.
- Your onshore professionals, who know little or nothing about going offshore, will discourage you to protect themselves and to retain you as a client.
- The Internal Revenue Service. As funds legally flow offshore, the IRS loses its ability to monitor and audit the day-to-day activities of people who are wrongfully perceived to be evading taxes by the mere act of going offshore.
- Credit reporting bureaus (there are three major services), databases, and credit card issuers. There is also money to be earned by selling demographics; your credit report and your buying habits at supermarkets are salable data and assets. As more and more transactions go offshore, the database on you becomes less accurate and complete. You have partially beaten Big Brother—the system doesn't know *all* about you.
- Plaintiff's counsel. To sue or not to sue, that is their question. It has got to be worth their while. The best way to find whether you are the next victim is to run an asset search on yourself to determine whether you're worth suing. If your assets are not in your name, that

might discourage litigation against you. If the assets are not in your name and are offshore, those assets could probably not be sold to satisfy a judgment against you.

- Law enforcement officials who abuse the asset forfeiture laws (with the full support of the courts, based on the English common law) to generate "funding" for their agencies. When your assets aren't in the U.S., they aren't available to be seized. I know of no asset protection structures solely in the U.S. that will protect assets against asset forfeiture. You must move the assets offshore.

In short, there are many reasons to look for alternatives to on-shore assets and investing.

Endnotes

1 Some people believe that the FDIC and FSLIC insurance encourages banks to take higher risk investments. This reduces reserves and causes excessive disintermediation. This in turn puts more pressure on bankers to offer depositors higher yields and assume higher risks.

2 The $100 bill is the de facto currency of Russia, where it is estimated that $16 billion worth of the bills circulate. *Forbes* reported in May 1999 that about US$260 billion circulate offshore.

4

Where Do I Place My Assets?

Sunny climes are for shady people.

F. Scott Fitzgerald, in
Tender Is the Night, in
reference to Monaco

The offshore location you select is called by different names by different people: the situs, the tax haven, the jurisdiction, the venue, or the international financial (or banking) center (IFC). All of these terms mean essentially the same thing. However, IFC is certainly more prestigious a term for a situs than a tax haven in a third-world or third-tier country.

The title of this chapter poses one of the four questions I am most frequently asked:

1. Where is the best location for my offshore assets and business operations? (This is usually the first question from the client. The only appropriate answer is that it depends on one's unique objectives.)

2. How do I trust the offshore service providers?

3. What if something happens to my trusted service provider?

4. How do I retrieve offshore assets if I need them?

There is no best answer as to where to go, because that depends upon the client's needs. Is it for personal reasons, business reasons, or both? Is it for a trust and/or an IBC? For creating and managing an offshore captive insurance company and mutual fund, you should split the two functions between two jurisdictions.

Guidelines for Evaluating Offshore Options

Here is my set of situs evaluation yardsticks, presented in no special order of priority.

General Reputation or Quality of the Tax Haven

Choose a haven that has a good reputation worldwide for providing quality international financial services. Some countries had successful economies before the U.S. was formed. Look for the well-regulated local institutions and professionals and sufficient safeguards to monitor the quality of banking services and professionals. Further, choose a country that provides business-friendly legislation and that has been a haven for many years, not a newbie to the field. Select a haven in which only "clean" business is encouraged and banks operate under strict rules. You might find yourself scrutinized and stigmatized based on the situs you have chosen. The U.S. government issued an alert to the U.S. banking system with respect to Antigua in 1999. This was in response to increasing levels of banking privacy and secrecy, which the U.S. government suggested might be an attempt to cover up money laundering.

Because the level of flight capital is increasing worldwide, offshore business has become very competitive. Capital flight occurs concurrent with social destabilization. If you threaten people and capital, they will leave! Around the world, many countries continue to inspire fear in their middle and commercial class through unstable governments, high taxes, burdensome regulations, or wealth redistribution through litigation. The prime candidates for capital flight in 1999 include:

- **Canada**. Renewed secession calls are being heard from Quebec, a French-speaking province of Canada that consumes more in tax dollars than it generates and will have no trade treaties with anyone, including Canada and the U.S. While Quebec is a mineral-rich province, the minerals will stay in the ground due to the cost of environmental regulation and the taxes on employees and labor.
- **Ireland, Italy, Spain, and Greece**. High taxes and a gross domestic product (GDP) disparity with other European Union nations will drive prices up and job growth down. The new EU currency will only aggravate the situation.
- **Venezuela**. Hugo Chavez, who led an unsuccessful coup several years ago, is now a democratically elected president with big social program ideas. Enough said.
- **Australia**. Because of the government's seizure of legally registered guns from gun owners, the criminals now know that nobody is armed—and crime is rising rapidly. The middle class and upper class are looking to hide assets abroad to protect against the growing civil unrest.
- **South Africa**. For fifteen years, money has been leaving South Africa illegally in bags, cars, stuffed animals, and other creative vehicles. Now that currency controls have been relaxed, many of the bourse-listed companies are seeking listing elsewhere— London, New York, Toronto, anyplace but South Africa. This nation leads the world in murder per capita, burglaries per capita, and carjackings per capita, and has designed an anti-carjacking device that will immolate any would-be carjacker with flame throwers from underneath the car.
- **United States**. The U.S. will also see its share of capital flight, primarily due to increasing regulations, socialization of medicine, out-of-control tort litigation,

and a government perceived as trying to exercise restrictive powers over its citizens.

New tax havens are springing up like mushrooms after the rain. How many of you have ever heard of the following jurisdictions, let alone tried to find them in a world atlas without an index: Vanuatu (1,300 miles northeast of Sydney, Australia, and northwest of Fiji), Niue, Cook Islands, and Anguilla? They all compete with each other for the economic gains from your money going into their tax havens. As businesspeople, the local politicians appreciate how your money can improve their banking industry, GDP, local economy, and employment opportunities for their citizens.

Choice of Governing Law

I prefer tax havens that utilize a legal system based upon British common law, precedents, and the doctrine of equity. This system is called the *Westminster model*. I find these havens preferable to countries that alternatively use statutory adaptations—a highly codified body of civil laws—such as Liechtenstein and the French Territories. These, I admit, are subjective criteria. It is your comfort level that needs to be satisfied.

For asset protection purposes, you should select a haven that will not enforce U.S. judgments and U.S. bankruptcy court orders, does not have forced heirship rules (permitting you to exclude U.S. statutory heirs (+)), avoids the rule against perpetuities allowing your trust to endure longer than in the U.S., and will not honor a tax claim from another country.

Principal Language

What is the principal business language of the country? My personal preference is that English-speaking Americans who can't converse at a highly sophisticated legal and technical level in another tongue remain in the English-speaking jurisdictions. I can be swayed, though, under the right circumstances. Can you read legal documents drafted in another language? If not, stay in the English-speaking havens; there are many high-quality jurisdictions to choose from. If you speak fluent Spanish, you could use Costa Rica, Panama, or the Canary Islands. Otherwise, don't add to the complexity of your education and decision-making process by considering a situs where language is an impediment to achieving your offshore goals. If Dutch is your language, try Curaçao ("Island of Business") in the Netherlands Antilles, or Aruba (where Papiamento is also spoken).

Use an Independent Country or a Very Stable Overseas Territory

There are conflicting views on this subject. Some say you should select an independent country that cannot be pressured by its parent jurisdiction to comply with an offshore court order. They think it's best to avoid jurisdictions that will be required by the parent country to implement laws that are unfavorable to the settlor (although I find this unlikely because of the fierce competition among the tax havens for flight capital and a desire to provide profitable banking services).

Others prefer the protection afforded by the Queen, that is, British territories; they feel the "British colours" provide stability to the country. For example, the Cayman Islands and the Turks and Caicos Islands have their military defense guaranteed by the Crown (+) and their banking systems are subject to review and audit by the Bank of England (+), making them much stronger than Antigua.

Seek Excellent, High-Quality Communications

Nothing is as frustrating as working late to send an E-mail message to Costa Rica before you leave for home, only to find out the next morning that it bounced back because of an Internet server being unable to connect or the connection timing out—or getting a fax from the Cook Islands with its most important copy garbled from noise on the line. Communications problems such as these can cause a full business day delay. One could always telephone, but at times the terms or conditions must be in writing. This is not the place to skimp on costs. Always go with first-class, high-quality equipment and long-distance telecommunications service providers.

You will need varied forms of telecommunications to transact your worldwide business offshore, including the following:

• **Voice communications by telephone.** If you feel compelled to use a "roam" phone, use a high-quality 2.4 GHz digital phone. The older, cheaper analog phones operate at 900 MHz and are very noisy. They can easily be monitored with inexpensive equipment; like the old party lines, they are not secure. The 2.4 GHz units are not easy to invade and are getting quite inexpensive. If you are willing to pay, you can get high-quality voice encryption from various suppliers.

• **Facsimile (fax) communications.** Always use the fine mode to assure higher-quality reception. Although it seems more expensive, in the long run it will save you money and time.

• **Modem-to-modem data transmission.** Don't push the curve— offshore lines are primarily satellite links of poorer quality than those in the U.S. Even though you may have just installed this red-hot 56K modem or you now have an ISDN or DSL connection, if you run at slower modem speeds (under 56K) you'll be happier with your connections, with fewer dropouts. (Exceptions do exist—Nassau, for example, has fiber optics lines run in its downtown area.)

• **Internet communication.** This includes encrypted E-mail using Pretty Good Privacy (PGP) over the World Wide Web. PGP is omnipresent on the Internet and has become the de facto standard for private, secure E-mail communications. If you are computer savvy, you can download PGP off various websites. If you're not, you need a relatively user-friendly PGP program.

The 1,024-bit PGP encryption system should be safe from the so-called "brute-force attacks" for several more years because of how costly it is to break this encryption. This is based on the current accelerating rate of technological advances in this field. If the government is willing to spend the money, they can break 1,024-bit encryption for around $750,000 a page in Arlington, Virginia. There is a publicly traded U.S. company that provides software that uses super-high levels of logic with a computer system that can teach itself to break the message in any language. Are you worth it?

• **Voice scramblers and encryption.** Voice scramblers provide some degree of privacy against eavesdroppers and hackers, but not at the same level obtained by full encryption. Don't confuse a voice scrambler with encryption—encryption is much better. High-quality, very secure, full encryption devices for voice communication, land line and cellular, are available from such firms as Transcrypt International in Lincoln, Nebraska. Phone: (402) 474-4800; fax: (402) 474-4858; website: www.transcrypt.com.

• **Wire transfers.** These fulfill the need for expedient money transfers and are available in most major world currencies. U.S. dollar wire transfers are all consummated in New York City.

Seek Tax Havens in a User-Friendly Time Zone

Consider the advantages of a convenient time zone. Do you want to get up during the middle of the night to call your offshore trustee or asset manager? How many hours are you willing to fly to visit your offshore banker? Summer is only "one day long" on the Isle of Man, but generally all year long in the Turks and Caicos, the Cayman Islands, the Bahamas, the Canary Islands, and the Caribbean.

Political and Economic Stability

What is the strength and stability of the central government? The Caymans, the Bahamas, and the federation of St. Kitts and Nevis are clear examples of stable democratic systems. Will a change in the governing political party affect the stability of your offshore structure or the safety of your money? Is the country susceptible to violent political swings, military coups, or invasion? Does it have a reputation for massive corruption?

A carefully drafted APT will provide for these contingencies with appropriate language in the trust deed. Several events may occur. The trustee may resign and/or the trust may be recandled (moved and reactivated) in another tax haven. The precipitating conditions could be enumerated in the trust deed, expressed in the letter of wishes (sometimes referred to as a *side letter*), or be discretionary with the trustee. Most tax havens welcome and will adopt "clean orphan" trusts, or those trusts in good legal standing moved from their original jurisdiction and in need of a new jurisdiction.

Information Exchange and Privacy

What are the levels of banking and financial privacy mandated by local laws? What are the disclosure requirements as to an IBC made a public record? What is the level of information exchanged between the U.S. and your tax haven for routine tax matters? What tax and assistance treaties exist between the U.S. and the tax haven? The Mutual Legal Assistance Treaty (MLAT) provides for the exchange of information among member countries for suspected criminal matters, but it excludes tax crimes such as U.S. tax evasion. The principal MLAT is between the U.S. and the U.K., and because of that, the U.K. exerts influence throughout the former British colonies and the current overseas territories. The U.S. exerts great direct economic pressure upon Caribbean jurisdictions to enter into special "drug trafficking" treaties.

The issue of tax treaties is extremely complex, requiring the assistance of a tax expert or an international tax specialist. Your CPA is unlikely to be really familiar with this topic (see Chapter 11 for detailed information).

Currency Regulations or Exchange Control

It's preferable to have no regulations, but minimal regulations might be acceptable. Look for the ability to obtain asset preservation by using currency diversification, as is done with Swiss annuities, Swiss francs, Euros, and so on. Countries such as the Bahamas, the British Virgin Islands (BVI), and the Turks and Caicos Islands (TCI) use U.S. dollars freely and with U.S. dollar–designated banking accounts. Euro accounts are available, as well as accounts in other G-7 currencies, with a corporate resolution authorizing such. Check with the bank, or use a bank that provides accounts in the best currencies for your application.

After countless years of currency controls, in May of 1998 Israel lifted controls on its currency, the shekel, and made it freely convertible. No calamity followed. Its citizens could freely invest offshore and open foreign bank accounts. The most interesting and unexpected consequence is that Israeli investors began to use the U.S. as their tax haven and have invested in U.S. real estate (in New York and Florida, for example) as a safe haven for their money. They also have provided for possible expatriation in their future or perhaps for their family use.

In early 1999, the Malaysian central bank lifted its six-month ban on capital flows (flight capital). A rush by foreign investors prompted it to impose a flight tax of up to 30 percent, only exacerbating the outflow problem.

Tax Regimen

Tax treatment on income tax, foreign source income, nonresident treatment, and special tax concessions are complex issues; see Chapter 11 for detailed information.

Quality of Local Professionals and the Financial Services Industry

Your OS structure is only as sound as the professionals who create and manage it and its tangential infrastructure. Look for an educated workforce: an abundance of fairly priced, qualified attorneys, banking facilities, chartered accountants, asset and portfolio managers, consultants, company managers, and trustees. Clearly, if you need the U.S. privacy afforded under the attorney-client communication privilege, you should limit your communications in the United States to your attorney. CPAs and others (such as financial planners) do not have such a complete privilege. You don't shop offshore for professionals by letting your fingers do the walking in the Aruba yellow pages—you use referrals through existing personnel and other trusted professional relationships.

I suggest that you use residents of the jurisdiction who have been there so long that they are no longer considered outsiders. They don't want to lose their work permits and become exiles, so they are more likely to be trustworthy. This is an extreme statement, but I avoid people with an alcohol or gambling problem or those who are preoccupied by the details of a bitter divorce. My sympathies go out to them, but my clients' assets are my highest priority.

Long-Term Economic and Social Stability

Select a jurisdiction with a high per-capita income, providing for a happier populace. Look carefully at the business and political climate to see how it might affect you. Even the Cook Islands had a political scandal in 1995 that made some offshore consultants nervous, including me. Haiti was a stable economy until the clampdown on U.S. importation of foreign-made goods that used child labor, and the takeover (invasion) of Haiti by U.S./UN forces in 1994. Now its economy continues in shambles. The EU constantly puts pressure upon the world's tax havens and the U.K. to pressure their overseas territories. The U.S. government continues to pressure the U.K. in the same manner. We see ever-so-slow erosion in the privacy of the world's banking system. In a balancing of interests between privacy and terrorism or money laundering, the individual's right to privacy will fail.

Local Customs and Social Environment

Religion, politics, labor movements, social life, work ethics, business customs, crime, and drug involvement are further factors to consider. You can find out whether these issues are important in your jurisdiction by reading the local newspapers, speaking with local citizens, and, best of all, living in the country during an evaluation period.

Acquisition of Second Passport or Citizenship

A second citizenship, second passport, tax residence, tax domicile, real estate ownership, work permit, operating a "local" business, or ultimate retirement site are essential considerations that would have an effect on the selection process. If you intend to become an expatriate, a second passport could be beneficial. (See Chapter 10.)

OS Operating Entity

What you require from your OS structure determines where you go. Clearly, if it is a self- or captive insurance company (see Chapter 13), one uses Bermuda, the Caymans, or Guernsey. Even the Turks and Caicos Islands are seeking to emerge[1] in this area.

For example, some havens encourage specific types of companies to locate there by enacting special preferential laws. Businesses that will help develop their infrastructure or create local jobs are highly desirable. These jurisdictions are generally in Switzerland, Luxembourg, the Netherlands, and Liechtenstein. Similarly, the Caribbean and the Netherlands Antilles, as holding company sites, attract IBCs.

Banking

Which international banks have correspondents in your other operating countries to facilitate transactions? Which banks don't have operating branches in the U.S.? For the ultimate in privacy, do not use those with U.S. operations. Statements should be sent to you by mail fowarding services to avoid foreign mail being posted directly to you.

Real Estate

What are the acquisition and annual costs of offshore real estate ownership? While the costs are outrageous in the Caymans, in Costa Rica you get more for your money. What are the limitations as to ownership? Who can take title?

Local Politics

What anticipated trends in future local legislation may affect what you are doing? Is the tax haven stable, with conditions changing slowly, or is it on the leading edge? Is the haven subject to outside (U.S.) influences and pressures of "cooperation" with U.S. authorities?

Currency

Select a haven with a stable currency, U.S. dollar or pegged to the U.S. dollar (Bahamian dollar, Eastern Caribbean dollar, or Cayman Islands dollar, for example).

Legal Issues and Terminology

Without at least a cursory knowledge of legal terminology, you will be at a disadvantage in the site selection process. For further elucidation on these terms, read Appendix A or *Black's Law Dictionary* (at your local library). For a comparison of features among the various jurisdictions, see Figure 4.1, provided courtesy of Barry S. Engel, Esq.

Spendthrift Clause

A *spendthrift clause* is language in a will or trust that is intended to protect the assets of the estate against the imprudent spending habits of a beneficiary. Distributions to the beneficiary will shift to the discretion of the trustee and may even cease if the beneficiary is insolvent.

Some exceptions where a spendthrift trust will not work are:

1. Where the grantor names himself as the beneficiary.

2. In states that do not enforce such trusts (Mississippi in tort law matters and New Hampshire). Always check with your local counsel.

The Statute of Limitations

The *statute of limitations* (s/L) is the deadline date after which a party claiming to be injured by the settlor should no longer file (but still may file) an action to recover damages. In California, the statute for fraud is one year from the discovery date, and the discovery period can be as long as seven years. If the settlor would file a bankruptcy during that period, the bankruptcy trustee is granted an additional two-year period to file a recovery action, extending the statute of limitations to nine years.

The statute of limitations prohibits creditor claims against the APT if brought too late (filed too late in the court of competent jurisdiction). Generally, the statute begins to run when the fraud was discovered or should have been discovered by the party who claims to have been damaged by the settlor. The Bahamas, Cayman Islands,

Figure 4.1: APT Jurisdictional Comparison (As of 1 August 1997)

Provisions (6 most important assest protection provisions appear first)	(1) Statutory certainty regarding non-recognition of foreign judgments	(2) "Beyond Reasonable Doubt" standard of proof required in establishing fraudulent intent	(3) Statute of limitations on challenging an APT	(4) Statutory certainty that settlor can be a beneficiary	(5) Statutory certainty that settlor can retain some degree of control	(6) Burden of proving fraudulent intent is always on creditor
Jurisdiction						
Anguilla				×	×	
Bahamas		×				×
Barbados		×		×	×	×
Belize	×			×	×	
Bermuda		×				×
Cayman Islands		×				×
Cook Islands	×	×	×	×	×	×
Cyprus			×	×		×
Gilbraltar			*			
Labuan	×	×	×	×	×	×
Marshall Islands		×	×	×		×
Mauritius		×	×	×		×
Nevis	×	×	×	×	×	×
Niue	×			×	×	
Saint Vincent and the Grenadines	×	×	×	×	×	×
Seychelles		×	×	×		×
Turks and Caicos						×
Alaska		×	×	×		
Colorado		×	×			
Delaware		×	×	×		

Figure 4.1: APT Jurisdictional Comparison (As of 1 August 1997), continued

Provisions	(7) Statutory recognition of different classes of creditor	(8) Specific Statute of Elizabeth override provisions	(9) Statutory certainty that trust remains vaild if fraudulent transfers determined to have taken place	(10) Retroactive protection afforded immigrant trusts	(11) Statutory certainty regarding requirements for freezing assets for an APT	(12) Presumption against fraudulent intent if transferor remains solvent following transfers
Jurisdiction						
Anguilla						
Bahamas	×	×	×			
Barbados			×			
Belize						
Bermuda	×	×	×			
Cayman Islands	×	×	×			
Cook Islands	×	×	×	×	×	×
Cyprus	×					
Gilbraltar	×	×	×			×
Labuan	×		×	×		×
Marshall Islands			×	×		×
Mauritius	×	×				
Nevis	×	×	×	×		×
Niue						
Saint Vincent and the Grenadines	×	×	×	**		×
Seychelles						
Turks and Caicos	×					×
Alaska	×	N/A	×			
Colorado	×	N/A				
Delaware	×	N/A	×			

Figure 4.1: APT Jurisdictional Comparison (As of 1 August 1997), continued

Provisions	(13) Binding effect of choice of law	(14) Forced heirship override provisions	(15) Community property provisions
Jurisdiction			
Anguilla		×	
Bahamas	×	×	
Barbados	×	×	
Belize	×	×	
Bermuda		×	
Cayman Islands	×	×	
Cook Islands	×	×	×
Cyprus	×	×	
Gilbraltar	×		
Labuan	×	×	
Marshall Islands	×	×	
Mauritius	**		
Nevis	×	×	×
Niue	×	×	
Saint Vincent and the Grenadines	×	×	×
Seychelles	×	×	
Turks and Caicos	×	×	
Alaska	×	×	
Colorado			
Delaware			

* While some believe Gibraltar law provides "instant" protection if transferor or is solvent following transfers, post-transfer solvency of transferor and hence validity of transfers can be challenged.

** Indicates nonspecific treatment in the law

Note: Local bank secrecy and other nondisclosure provisions do not appear because of the author's view that such provisions are not material considerations in asset protection planning.

Cook Islands, and Mauritius, for example, have specific statutes of limitations on challenging an APT.

Most tax havens have abrogated the time period of the statute. The S/L clock can start to run when an APT is created or an asset is transferred to the APT. Most jurisdictions typically have a statute of limitations of two years or greater—for example, the Bahamas has a two-year S/L, sometimes referred to as a *Fraudulent Disposition Act,* which limits the period in which a transfer or disposition of an asset can be attacked by a creditor.

The Cook Islands is unique in this area—it has by far the shortest S/L, only one year from the date of formation of the APT (under one interpretation), whether the creditor has knowledge of the APT or not. Adding insult to injury, even when a creditor is successful in attacking the transfer, it is only beneficial on that creditor's behalf and not for the benefit of all the creditors.

Choice of Governing Law

A significant issue to ponder is the governing law for your structure or entity. For example, the Bahamas' Governing Law Act states that if a trust is clearly governed by the laws of the Bahamas (in language to that effect contained in the trust deed), then the courts of the Bahamas have the exclusive jurisdiction with respect to any disputes over the trust. A foreign judgment regarding assets or rights as contained within the trust would not be honored by the Bahamian courts. Nothing precludes the party claiming to have been harmed from filing an action in the Bahamas, but cost and geography are usually deterrents.

Some U.S. cases have reflected the views of U.S. judges angered by assets moved offshore or trying to retain their broad jurisdiction (called "long arm") over the assets. They have ignored the foreign jurisdiction election because of the nexus of the assets to their venue. In a 1999 federal case (referred to as the Anderson case), the judge failed to accept the position of the defendants, that the assets they sent offshore were out of their control. The judge held the defendants in contempt and jailed them until they returned the money—

six months later. This type of judicial conduct sent chills through the offshore community.

One other issue to consider is the Mutual Legal Assistance Treaty (MLAT), an agreement among the U.S. and many Caribbean countries for the exchange of financial and banking information for the enforcement of criminal laws. U.S. tax evasion is excluded as not being a crime to the offshore countries. The United Kingdom has similar agreements with the Cayman Islands, Anguilla, British Virgin Islands, the Turks and Caicos Islands, Montserrat, Uruguay, Morocco, Spain, and Thailand. MLAT is intended to improve the effectiveness of law enforcement authorities of the U.S. and other treaty nations. MLAT provides for the establishment of a "Central Authority"; the Central Authority for the United States is the "Attorney General or a person designated by him [or her]." The Central Authority, for example, for the Cayman Islands is the "Cayman Mutual Legal Assistance Authority or a person designated by it." Requests for assistance under the Cayman MLAT are made by the "Central Authority of the Requesting Party to the Central Authority of the Requested Party." The assistance provided by the Cayman MLAT includes the following:

- taking the testimony or statements of persons;
- providing documents, records, and articles of evidence;
- serving documents;
- locating persons;
- transferring persons in custody for testimony;
- executing requests for searches and seizures;
- immobilizing criminally obtained assets;
- assistance in proceedings related to forfeiture, restitution, and collection of fines;
- any other steps deemed appropriate

The assistance provided to the United States by the Cayman MLAT, however, is limited. Significantly, the assistance afforded by the Cayman MLAT does not apply to:

(a) any matter which relates directly or indirectly to the regulation, including the imposition, calculation, and collection, of taxes. . . . Accordingly, the assistance provided by the Cayman MLAT does not extend to providing information on "pure tax matters." The Cayman MLAT further provides:

2. The Central Authority of the Requested Party may deny assistance where:

(a) the request is not made in conformity with the provisions of [the Cayman MLAT];

(b) the request relates to a political offense or to an offense under military law which would not be an offense under ordinary criminal law; or

(c) the request does not establish that there are reasonable grounds for believing:

(i) that the criminal offense specified in the request has been committed; and

(ii) that the information sought relates to the offense and is located in the territory of the Requested Party;

During negotiations between the United States and the governments of the United Kingdom and the Cayman Islands leading to the Cayman MLAT, the government of the Cayman Islands "refused the requests of the U.S. delegation that pure income tax offenses, i.e., tax offenses based on income from legal proceeds, be included within the scope of the [Cayman MLAT]." Springer Decl., ¶ 5.

The Treaty with the United Kingdom on Mutual Legal Assistance on Criminal Matters, 6 January 1994, S. Treaty Doc. No. 194-2, 1994 WL 855115, does not contain a similar provision limiting assistance to non–tax related offenses.

Transferring Assets

The usual way to transfer funds is by cashier's check or wire transfer. Cashier's checks are not preferred in most of the world because of concern about counterfeiting. In Nassau, for example, there is a twenty-one banking day hold on a cashier's check. The wire transfer provides almost overnight transfers of funds.

The wiring of U.S. dollars globally and electronically on the SWIFT banking system appears to be done by electronic book transfers among member banks in New York City. Other secure and dedicated communication systems used in the offshore banking system are called Cedcom, Euclid, and Microwire. The transferring of U.S. dollars with SWIFT is done in the U.S. banking system, which appears to be vulnerable to snoops and not secure.

Note the following E-mail message appearing on the "net-lawyer" mailing list (net-lawyers@lawlib.wuacc.edu) on the Internet:

From: [address withheld]
To: net-lawyers@lawlib.wuacc.edu
Subject: Asset Locators

A while back, someone posted a listing of asset locator services, but for some reason I cannot find that post. Would someone post the names of some of these companies for me? I am particularly interested in companies that can trace electronic fund transfers. Thanks.

What is surprising is that even if U.S. dollars were to be wired from Zurich to the Cook Islands in the South Pacific, they would go through New York City. The process involves sophisticated encrypted electronics (the SWIFT system) without any exchange of paperwork by the correspondents. There must be a clear audit trail to protect member banks, but no cash changes hands except for final accounting. The expressed goal is to reduce banking errors to a minimum, but the end result is to provide little privacy to the parties involved. *The U.S. Federal Reserve wire transfer system is not a very private system.*

For privacy, clients have reported exchanging their currency to yen or deutsche marks for wire transfers with more privacy and then staying in those currencies.

APT Costs

For a turnkey APT with trustee and trust protector in place, the formation costs could be two to four times the cost of an equivalent U.S. trust structure.

Endnotes

1 Reports indicate that a far greater number of new captives are being formed in the Turks and Caicos Islands than in Bermuda, as TCI takes a low-fee approach and targets the smaller captives.

5

Which Structure Do I Use?

ONCE AGAIN, there are multiple answers to the question posed in the chapter title. Each person's needs are unique. Steer away from offshore consultants who offer only one solution—for example, an offshore private bank in Nauru for everyone, including your dog. Why are you going offshore? What are you trying to accomplish? Is it achievable? Does your OS structure have flexibility to accommodate future personal or business changes?

The following are the factors that lead up to the creation of the operating structure. They are not presented in any particular order of priority.

- **Your age.** If you are in your 40s, your prime earning years, you can afford to take more risks and be more aggressive. You have the time to make some of your capital back if you lose it, and consequently you can seek a higher return on your money. On the other hand, if you are close to your retirement age, you want safety because you don't have the time and energy to earn it back again. You may also want to provide for your grandchildren or fund a family dynasty or private foundation.

- **Your occupation and skills.** The farther removed you are from the day-to-day financial community, the more you should rely upon investment professionals. I don't think you can be the world's foremost cardiac surgeon and also know if and when to sell stock short.

- **Nationality, citizenship, domicile, and residency.** All four are quite different and generally have tax implications that affect the operating structure. If you have active offshore relatives and trusted friends, you may be able to use them to assist in creating and managing those offshore structures. Are you a resident alien or nonresident alien (NRA) or married to a resident alien? As a resident alien, the IRS treats you as a U.S. person with some disadvantages. As a nonresident alien, you have many tax breaks in the U.S.

- **Investment philosophy.** Are you conservative or aggressive? Do you want to give total discretion to your asset manager, or retain investment decision powers?

- **Preexisting offshore entities and offshore funds.** Do you already have an OS presence? Do you remember what it was for? Is it now obsolete because of major changes in your family (divorce, children, grandchildren) or because of changes or proposed change in the U.S. tax code? Is it tax compliant? Did you accumulate millions offshore and don't know how to get it back into the U.S. legally?

Basic Offshore Entities

One of the most fundamental OS entities used as a building block for OS structures is the international business company (IBC), known in other jurisdictions as the *exempt company*, the BVI or Caricom model, or the Channel Island model. The typical IBC is used as an *operating* or *holding company*, as shown in Figure 5.1. Offshore it is referred to as a company because it is created under a *company act* or *ordinance*. The IBC, like any corporation, has beneficial owners called *members*—the equivalent of shareholders, officers, and directors. The vertical line in Figure 5.1 is the offshore line, designated "OS." (*Offshore* would be defined as *foreign* under the Internal Revenue Code.) (See Appendix A for the critical definitions of *foreign* and *offshore*.) *Foreign* denotes any location other than the U.S. and its territories and possessions. To the left is the U.S., and to the right, offshore. We see that the OS IBC has opened up a brokerage account with a U.S. stock brokerage firm. The assets can be managed and traded under a full discretionary account by the brokerage firm or by using an onshore or offshore portfolio manager. The IBC has entered into a written engagement with the portfolio and asset managers to provide for compensation—commissions, fixed fee, or performance-based fee. Trading could be over the Internet with a brokerage firm that provides such services.

Under current U.S. tax laws, the IBC pays no capital gains taxes to the U.S., providing it is not a *controlled foreign corporation*[1] (CFC). It is extremely difficult to avoid controlled foreign corporation (CFC) status! It may pay income taxes on U.S. source income or income effectively connected with the U.S. If the IBC is located in a zero- or low-tax haven, it also pays little or no capital gains tax in the tax haven. (A withholding tax is assessed on any U.S. paid dividends on stock and withheld at the source.) This is not a tax windfall. Although the OS funds grow more rapidly because of the compounding effects of utilizing untaxed resources, when the money is ultimately repatriated to America, the taxman gets his due. That's what makes it tax compliant. The distribution is the taxable event. Remember that tax-compliant offshore tax deferral is very difficult to achieve.

Figure 5.2 takes Figure 5.1 a step further, building upon the concept of the holding company. Holding companies are generally created for a specific purpose—for example, to hold real property, to hold the bearer shares of operating companies, to manage and trade

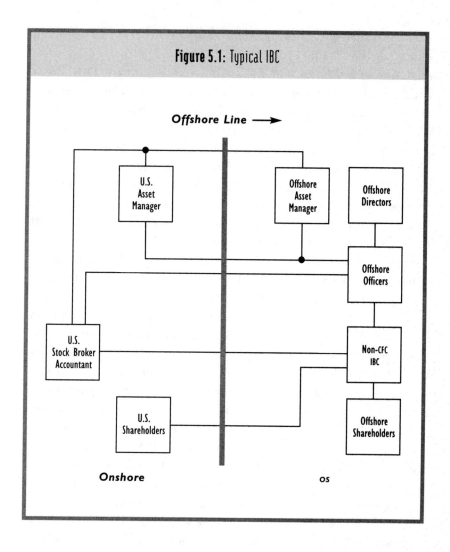

Figure 5.1: Typical IBC

stocks and bonds, for currency or commodity trading, or to own a U.S. business. The holding company may be an excellent vehicle for owning a company with high environmental risks or contaminated and polluted real property. It could be used to circumvent the prohibition against a trust owning or having an interest in restricted forms of investments (including real property).

Notice that we now have four operating IBCs, each being the shareholders or owners of the U.S. entities. I have intentionally made

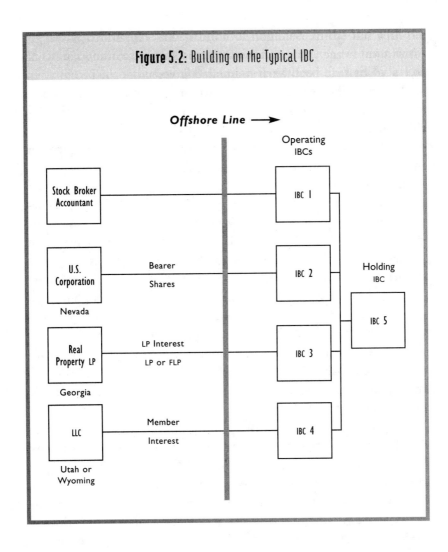

Figure 5.2: Building on the Typical IBC

it quite complex to use it as a teaching tool. IBC 1 is the same operating company as in Figure 5.1, but now it is 100 percent owned by the holding IBC, IBC 5. In our example, IBC 2 is a shareholder of an American corporation.

IBC 3 is involved with U.S. real estate. It could be the sole general partner of a U.S. limited partnership holding environmentally contaminated real property with an uncertain liability for cleanup. It could hold U.S. real property in its own name, but if it did it would subject itself to the Foreign Investor in Real Property Tax Act of 1980 (FIRPTA) and the Economic Recovery Act of 1981 and have U.S. capital gains taxes withheld in escrow upon sale of the property in the U.S. It could also be a limited partner in a limited partnership.

In Figure 5.2, IBC 4 is a member (owner) of a U.S. limited liability company.

All four of the operating IBCS have central management through an OS holding company, IBC 5. So long as it is not prohibited in the jurisdictions where established, there can be total commonality of management—the same directors and officers for all five IBCS. Further privacy could be achieved by placing the operating companies in the Bahamas and by establishing the holding company in the Netherlands Antilles. If money is no object and privacy is of utmost importance, or you are just plain paranoid, each IBC could be incorporated in a different tax haven. Further, each IBC could have different officers and directors. No one but you would know what was happening. If you arrange such a complex structure, make sure to leave good notes in case of your disability or premature death, or no one will be capable of running it. I suggest that you have a master book in any case, updated as necessary, held offshore, sealed and in escrow, for that ultimate day.

Figure 5.3 is a variation of Figure 5.1. It is a simpler structure than Figure 5.2 in that the holding company is replaced by a family trust, called an *asset protection trust* (APT), where the APT provides insulation for the settlor and his or her family.

Note in Figure 5.3 that the prior roles of the IBCs' directors and officers have been taken over by a pair of administrators and fiduciaries called the *trustee* and the *trust protector*. The trustee and the protector manage the trust on behalf of the three beneficiaries identified as Beneficiary 1, 2, and 3. Figure 5.3 is a popular OS combination, combining the features of the IBC for asset management and the trust as an *inter vivos* and/or testamentary vehicle. The trustee could also act as the asset manager or hire an asset manager for the IBC.

A structure for handling the "problem" of excessive equity in U.S. real property is the *equity stripping company* (see Chapter 10, page 144). In Figure 5.4, the domestic real property is an attractive

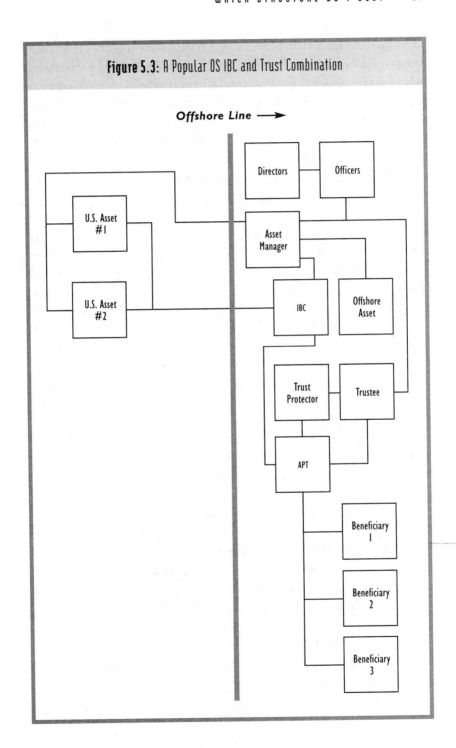

Figure 5.3: A Popular OS IBC and Trust Combination

plum inviting litigation because you have assets (equity) that your prospective plaintiff and his or her attorney want to take from you. In an "arrangement," for example, a loan is made by you, and your real property is given as security, the collateral for the loan. This is not a taxable event in the year taken. A second mortgage or deed of trust is recorded against the real estate, reducing your equity. Perhaps, in the case of your residence, the equity is reduced down to the homestead[2] value, making the house unattractive as a means of satisfying a future judgment against you.

Referring to Figure 5.4, first, an escrow account is opened with an attorney or escrow company. A preliminary title search is performed and provided for the IBC. The officers of the IBC decide independently whether they wish to make a loan on your real estate. If so, they fund the escrow, which in turn distributes the money to you and records the second mortgage on behalf of the IBC. Because the IBC is a corporation, there generally is no usury limitation on the interest rate it can charge you, but it should be in line with the going rate for similar domestic loans so as not to be conspicuous. Proposed new laws may mandate a minimum interest rate. The new promissory note is due as a balloon in five or ten years or upon sale of the real property. Or, for an administrative fee (perhaps one to five points), it can be rolled over for another term. What you do with the money received is only limited by the lack of imagination on the part of you and your OS consultant. Perhaps you buy a lump-sum, irrevocable offshore annuity due at age sixty-five.

One of the few remaining tax shelters available to Americans is the *annuity* (see Chapter 9). With the blessing of Congress and the IRS, it is a method to defer capital gains and taxes until funds are actually received by you, the *annuitant*, hopefully at a time when you are in a lower tax bracket and have more need of the money. The annuity should be irrevocable and noncancelable if it is intended primarily for asset protection purposes. The RA can buy the annuity domestically or even go OS to a Swiss insurance company and convert his or her weak U.S. dollars into stronger currencies when the annuity is purchased.

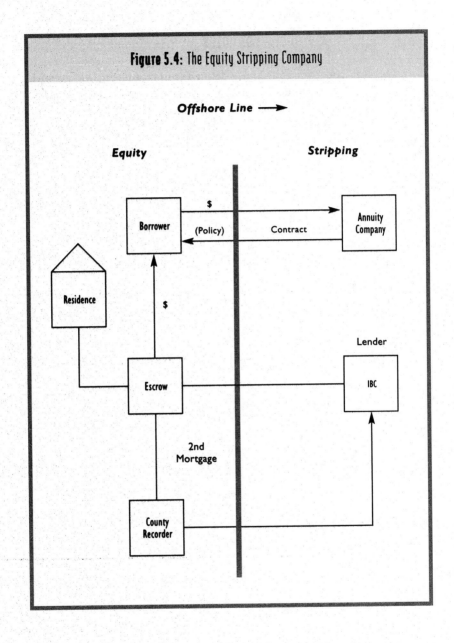

Figure 5.4: The Equity Stripping Company

Endnotes

1 IRC §951 and §957 collectively define the CFC as one in which more than 50 percent of the total voting stock is owned by five or fewer U.S. shareholders.

2 For a detailed explanation of the homestead allowance on your residence, see your own state's laws.

6

The International Business Company:
An Exempt Company

THE INTERNATIONAL business company (IBC) is an entity not customarily familiar to Americans (except perhaps to those living or operating in the U.S. Virgin Islands, which permits a restricted form of an IBC). It is created under a model of a *company act*. The *Caribbean-style company act*, also called the *Caricom model*, has been adopted as a model act throughout the world's tax havens, but is not used universally. The alternative model involves forming a company under an *exempt company act* in the tax haven, as is done in Europe, St. Kitts, and the Turks and Caicos Islands. This is called the *Channel Islands model*. It does not actually create an IBC, but an exempt company with characteristics similar to an IBC.

A simplistic definition of the IBC is a corporation that is referred to as a company, generally created in a tax haven that is authorized to do business worldwide *excluding the country of incorporation*. It can't directly hold title to real property (except for renting local office space) or even operate a local flower stand. Bermuda permits an IBC to lease land for a period up to fifty years. Local banking is permitted (of course), as is dealing with other local IBCs. The IBC is an international operating company as opposed to a domestic company. It is readily accepted in the worldwide banking community as a proven structure to carry on financial or business interests. As such, many offshore trusts carry on their financial and business transactions using one or more entities such as IBCs or limited liability companies (LLCs), both totally owned by the underlying trusts and operated under the direction of the trustee. More complex and ambitious structures may even include a private foundation to pursue altruistic goals or permissive family interests worldwide. Under current U.S. tax laws, so long as the IBC is not a controlled foreign corporation (CFC), personal foreign investment company (PFIC), or foreign personal holding company (FPHC), there are significant tax deferral features available from this structure because a foreign corporation pays no U.S. capital gains taxes as the incentive to invest money in the U.S. But, capital gains realized by the IBC are eventually converted into ordinary income when repatriated.

What Can an IBC Do?

Since many of you are already familiar with American corporations, the following is presented in the form of a comparative discussion of the distinctive similarities and differences between them and IBCs.

Engage in Commerce

The IBC can promote and market goods and services worldwide except as may be restricted under the company act of the country of formation. Some of the types of services that are generally restricted or expressly prohibited in most havens include:

- **Banking services.** The creation of a bank (generally a Class A license) or a private bank (generally a Class B license) is accomplished by a procedure separate from and different than the formation of a company and is quite expensive and time consuming in the better tax havens.
- **Trust services.** A separate license is required for a trust company.
- **Insurance or re-insurance services.** Formation of an insurance or captive insurance company (Chapter 13

describes this type of company in greater detail.) An interesting exception pointed out to me by E. L. Bendelow of Basel Trust Corporation is that under Jersey law, their IBC can participate in insurance.

- **Act as an investment, stock, or commodity trading company.**

Act as a Holding Company with Ownership in Other Entities

This is one of the more complex topics and is far beyond the scope of this book. Since it may encompass controlled foreign corporation (CFC) treatment, investment companies, intercompany transfer pricing, and subsidiaries of CFCs, I refer you to your qualified tax consultant.

Act as a Lender, Accounts Receivable Factorer, and Lessor

An IBC can make its money work by providing loans. Conversely, it can borrow. It can pay finder's fees and commissions. For example, in the U.S. movie industry, it can extend credit based on accounts receivable in another country. Again, this topic is beyond the scope of this book; but I recommend Melvin Simensky and Lanning G. Bryer's *The New Role of Intellectual Property in Commercial Transactions* (John Wiley & Sons, 1994). Another good source of information is the Export Import Bank.

Hold Real Property

Other than where locally restricted, an IBC can take title of (own) real estate and other interests in nonmobile assets worldwide, but not in the country of incorporation. However, many jurisdictions permit the IBC to lease or rent real property for local office space.

Enter into Leasing

An IBC may enter into leases for real property interests and personal property, such as vehicles and equipment, worldwide. My associates report that there are excellent vehicle leasing opportunities offshore for leasing companies.

Act as a Trading Company

As the level of worldwide exporting and importing skyrockets, the IBC can participate by performing the function of a trading company. The IBC can use a fulfillment company to take orders from the customer, do invoicing, drop-ship orders, and collect on irrevocable letters of credit. Profits would then be captured offshore in a low- or no-tax regimen. The IBC could also license intellectual property. High-quality communications is essential for this type of function. Also, watch out for transfer pricing problems.

Probate Avoidance and Privacy Tool

An IBC can be used on behalf of an APT as a probate and privacy tool. Through the medium of a holding company, it could indirectly manage the APT's offshore assets, without it becoming part of the probate estate upon the settlor's death. This would save on legal fees and probate (the same rationale for using a living trust) and provide greater privacy since the probate of a will in the United States makes it a public record.

As a general rule, the IBC may participate in any lawful activity not restricted by the country of incorporation or the jurisdiction in which it desires to operate. This would include shipping companies, consulting companies, offshore manufacturing, shipping and air transportation companies, and licensing and sublicensing companies.

Some of the more popular IBC jurisdictions are the Bahamas, the British Virgin Islands (where the concept of the IBC was created), the Cayman Islands, the Isle of Man, Panama, the Channel Islands, Hong Kong, and Gibraltar.

Now let's consider some desirable features of the IBC and factors that must be weighed in selecting a location for the formation of the IBC.

IBC Features

As a fundamental proposition, an IBC that essentially runs almost automatically without the U.S. corporate formalities would be most desirable for the following reasons:

1. There is no requirement for a formal annual meeting. All meetings can be informally fulfilled by telecommunications (telephone, E-mail, mail, or fax), by proxy, or even by ratification after the fact.

2. Multiple classes of stock may be issued, and there is an option for bearer or nonbearer stock.

3. It permits a minimal number of directors, preferably only one, who may be a nominee—for example, the APT's trustee. (Compare this with the higher requirement of company formation for Panama—three nominees/directors—in Chapter 15, page 241).

4. There are no limitations or restrictions upon the nationality, citizenship, or residency of its officers, shareholders, or directors.

5. It is not required that the officers or directors also be shareholders.

6. Officers and/or directors may be other entities; for example, a trust, another IBC, an LLC, or a partnership may act as an officer or director when permitted by law. (Again, compare this with Panama.)

7. It is not required to publicly file the names of the directors and officers, as it is in all U.S. jurisdictions.

8. The books of the IBC may be maintained in another jurisdiction.

9. Simplicity of operations and reduction in professional fees saves time.

Tax Regimen

At first blush, a no-tax jurisdiction appears preferable to a low-tax one, but taxes are not the only factor that one must consider. It is essential to have a competent analysis performed of the dual-tax treaty aspects, called *treaty shopping*. (For more on taxes, see Chapter 11.) Select a haven that has no or minimal taxes on the capital account and no corporate income taxes.

Quality of Communications

Time means money, and poor-quality communications can cause delays in transmitting essential instructions. I don't own AT&T stock, so I can say (from personal experience, and without accusations of deriving insider benefits) that I consider AT&T the best for offshore communications. But don't overlook the lower-cost (almost free), more private option of using E-mail over the Internet (using PGP encryption).

Language

Unless you are fully conversant (that is, truly fluent) in another tongue, stick to an English-speaking jurisdiction. Otherwise, you add a level of delay and complexity by requiring certified translations of each document.

Legal System

Unless you are fluent in its language and understand a given country's unique legal system, stick to those using the traditional English common law and the standard form of a company act. It appears that all the English-speaking, British-based jurisdictions are improving upon each other with their own form of a company act (as well as their trust, mutual fund, and LLC acts). Minimal capitalization should be required. The level of company capitalization may affect the cost of the filing fee.

Costs

Low formation costs are not the only factor—consider subsequent annual fees as well. Also, get full disclosure on the costs for day-to-day transactional fees, further services available, the hourly rate, and any other anticipated extraordinary fees or costs. Inquire as to the OS consultant's associates (for example, a chartered accountant or attorney) and their charges. See Figure 6.1 for an example of a typical quote.

Figure 6.1: Typical Costs of Incorporating an IBC

Preparation of the Memorandum of Association	$350.00
Preparation of the Articles of Association	$350.00
Preparation of the Resolution	$250.00
Total cost of incorporating an IBC	$950.00

Other Charges

Corporate seal	$40.00
Government fees	$310.00
Annual registered agent fees	
• Bahamian business address	
• Telephone number	
• Mailing address	$600.00
Subscription fees	$300.00
Assistance with establishing a bank account	
• assistance with completing the necessary bank forms	
• introduction to an offshore bank officer	
• following up to ensure that the bank account is open	$300.00
Total other charges	$1,550.00

Privacy

One of the principal reasons the RA has for going offshore (along with asset protection) is the quest for enhanced privacy. Concerned with the monster computer databases in the U.S. and the apparent ease of eavesdropping on the U.S. banking system and even the Federal Reserve wire transfer network, RAs seek confidentiality and privacy with respect to financial matters by selecting a jurisdiction that has no requirement to file public or private annual returns in the country of incorporation. Our civil justice system can also be emotionally painful to the innocent defendant expending large amounts of money and precious time on defense of frivolous litigation.

Choice of Name Restrictions

A name you prefer or are currently using in the U.S. may not be available offshore. For optimal privacy and asset protection, the name of the offshore company or entity should be different than the one used onshore. In cases where a business name carries goodwill, the benefits of using the same name offshore might outweigh the disadvantages.

I am aware of various restrictions on IBCs using the words *trust*, *insurance*, *assurance*, *trustco*, *bank*, *bancor*, *bancorp* (anything suggesting you are a bank), *sovereign*, *royal*, *imperial*, *financial*, *building society*, *chartered*, *chamber of commerce*, *cooperative*, and *foundation*, to name a few. Other jurisdictions limit names ending with *S.A.*, *Inc.*, *Ltd.*, *Corp.*, and so on. Bermuda defines "restricted business activities" for the IBC and prohibits it from providing financial services where that is defined as:

- Banking
- Deposit taking
- Trust business
- Insurance business
- Custody and administration of securities

In summary, I strongly recommend against incorporating offshore using the same name as your onshore corporation. It ties the two together, destroying the very privacy you wish to achieve by using a common name. The overriding factor is where the goodwill of the name is very significant in the worldwide community.

Monetary Controls

Select a haven that has no or minimal exchange controls, one that affords the ability to transact business in any major world currency.

Applying for Company Formation and Agreement

A typical application to form and manage a basic IBC structure is shown in Figure 6.2. Figure 6.3 is for a more complex personal plan, a three-company structure being offered by some offshore consultants, but is not recommended. It is presented only for your information. The structure of Figure 6.3 consists of three boxes representing an IBC and two OS trusts. Initially, the IBC is formed. The IBC then is the settlor of an OS trust (a foreign self-settled trust) called Trust 1; the IBC is the sole beneficiary (no U.S. beneficiaries) of Trust 1. Trust 1 (must be a foreign grantor trust) is the holder of more than a 50 percent equity position in the IBC. The settlor is taxed on all income of an APT under IRC §679. As owner of the trust, the settlor owns the IBC.

You should not just buy an IBC—you need to have a sense of the selection process. That is, who to contact and where to locate for what you are trying to achieve. Each item is discussed in greater depth throughout the book.

An IBC Comparison Checklist

1. Total out-of-pocket costs for incorporating a turnkey IBC, including all nominees' fees, registrar fees, agent's fees, share certificates and corporate seal, bank account establishment, banking services, remailing services, local presence (if you require), and so on.

2. Subsequent years' costs, including company management and transaction costs.

3. Availability of bearer shares.

4. Requirement to keep books in local jurisdiction.

5. Requirement for local directors.

6. Requirement for local meetings.

7. Public records of directors at company registrar, which is database of registered companies maintained by a government office.

8. Disclosure of beneficial owner(s).

9. Requirement of annual audit.

10. Tax imposed on offshore profits.

11. Company name restrictions.

12. British-based common law legal system.

13. Total privacy of banking information.

14. Total privacy of records at company registrar.

15. Criminal penalties for the disclosure of banking records by bank personnel.

16. Criminal penalties for the disclosure of corporate records at registrar's office.

To illustrate this comparison, let's take a close look at a Bahamian IBC, which some think has major advantages:

1. Only one director is required.

2. A minimum of two subscribers for shares is required, however, these may be bearer shares.

3. A director may be another corporation.

Figure 6.2: Company Formation Application Form

CONFIDENTIAL & PRIVATE
COMPANY FORMATION INFORMATION FORM
The Bahamas

1. Proposed Company Name: (Give first choice and two alternatives)

    (1) _____

    (2) _____

    (3) _____

2. Type of Company:

    ☐ International Business Corporation   ☐ Regular Corporation

3. Capital & Types of Shares:

    Capital: (1) U.S.$5,000 divided into 5,000 shares of U.S.$1.00 each

    (2) Other (Specify)_____

    Shares: ☐ Regular   ☐ Bearer   ☐ Other (Specify)

    _____

4. Shareholders:

    ☐ Nominees to be provided

    ☐ Issued to: (Provide a list, if necessary)

Name	Address	No. of Shares	Type of Shares

5. Beneficial Owners (For Internal Use Only):

Name	Addresses	Percentage of Capital

Figure 6.2: Company Formation Application Form, continued

6. Registered Office in the Bahamas:
   Unless otherwise specified, it will be a nominee. If otherwise, give specific name and address:

   _____

7. Registered Agent in the Bahamas:
   Unless otherwise instructed, this will be a member of a legal firm in the Bahamas.

   _____

8. Directors and Officers:

   ☐ Nominees to be provided   ☐ Other, please supply:

   Name   Address   Position/Officer

   _____

   _____

9. Proposed Trade or Business:

   _____

   _____

10. Special Requirements for Memorandum or Articles of Association (Specify):

    _____

    _____

11. Special Services (opening bank accounts, communications, etc.):

    _____

    _____

12. Other Services (reinvoicing, escrows, etc.):

    _____

    _____

    Signed:_____ Dated:_____

Figure 6.3: Company Information and Agreement Form

COMPANY FORMATION INFORMATION AND AGREEMENT

By this agreement_____ ("Client")

of _____
Street   City   State   Zip

do/does hereby agree to the creation of a company structure consisting of one Bahamian international business company and two Bahamian trusts.

CORPORATE INFORMATION

Name of Corporation: _____(First Choice)

_____(Second Choice)

Name(s) of Director(s):_____

_____

Name(s) of Officer(s): _____(President)

_____(Secretary)

TRUST #1 INFORMATION

Name of Protector: Primary _____ Secondary _____

TRUST #2 INFORMATION

Name of Protector: Primary _____ Secondary _____

Beneficiary of Trust:

Primary Beneficiaries & %: _____

Secondary Beneficiaries & %: _____

BANKING INFORMATION

The Client should be prepared to make an initial bank deposit of U.S.$10,000. In addition, determine which additional banking services you want. Additional services, such as debit cards, may require additional deposits to this or a separate bank account.

☐ MasterCard or VISA debit cards   ☐ Personal   ☐ Corporate

☐ U.S. checkwriting ability   ☐ Securities trading   Other:_____

No representations, warranties, or guarantees are offered or implied that any company or company structure will be successful for any purpose whatsoever. No representations, warranties, or guarantees are offered or implied regarding the tax effects, benefits, or implications involving any company or company structure. All persons are encouraged to seek competent legal and tax counsel in the particular jurisdiction where they reside.

Agreed to by the undersigned this _____ day of _____, [year].

Client_____   Client_____

4. Board of directors' and shareholders' meetings may be conducted by electronic means such as telephone, fax, and E-mail.

5. The IBC may trade in its own shares.

6. The IBC may hold treasury shares.

7. There is no record of the names of the shareholders and directors in the public registry.

8. There is no requirement for filing financial statements or annual tax returns.

9. The government has guaranteed an exemption from taxes for twenty years.

10. No rule against *ultra vires* activities. The IBC may be established for any purpose not prohibited by Bahamian laws.

11. The IBC may transfer its domicile, and conversely, an existing offshore (foreign) IBC may transfer to the Bahamas.

12. No prohibition concerning transferring assets to a trust.

13. Registration and annual governmental fees are considered low.

14. The IBC may act as a guarantor of third-party obligations.

15. The IBC is not subject to Bahamian exchange control legislation.

16. A foreign government may not nationalize the shares of a Bahamian IBC.

17. A foreign government may not seize the shares of the IBC to satisfy a tax claim arising in the foreign country.

Bahamas does limit the IBC from the following activities:

1. Cannot carry on business with residents of the Bahamas.

2. Cannot own an interest in Bahamian real property other than leased office space.

3. Cannot carry on a bank or trust business.

4. Cannot carry on an insurance or re-insurance business.

5. Cannot carry out the business of providing the registered office for companies in the Bahamas.

Other Forms of Companies

Although our major emphasis in this chapter is on the international business company, other forms of offshore companies are also available. These include:

1. Local companies (the traditional corporation)

2. Exempt companies (see the jurisdictions using the Channel Islands model for further details)

3. Special companies

   • Local banking, with deposit-taking privileges
   • Insurance
   • Mutual funds
   • Ship ownership
   • Investment management

These types of companies are discussed throughout the book.

Endnotes

1 IRS Revenue Ruling 69-70 provides that a foreign trust may make certain types of gifts to an American recipient without the recipient being taxed.

7

The Offshore Asset Protection Trust

When I go into any business deal, my chief thoughts are on how I'm going to save myself if things go wrong.

J. Paul Getty

In the offshore community, the buzzword for the next millennium is APT. APTs, when properly conceived, designed, and implemented, can be reasonably expected to create far better asset defense and wealth preservation than the absence of planning.

The current OS or foreign asset protection trust (APT or FAPT) is a sophisticated, modern mutation of the basic trust established principally for a specific purpose—asset protection. A basic trust is defined as a legal structure in which title to and right of possession of property (the trust "corpus") is in the hands of a trustee. The trust is established by the settlor, creator, or grantor. (I prefer the terms *grantor* and *settlor* and use them synonymously[1] in this book. *Creator* is a term unique in the U.S. lexicography and is used in the areas of pure trusts and business trusts.) Surprisingly, *you* need not be the grantor—some other entity or person may create a trust on behalf of your beneficiaries. This is commonly known as a *nongrantor trust*. The person or entity creating the trust and transferring assets to the APT by way of a testamentary disposition or gift is the settlor.

With a *discretionary* APT, the trustee has been granted a power, the discretion as to whom from the identified schedule of beneficiaries distributions will be made. Distribution may be made from principal, income, or both. This discretionary power creates the needed element of asset protection. The trustee may be guided only with a mission or purpose for the trust, hence we get the term "purpose trust."

If the settlor of the foreign APT is a nonresident alien (NRA), if it is sited offshore, and if the assets are owned offshore, it will be characterized as a foreign nongrantor trust under the IRC. This characterization is true even if one or more of the beneficiaries include U.S. persons.

The trustee has the right to manage, hold, and use the asset, and the duty to protect it on behalf of the beneficiary. A commercial trustee is usually required to be licensed by the jurisdiction. The trustee has a fiduciary obligation to deal with the trust assets fairly on behalf of the beneficiaries. A trust is a legal entity, having the ability to deal with banks in its own name and being required to file a trust tax return with the IRS and with the states in which it does business or has a nexus. It is an extremely flexible structure and may serve many functions, so long as they are not specifically prohibited by statute or law and are not in contravention of public policy. (Public policy varies from country to country. Ask your counsel about specific prohibitions of trusts in your jurisdiction.) Some of the powers of a trust (acting through its trustee) are:

- Taking title to or acquiring an interest in real property for any lawful purpose
- Managing the real property owned by the trust
- Taking title to or acquiring personal property, such as cash, stocks, bonds, art, antiques, businesses, promissory notes, and other negotiable instruments
- Managing the business interests of the trust
- Providing better spendthrift provisions than are generally provided under U.S. laws
- Acting as a substitute for probate or a tool to avoid probate

- Providing the offshore role of a trust protector for better trust administration. A second trust may act as a trust protector instead of using an individual. Some trusts use corporate trust protectors.
- Use in lieu of a prenuptial agreement. I have seen instances where a party transfers some of the separate property into an offshore blind trust before marriage. The trust manages the assets independently from the transferor. This prevents the separate property from becoming marital property subject to a divorce settlement.

The trustee, as a fiduciary to the beneficiaries, has certain duties of professional competence:

- The trustee must validly settle (create) the trust.
- The trustee must act as a reasonable, prudent businessperson under any circumstances. He or she should know the nature and consequences of any trust transaction. The trustee must be properly equipped and qualified. If not, the trustee could be deemed negligent and held liable for losses to the trust.
- The trustee must take control over the trust assets from the settlor. Failure to do so could result in the trust being deemed a sham transaction. (How could there be a functional trust if the trustee does not have title to the trust assets?)

The offshore trust may not have been created for the primary purpose of hindering, delaying, or frustrating existing creditors or claimants of the settlor, but it may be implemented to achieve estate planning. You can't legally relocate your assets offshore to dodge collection on a judgment or avoid a lawsuit. Many trustees require an affidavit or declaration of solvency of the settlor to that effect (see Figure 7.1).

Where there is more than one trustee, such as one U.S. and one foreign trustee, certain tax issues may arise upon the resignation of the U.S. trustee. The IRC says a domestic trust, upon the resignation of the U.S. trustee, converts into a foreign trust, and that is a taxable event.

It is no longer the same trust, and the settlor may have a transfer that is subject to fraudulent conveyance rules. This may encourage a domestic judge to impose contempt penalties and force the money back to the United States. (See the Anderson case on page 93.)

The U.S. Living Trust

Most readers are aware of the attributes of the *living trust*, a variation of the revocable *inter vivos trust*, but let's review its features:

- No tax advantages to the settlor or the estate.
- No asset protection.
- Revocable by the settlor until death. (This defeats its efficacy as an asset protection tool since, during the lifetime of the settlor, a court can order the settlor to revoke the living trust under a threat of contempt of court.)
- Settlor can be a trustee of the trust. (Although it's permitted, I believe this should *never* be done for the APT.)
- Can provide for your possible future disabilities and avoid a costly conservatorship hearing in court and avoid the "public" conservator being appointed to manage the corpus of the trust.
- Created and effective while you are alive, but not effective upon your death.
- The beneficiaries are "residual" beneficiaries—they take what is left after the death of the settlor.
- The trustee has no duty to the creditors of the grantor, as would the executor of your will.

The Evolution of the Trust

Legal historians report that within an Egyptian tomb, vestiges of a last will and testament dating to 1805 B.C. were discovered. Trusts

---

Figure 7.1: Declaration or Affidavit of Solvency

1. At the time of the transfer, you are not insolvent, nor would transfers to the trust make you insolvent. You are able to meet your debt obligations and discharge your liabilities.

2. You are not named as a defendant (cross-defendant) in any legal action, in a divorce or family law matter, or in any administrative proceeding.

3. You are not using the APT to try to avoid any federal or state tax obligation.

4. The assets being transferred are not more than_____ percent (settlor to insert an appropriate percentage here) of your total assets.

5. The assets being transferred do not have as their origin any criminal activities under the laws of any country through which the assets passed, are not the product of or in violation of the bankruptcy laws of any connected country, do not violate the FDIC and RTC rules, are not the product of any fraud, drug trafficking, espionage, RICO violations, counterfeiting, kidnapping, hostage taking, or smuggling, and are not in anticipation of an action for environmental pollution or copyright, patent, or trademark violations. [*Author's comment:* In other words, it is "clean" or "white money."]

Date:_____   Signature of settlor:_____

---

were also used under Greek and Roman law. It is reported that the trust was so popular during the reign of Augustus Caesar that Rome had a trust court. Trust concepts continued to evolve under Islamic, German, and French laws, but the roots of primary interest to us derive from the English common law. The law of trusts has been established since the Statute of Uses was adopted in England.

The basis of American law is the English common law. With respect to offshore trusts, since we are going offshore, an understanding of the law of trusts is essential. However, U.S. judges tend to interpret OS trusts under U.S. laws. I encourage you to study the Anderson case (see p. 93) to understand current judicial thinking.

The offshore islands of Western Europe (such as the Channel Islands) were among the first used for offshore trusts. To attract this type of business, they provided some of the following desirable characteristics:

- No taxes or low taxes
- Tax exemptions
- No tax status
- Simpler regulatory requirements than the mainland
- Active financial centers capable of providing the needed services

Although the APT has its roots in the English common law, it is not being taught in U.S. law schools and is generally learned from attending special postgraduate seminars. The concept of going offshore for business is glamorous, romantic, and, from a practical standpoint, quite necessary for survival. Because of the globalization of institutions, I foresee a world soon to be managed (or very heavily influenced) by the multinational conglomerate more than by the professional diplomat. World economics and individual needs break down and transcend Berlin walls, Iron Curtains, and artificial political barriers. The world leaders of the future will be the heads of major multinational conglomerates. Will this global change be part of the "new world order"?

Perhaps what most precipitated the growth of the use of APTs in the U.S. is an exponential growth in litigation: you don't talk it over anymore, you sue! Every day we read about the runaway jury awards for hot coffee spills, teachers getting sued for giving a student a C in mathematics, allegations of sexual harassment, recovered memories, New York City being sued by a firefighter for $5 million for a flea bite, a landlord assessed $1 million in damages, and on and on. This environment of frivolous litigation feeds upon itself and creates more and more copycat litigation, or even more "creative" litigation. When will *you* be sued? I didn't say *if*, but *when*. It may be only a matter of time. State Farm Mutual Automobile Insurance Company paid out $58.7 million for dog bite cases in 1994. One runaway jury returning a catastrophic judgment against you can wipe out your life's savings. Only the state and federal government can stop it by placing caps on the levels of the jury awards. I don't expect to see legislators (many of whom are attorneys) being able to do very much to protect defendants in the near future; *you must protect yourself*. As one attorney was reported to have said, "If people did to me what I do to them every day, I would be offshore with my assets."

The APT doesn't differ in many aspects from the traditional trust, except that it is traditionally offshore and irrevocable. The recognized purpose of such a trust is to be able to transfer assets out of reach of creditors! However, the same litigious environment that encourages use of the APT may also create a higher risk of litigation because of your use of the APT. There still is a mentality that if you have an offshore APT you must be "guilty" and hiding something in the Caymans.

As a general proposition, your expectation should be that the APT is a vehicle for protecting your assets by holding them offshore; you should not assume that it is a guaranteed method for protecting assets in our litigious society. To avoid allegations of fraud with respect to current creditors or claimants, you must be solvent at the time you transfer the assets to the APT. I would conservatively measure solvency by two different tests, both of which you should meet.

1. **Bookkeeping test.** The value of your assets should exceed the level of your liabilities. For valuation purposes, assets are valued at liquidation values (FMV), *exempt assets are excluded*, and all contingent debts must be included. Assets to be transferred to the APT are excluded.

2. **Bankruptcy insolvency test.** You must have the ability to pay your debts as they mature. Many offshore trustees require an affidavit or declaration of solvency to that effect (see Figure 7.1).

The asset protection trust is not necessarily used for tax considerations and privacy. It is used primarily for what the name suggests: protecting one's assets.

Who Needs an APT?

Some time back, the Oxford Club defined some guidelines for determining asset protection need. Following is a paraphrased version of

their list. If you say yes to two or three questions, you might need
an APT.

- Are you in a profession with a high risk of litigation,
  such as physician/surgeon, manufacturer, commercial
  architect, or CPA? You know who you are by what is
  happening to your peers.
- Do you have a net equity of more than $500,000 free
  and clear in your residence?
- Do you have liquid personal property or assets with a
  value of more than $500,000?
- Are you a general partner in a real estate or other
  high-risk partnership?
- Are you an officer or director of a U.S. corporation?
- Are you a high net worth person contemplating
  marriage or remarriage?
- Do you have a teenager with a heavy foot on the gas
  pedal?
- Do you have a high financial profile or perception of
  high net worth that would attract litigation?
- Do you lease out equipment or rent out commercial
  property, or are you an apartment owner?
- Have you been underinsured or uninsured for a period
  of time?

Some of the major reasons to consider a discretionary offshore
APT:

- It responds to your reasonable suggestions (through
  "letters of wishes") while you are still alive and have your
  full faculties. (Of course, this would be with the consent of
  the committee of advisors and/or trust protector.)
- It provides for testamentary distributions offshore as
  an alternative to U.S. trusts. It generally insulates your
  provisions for future protection of your family after
  your death. It can pass assets on to your beneficiaries.
  It could reduce or avoid probate costs and may save on
  estate taxes.

- It enables asset managers or trustees to take positions in investment opportunities not available to U.S. citizens. There is a virtually unlimited worldwide marketplace in which to invest.
- It is a substitute for or supplement to a U.S. living trust.
- It provides privacy—assets are not part of the U.S. banking or reporting system.
- It can discourage litigation (which may need to be offshore in a pro-settlor environment) and encourage earlier and less expensive settlements.
- It gives you an onshore advantage in negotiating claims against you.
- Coupled with insurance, it can be a powerful estate planning device.
- It can provide for your children's and grandchildren's education.
- It can be structured to provide tax deferral and tax avoidance and minimize current tax liability.
- It provides private retirement income in anticipation of the demise of the Social Security system.

To protect assets, they must be *custodied* or *custodialized* (entrusted to a person who has possession of an asset and authority to manage it) offshore. For APTs, all of the trusts' assets must be either transferred outside of the U.S. or invisible to any U.S. asset search. If the assets are in the U.S.—even if owned by an offshore entity—and if the U.S. court can link them to you, the court can find a way to assert jurisdiction over the assets. Even if some doubt exists in the mind of the judge, he or she could still tie up the assets with a temporary restraining order or a Mareva injunctive order[2] until the issue is ultimately resolved or you give up. Or a judge can issue an order that requires you to return assets to the U.S., and incarcerate you until it is done. And you thought there was no debtor's prison in the U.S. (see p. 93 for a discussion of the Anderson case.)

Although known by different titles in different jurisdictions (family settlement trust, family protective trust, trust deed, and trust indenture), all APTs essentially serve the same purpose, and I treat them collectively in this book as APTs.

The Parties to the APT

The parties to the APT are the same parties as in the basic trust (except for the trust protector and the agent).

1. The **creator, settlor, or grantor** is the person who created or settled the APT. (The word "person" as used in this book refers to an individual [including a third party or "straw man"], business, company, partnership, corporation, IBC, LLC, or any other entity with legal standing recognized in the jurisdiction of its creation. A sole proprietorship is not a person, as it "speaks" through its owner.) I prefer the term *settlor*. I believe that the settlor should not have the right to directly replace the trustee. The settlor could encourage the trustee to resign by expressing his or her dissatisfaction with the way in which the trust corpus is being managed in a private letter of wishes. If a reasonable trustee could not remedy the concerns, I believe that he or she would likely cooperate and resign. He or she doesn't need or want adversarial scenarios with the settlor. The trust protector then could appoint a substitute trustee. Or there could be a previously appointed "standby trustee" waiting in the wings to take over the role. Others appoint three joint trustees at the onset so that the resignation or temporary absence of a trustee does not create a problem.

Trust language may not provide binding advice to the trustee and trust protector, but advisory language instead. It can come from the settlor or the committee of advisors. A settlor who desires to provide an indication of his or her inclinations traditionally delivers a letter of wishes to the trustee. Communications by letters of wishes may be an ongoing process with a discretionary APT as circumstances change (a birth, death, wedding, divorce, or separation; a provision for a person with disabilities; education and health care for beneficiaries; changes in the U.S. tax laws or dual-tax treaties). The settlor is already deemed to be the owner of the IBC under the IRS attribution rules. All income earned by the IBC, whether distributed or not, is taxable to the settlor as the owner. The settlor is deemed to be the shareholder of the CFC.

The settlor may perform indirectly by acting as director or officer of an offshore IBC that was created for the purpose of managing the assets of the trust. He or she could receive compensation, deferred compensation, perks, or expense reimbursement, some of which would be taxable upon receipt by a U.S. person.

2. The **trust protector**, the watchdog over the trust, oversees the trustee and the trust corpus to assure that the trustee fulfills the objectives of the APT. There may be more than one protector. The protector's duties include providing legally binding counsel and advice to the trustee on interpretation of the trust deed, construing the settlor's letter(s) of wishes, and deciding upon the appropriate action after receiving advice from the committee of advisors (if one was authorized and in effect). The protector is not a trustee and does not manage the APT, but is an advisor to the trustee. The trustee recognizes the veto power of the protector. In an efficient APT, there is an ongoing dialogue between the two parties, both attempting to fulfill the wishes of the settlor with concern for treating all beneficiaries fairly and equitably under the terms of the APT.

3. The **trustee** is charged with the duty of capital conservation and income accumulation for the beneficiaries. It is generally recommended that the trustee not be a U.S. resident or citizen. Ideally, the trustee should be a U.S. nonresident alien. This precludes the U.S. courts from issuing court orders to the trustee. In larger estates (with a larger corpus) there could be multiple trustees, all with trust powers, and even a U.S. trustee among the group of joint trustees. Use of a U.S. trustee should be carefully researched by the service provider or personal planner because there may be express prohibitions in the tax haven. Many offshore trust companies may not want a U.S.-based trustee. Some APT legislation specifically prohibits U.S. trustees. Furthermore, the Statute of Elizabeth (see p. 87) override provisions may not apply with a U.S. cotrustee. If an APT with a U.S. cotrustee were under attack within the U.S., the U.S. trustee should resign. The trustee is usually given full discretion with respect to treatment of the beneficiaries and asset disposition with

the consent of the trust protector. Choose someone you know to be the trustee, or let your consultant or planner (if trusted absolutely) choose the trustee.

4. **Beneficiaries** could include a family foundation, a favorite charity, or children born or unborn of the marriage(s) or future marriage(s) of the settlor. A discretionary trust with full powers in the trustee grants the trustee the right to add new beneficiaries and substitute assets of equivalent value. Although the beneficiaries can request distributions, the distributions are at the sole discretion of the trustee and his or her interpretation of the trust.

The beneficiaries should not generally include the settlor. (Note that some lawyers believe that if an APT is truly discretionary, the settlor can be a beneficiary.) If the settlor is a beneficiary, there is little asset protection. However, it could serve alternatively as an offshore living trust or testamentary trust.

5. Behind-the-scenes **service providers and offshore consultants** may be known only to you, for your privacy. They know the U.S. and offshore technicalities and APT requirements. Further, they have the ingenuity to formulate a structure that won't become obsolete and fully takes into account your personal situation and present and future needs. You may wish to pay by cashier's check to avoid having a permanent banking electronic record of a check drawn on your personal or business checking account.

6. Is the **asset or portfolio manager** for the trust's assets given full discretion as to investment decisions? If not, is there a committee of advisors to guide him or her?

7. A **committee of advisors** to the trustee is optional. When one is established, the settlor can be its chair. The committee's opinion is not binding upon the trustee and is treated as advisory. It is not legally incumbent that the trustee honor the advice of the committee because the trustee must act in the best interests of the beneficiaries.

8. The Small Business Job Protection Act of 1996 established an IRS reporting requirement and party to the trust, the **agent** for the foreign trust. Since a foreign trust is now required to provide

annual reports to the IRS about the trust's income and assets, the trust is required to appoint someone (usually the grantor) to serve as an agent to whom the IRS can send legal notices and questions. See Figure 7.2 as a typical appointment form.

The APT is very private; it is generally not filed, registered, or recorded. (But some jurisdictions do require the filing of an APT, sometimes because they want to collect filing fees.) There is no general requirement to register it with any regulatory body. Some jurisdictions, however, require that a trust duty be paid and even affix a stamp to the trust, but it has no local reporting requirements. Treat the APT as an unrecorded, written contract among persons. When sited in a tax-free jurisdiction, there are no local tax filing forms, reports, or other requirements. Of course, if the trustee is served with a valid court order from the local jurisdiction, he or she is compelled to disclose the content of the trust deed and the assets of the trust.

A Trust with a Dual Nationality

How may an advisor effectively structure a trust domiciled in a foreign country so that it would be considered a domestic trust for U.S. tax purposes? Some of the international trust lawyers are initially creating the trust with two U.S. trustees and one foreign trustee. The trust deed then includes a provision that upon the resignation of the two U.S. trustees, the trust would cease to be domestic, and the trust would become a foreign trust for U.S. tax purposes. When the domestic trust becomes a foreign trust there may be a taxable event, specifically a capital gains tax.

Costs

The APT and its companion entities comprising your offshore plan are complex to formulate. You must select a professional (or even multiple professionals) to assist you, and you must be willing to pay

Figure 7.2

AUTHORIZATION OF AGENT

_____PRUDENCE TRUST_____ hereby expressly authorizes
_{Name of Foreign Trust}
_____WILLIAM B GRANT_____ to act as its agent solely for purposes of
_{Name of U.S. Agent}
section 7602, 7603, and 7604 of the Internal Revenue Code with respect to any request
to examine records or produce testimony related to the proper treatment of amounts
required to be taken into account under the rules of section 6048(b)(1)(A) or to any
summons for such records or testimony. I certify that I have the authority to
execute this authorization of agent to act on behalf of _____PRUDENCE TRUST_____.
_{Name of Foreign Trust}

_____William B. Grant_____ _____Agent_____ _____2/1/98_____
_{Signature of trustee (or other authorized person)} _{Title} _{Date}

Type or print your name below

_____WILLIAM B GRANT_____ _____123-45-6789_____
_{TIN (if any)}

_____123 MAIN STREET_____
_{Address}

_____GRANOLA, CA   91234_____

_____WILLIAM B GRANT_____ accepts this appointment to act as agent for
_{Name of Agent}
_____PRUDENCE TRUST_____ for the above purpose. I certify that I have
_{Name of Foreign Trust}
the authority to execute this authorization of agent to act on behalf of _____PRUDENCE TRUST_____
_{Name of Foreign Trust}
_____ and agree to accept service of process for the above purposes.

_____William B. Grant_____ _____Agent_____ _____2/1/98_____
_{Signature of agent} _{Title} _{Date}

Type or print your name below

_____WILLIAM B GRANT_____ _____123-45-6789_____
_{TIN (if any)}

_____123 MAIN STREET_____
_{Address}

_____GRANOLA, CA 91234_____

reasonable fees. Don't forget the cost of maintenance services and
annual reporting dictated by the IRC in the subsequent years.

Reasonable fees for setting up an APT are divided between
onshore and offshore and between the first-year setup costs and subsequent annual fees. Setting up your offshore structure properly will

not be inexpensive. But consider the extrinsic benefits. The larger the estate going offshore, the more cost effective going offshore becomes. The question is, How much will ultimately go into the structure? Measure costs in terms of value added as well as the subjective benefits—you *can* get ripped off.

Some typical ranges of offshore fees you may encounter for an APT are:

- First-year acceptance fee of $1,000 to $5,000 for setting up the trust
- Annual trustee's fees of $1,500 to $3,000, in addition to the setup fees

What should you get for your money?

- A professional acting in the capacity of trustee for the year.
- A brokerage account opened for investing by the trustee or asset manager on behalf of the trust, if required.
- A trust bank account opened.
- Extraordinary services charged at a flat rate negotiated with the trustee or at an hourly rate of $100 to $300.
- Out-of-pocket expenses—for example, air courier, private telephone lines, E-mail accounts, banking fees, or wire transfer fees.

Trust Terminology

This section of this chapter offers some legal and technical discussion.

The Rule Against Perpetuities (−)

In English common law jurisdictions, equity abhors the vesting and distribution to the beneficiaries that are too distant in time. Os tax havens have adopted longer and therefore more favorable rules with respect to remote vesting than those found domestically (+). For example, Bermuda, the British Virgin Islands (BVI), and the Isle of Man have the purpose trust or "dynastic" settlements, avoiding the rule against perpetuities. This rule traditionally requires the vesting period to be generally not later than "lives in being plus twenty-one years." To increase their attractiveness as tax havens, some jurisdictions have extended this period.

BVI now allows income accumulation by the trustee of the APT for any period up to 100 years (+). BVI has also abolished the concept that the trust is void if any beneficial vesting could occur beyond the 100-year vesting period. In addition, BVI has adopted a wait-and-see policy with respect to future beneficiaries. Because of these innovations and a lack of full trust legislation, some trust scholars in the offshore community are uncomfortable with BVI as an APT situs. I, however, have referred clients there, and I am still comfortable with the decisions.

Rights of Settlement

Basically, the law of the trust governs. Any prohibitions against certain transfers at the settlor's domicile are inoperative with respect to the trust. The rules of inheritance and/or succession of the settlor's domicile do *not* govern the offshore APT and the assets transferred into the trust. The situs remains the county in which it is located. Can a U.S. judge disregard the fact that it is owned by an offshore trust? The answer is yes, and that is why real property is the most difficult asset to protect. I refer you again to the discussion of equity stripping in Chapter 10 (page 144).

Classes of Creditors

Fraudulent transfer is the transfer of an asset intended to frustrate, hinder, or delay the ability of a creditor to collect a judgment. Alleged fraud (fraudulent transfer) with respect to a creditor or claimant falls into one of three classes based on *when* the asset transfer occurred. These three classes are unique to the area of fraudulent transfers:

1. Present

2. Subsequent

3. Future

Item 3, future creditors, is the most difficult to address. The statutory laws of the tax haven determine the prescribed treatment for future creditors. Get professional help with this blurred issue. For example, what is the difference between a subsequent and future creditor? A tough issue to put in black and white.

Some tax havens have recognized the different classes of creditors: Bahamas, Bermuda, Cayman Islands, Cook Islands, Cyprus, Gibraltar, Mauritius, Nevis, and Turks and Caicos Islands.

The Statute of Elizabeth

In 1570, the English common law jurisdictions began to contend with the restrictions imposed by the Statute of Elizabeth, which was intended to defeat and set aside transfers of assets and property where the transferor's intended purpose was to frustrate, hinder, or delay *future* but *unknown* creditors or claimants.[3] Tax havens that are more favorably inclined to trust business have enacted legislation with provisions to override the Statute of Elizabeth. An old English case[4] started the confusion by blurring the distinction between subsequent and future creditors, establishing the principle that there was no difference between the two. The override statutes of the more progressive tax havens remedy this problem. Clearly an immediate but subsequent creditor should be treated differently than a distant future creditor.

The following tax havens are known to have enacted override provisions (+): Bahamas, Belize, Cayman Islands, Cook Islands, Gibraltar, Mauritius, and Nevis.

Forced Heirship

As a settlor, you cannot deprive the heirs to your estate (your wealth and assets) of their rights according to local law (the state in which you reside), except where just circumstances may exist to disinherit them. Local laws may require you to pass certain percentages of your estate to certain heirs; check with local counsel. For example, you can't bequeath or devise your spouse's community property interest in the community (the assets owned by the spouses). The APT circumvents the forced heirship laws of your local jurisdiction (+).

Choice of Law

The jurisdiction's laws govern the APT. The trust deed should unequivocally state that the trust is to be governed exclusively by offshore laws. The trust records should be maintained there or with the OS trustee, usually in the same jurisdiction.

Even though the trust deed may specify that the laws of a certain jurisdiction may govern the APT, there should be some nexus with that jurisdiction. Where there are no contacts with the specified jurisdiction, problems may arise. At a late date, the court of the relevant jurisdiction may not believe it could carry out its equitable jurisdiction, and the APT may not be recognized by the jurisdiction. Choice of law should have a basis in the local precedent of the jurisdiction and general principles under international law.

Clearly, the following contacts should make for a sufficient nexus with the jurisdiction:

- A local trustee
- A local grantor
- Investment activity controlled locally
- Local meeting between the trustee and trust protector

In Rem Jurisdiction

When the assets are physically located in the United States (for example, real property), the local (U.S.) court has jurisdiction over the property. The mere fact that the title of the real property is in the name of an offshore trustee does not negate the power of the U.S. court to affect the property. If the trustee objects to the court's proposed action, he or she is free to appear in the U.S. to object. Unfortunately, once the trustee appears, the court then has jurisdiction over the trustee as well as the property.

What if the OS trustee is delivered a demand letter from a U.S. attorney, perhaps even one that includes a copy of a valid and enforceable U.S. court order with respect to the settlor? The trustee may ignore it (and usually does), because the foreign jurisdiction has no standing in the tax haven. The U.S. attorney is left with a difficult financial judgment call: Does he or she retain local counsel in the tax haven and file a new suit? If the statute has already "run," the attorney may be unable to effectively file. Does this give him or her the impetus to convince the judgment creditor to settle the matter?

Assuming you have a bulldog for counsel, a highly emotional plaintiff, and a "let's sue the bastards" attitude, what do you do? You exhaust them emotionally and financially bankrupt them to a point where they will settle with you. How? By using duress provisions, flight provisions, recandle provisions, "ransom" clauses, letters of wishes, and the "Cuba" clause, to name a few.

Actionable Fraud and the Badges of Fraud

The APT and the settlor may be attacked on the basis of transfers of assets made to the APT under circumstances alleged to be fraudulent. Fraud is considered under three different bodies of law:

1. The state's laws

2. The bankruptcy code

3. The offshore fraud laws of the applicable jurisdiction

The factual situation on the day of the transfer of the asset is to be considered. Was there an actual intent on the part of the settlor to hinder, defraud, and delay the creditor by the asset transfer? Is there a *cloud of fraudulent conveyances*? Was the fraud hard or soft? *Hard fraud* is defined as a finding that the settlor actually intended to hinder, defraud, and delay the creditor, whereas *soft fraud* is a constructive fraud ascertained by the facts. For example, soft fraud could occur if you rely on facts provided by others that turn out to be fraudulent assertions.

The so-called *badges of fraud* are also referred to as the *eleven commandments* and the *indicia of fraud*. In nonlegalese, they are summarized as follows:

1. The settlor made a transfer of an asset before the APT was created to an insider such as a family member, friend, close professional, or employee.

2. The settlor continued to assert control over the asset or retained possession of the "transferred" asset.

3. The settlor made the transfer to remove the asset from his or her estate or to conceal its existence.

4. The settlor failed to receive "fair" consideration for the transferred asset. It must be an equitable exchange or it fails the "smell test."

5. The transferred asset was concealed from the creditor.

6. The transfer was made while the settlor was being threatened with litigation or after actually being sued.

7. The settlor transferred almost all of his or her assets to the trust.

8. The settlor was insolvent or became insolvent at the time of the transfer or shortly thereafter.

9. The settlor had absconded.

10. The transfer was made just before or after the settlor accrued new debt.

11. The settlor transferred all of his or her business assets to a secured creditor, who in turn transferred them to an insider of the settlor.

How many badges of fraud give rise to a fraudulent conveyance? If they are major, only one or two are necessary.

Duress Provisions

Your well-drafted trust deed and/or letter of wishes provides direction and guidance to the trustee and protector. The condition of *duress* arises when a U.S. demand is made by a third party upon the OS trustee. The duress could be that of serving the OS trustee with a copy of a U.S. court order, or as little as a letter representing a claim against the OS trust from a U.S. attorney. A higher degree of duress is present if a copy of a U.S. court order is served upon the trustee or, even worse, served upon the trustee while he or she is in the U.S. In the latter case, the U.S. court has jurisdiction over the trustee and the trust. We will ignore this unfortunate case and stick to the legal obligations of an OS trustee (or trust protector) to "foreign" demands or court orders.

Basic trust language and the side letter provide sufficient guidance to the trustee to automatically ignore any "foreign inquiry, demand, or court order" creating a situation of duress. Some writers refer to this wryly as a *ransom clause*. Simply stated, the trustee and protector are bound and/or advised to disregard any demand for funds from any entity, including the settlor, in an environment of duress.

As a typical scenario, at the first sign of a creditor or claimant problem, the protector could direct the trustee to move the trust's assets to another jurisdiction—even Liechtenstein has been used by some. The trust is also rekindled (moved and sited) in another jurisdiction other than where the assets are located.

Settlor in Contempt of Court

Once the settlor has irrevocably transferred assets to the APT, he or she has voluntarily yielded control over the assets. Is the voluntary disposition of assets by a settlor with knowledge of the possibility of future claims against him an act of contempt?

One example of a condition of duress would be the settlor writing a letter to the trustee as shown in Figure 7.3.

What does the trustee do? With the appropriate clauses and language previously and unequivocally drafted in the trust deed and

---

Figure 7.3: Condition of Duress Sample Letter

Date

Name
Business
Address

Re: The Smith Family Protective Trust

Dear Trustee:

Unfortunately, as a result of frivolous litigation and a runaway jury verdict, there was a large judgment entered against me in the Superior Court in California on February 1, 1999, on behalf of an undeserving litigant.

The appeal failed and the judgment has become final. The judgment creditor is seeking to collect on the judgment. I have been served with the attached court order. My attorney advises me that it is a valid court order and I must comply with it. It orders me to repatriate my assets and direct you to return funds in the amount of U.S.$1,000,000 to satisfy the judgment. I have been ordered to satisfy this judgment with the assets offshore that are of a sufficient sum to do so.

I have no interest in being held in contempt of court with respect to this order and hereby direct you to liquidate any and all assets of the referenced trust to comply with this bona fide court order.

Your immediate and prompt attention to this order would be appreciated. Please advise when the funds will be wire transferred.

Sincerely yours,

[signature]

---

the letter(s) of wishes, nothing. Or even more to the point, what authority does a foreign person or court have in the APT's jurisdiction or situs? Answer: None. Are you going to be found in contempt? In the prior edition of this book, I had written "Not likely, as you have done all you can do; you provided immediate and unequivocal instructions to the trustee. If the trustee fails to act, it will be his or her judgment call. You did not obstruct the enforcement of the order." I no longer feel comfortable making that unequivocal statement.

In mid-1999, a chilling decision was affirmed on appeal to the Federal 9th Circuit. Although not binding upon the other Federal Circuits, it will have great persuasive influence on other judges throughout the U.S. Examine the facts in what is referred to as the Anderson case. A federal judge in the Las Vegas, Nevada, courts jailed a couple (the Andersons) for failing to pull $1.3 million from an offshore trust they had established. The trust was created about two years before their wrongful conduct. The couple operated a San Diego company that sold investments for the Sterling Group, a Las Vegas company facing allegations of a $50 million fraud. The couple claims they weren't aware the Sterling Group was cheating investors. They were ordered by the court to repatriate assets from offshore but instead they notified the OS trustee that they were under duress and should be removed as cotrustees. To add to the complexity, they were also protectors of their own OS trust.

The judge complained that the couple had for weeks failed to return an estimated $1.3 million from a trust in the Cook Islands. The judge ordered the couple jailed until the Cook Islands trust sent the money back to the United States. A provision in the trust agreement removed the couple as trustees automatically (duress clause) when they notified the trust that they needed the funds because of the FTC suit. FTC attorneys have argued that the couple didn't need to mention the FTC and did so to trigger the clause that disqualified them as trustees. The couple remained on as the trust protectors of the trust and used those positions to appoint replacement trustees overseas. The judge accepted the FTC argument that the couple controlled the offshore trust funds. The judge said he would release the couple from jail when they recovered the money. The judge criticized the couple's attorney for both allowing the couple to name foreigners as replacement trustees without his prior approval and failing to get prior commitments that the new trustees would return the funds.

The Andersons were held in contempt of court for failing to repatriate assets (the funds) from their offshore trust and jailed. The judge in this case remarked that there is nothing wrong with "immunizing" oneself (nexus of time test) but the facts here were egregious abuses of the asset protection system. So abusive that the judge considered referral of the matter to the Attorney General or to the FBI for possible perjury and suggested that the Andersons' bankruptcy attorney could be sued. This case is an example of much being done wrong, by the Andersons and by the judge.

Upon appeal, the contempt was upheld because the Andersons frustrated the orderly administration of the courts. A new concept!

If you would like to read more about the Anderson case, go to Jay Adkisson's website at http://www.falc.com.

Three cases from the bankruptcy courts are must-read cases. Bankruptcy judges are attacking transfers to offshore APTs as being transfers that "violate the public policy" of the state in which the creator was domiciled. The three important cases you can read in the law library are:

- Portnoy, cite: 201 B.R. 685 (1996) (Translation: Portnoy is the common case name, 201 refers to volume 201, B.R. means Bankruptcy Reporter, 685 is the starting page, and 1996 is the date the case was decided.)
- Brooks, cite: 217 B.R. 98 (1998)
- Lawrence, cite: 227 B.R. 907 (1998) and its progeny

Flight Provisions: The Fleet Clause or the Cuba Clause

One could provide for political instability, major changes in APT or IBC laws (very unlikely), or onshore duress with *automatic migration* or *discretionary flight* language. The language providing for these events is sometimes referred to as *fleet* or *migration for duress* or the *Cuba clause* for political instability causes. Flight results from one or two of these specified events:

1. Major changes in the political environment of the tax haven affecting banking laws, privacy, the APT, or the IBC, resulting in the trust being relocated or recandled in another IFC—typically, a coup, revolution, major change in political parties, anticipated changes to treatment of offshore parties, or severe currency controls.

2. The occurrence of a condition of duress, the trustee and/or trust protector resigning, and a standby trustee and/or trust protector in another jurisdiction assuming those duties.

For asset protection, many professionals are drafting APTs that are designed to be considered U.S. trusts but migrate offshore when events demand. Automatic migration clauses are likely to make the IRS consider the APT a foreign trust. The migration causes serious U.S. tax ramifications but some people believe it is still justified.

A principal test for determination of whether an APT is domestic or foreign hinges on the automatic migration provisions in the trust deed. A U.S. court is not considered to have primary supervision over the administration of the trust if the trust instrument provides that a U.S. court's attempt to assert jurisdiction or otherwise supervise the administration of the trust directly or indirectly would cause the trust to migrate from the U.S. An exception permits the trust to migrate only in the case of foreign invasion of the U.S. or if there is widespread confiscation or nationalization of property in the U.S. [Treas. Regs. 301.7701-7(c)(4)(ii)]

Enforcement of Foreign Judgments

Tax havens that don't automatically recognize foreign judgments (St. Vincent, for example) are preferable. They require that a new (*de novo*) legal action (a case) be filed. The settlor may benefit if the statute of limitations has run, precluding the filing of a new lawsuit in the tax haven. The statute with respect to fraud begins to run when it is discovered by the damaged party, when it should have been discovered, or when an asset is transferred to the trust with the intent to hinder, delay, or defraud creditors.

Conflict of Law Principles

Since most structures are multinational, when litigation arises, it must be determined which country's laws should be used by the court. In a Connecticut case involving two offshore spendthrift APTs, the judge held that Connecticut law applied. The judge disregarded the situs of the two foreign trusts, Bermuda and Jersey, which both provided that the laws of their respective countries were to be used. Instead, the judge ruled that Connecticut's conflict laws applied. In reality, the judge likely suspected that the transfers of assets to the two APTs occurred within eighteen months of the filing of the bankruptcy, probably created in anticipation of the bankruptcy filing. The lessons to be learned here are:

1. When a judge suspects the motives of the witness, he or she might shape the laws to suit the case and facts under his or her interpretation of what is equitable.

2. Transfers of assets that appear to have been principally done in anticipation of a claim by a creditor will be construed as an act to hinder, frustrate, and delay a creditor's rightful claim. This is called the nexus of time issue, and it will not be tolerated by a judge.

Technicalities

The following items are very complex technical issues that should be addressed with your OS planner and service provider; they are not suited for do-it-yourselfers. Although directed toward APTs, they may apply equally to other OS entities.

1. Settlor being a beneficiary, trustee, cotrustee, or protector of the APT. Automatic migration where duress, as well.

2. Level of control of settlor over the APT or IBC.

3. When the APT is under attack by a creditor:

- Degree of recognition by the tax haven of foreign judgments
- Local standards of law for the blocking or freezing of assets located there
- Standard of proof required in the local jurisdiction
- Upon whom rests the initial burden of proof? Does the burden shift, and if so, when?
- If the creditor is successful in setting aside the fraudulent transfer, does the APT remain valid?

4. Efficacy of the "choice of law" selection in the APT. Generally, factors to be considered in the choice of law analysis would be: English common law, Statute of Elizabeth abrogated, stable economy, and experienced professionals.

5. Where flight of the APT has resulted in a new jurisdiction, what level of protection will be afforded by the immigrant APT in the redomiciled jurisdiction?

In summary, you need a trust you can trust, a proven structure and shield and a base for operating other investment interests. It may be for asset protection, estate planning, or business planning purposes.

Statutory Improvements

As U.S. and IRS APT litigation tests the efficacy of offshore trusts, new issues must be addressed by the U.S. and foreign courts, many for the first time. For example, how does a foreign court handle a foreign judgment providing for treble damages or punitive damages? What are the powers of removal of the trustee vested in the protector? Are trust principal and trust income treated differently?

Endnotes

1 Previously, a fine distinction arose in the case of a foreign nongrantor trust created by a third person who was a nonresident alien, and called the "nominee settlor." Although the nominee (third person) settlor was the

"legal" settlor of the trust, he, she, or it must be distinguished from the "true settlor," some other person. Although this is not currently being used by U.S. persons, others continue to follow this practice. The current IRS standard is no longer who is the settlor but whether there are any U.S. beneficiaries or trustees or whether a U.S. court has exclusive jurisdiction over the trust.

2 A Mareva order is usually sought by the creditor against the settlor. It enjoins the settlor from removing assets from the jurisdiction to frustrate the enforcement of a judgment against the settlor by a judgment creditor.

3 The laws of approximately 19 U.S. states have the equivalent restrictions as in the Statute of Elizabeth. California, for example, looks for "badges of fraud." The elements of badges of fraud include: Was the transfer to an insider? Did the transferor retain control over the assets transferred? Was the primary intent to "remove" or "conceal" the assets? Did the transferor receive adequate or fair consideration for the assets? Was the transferor being sued? The Statute of Elizabeth was first codified in the U.S. as the Uniform Fraudulent Conveyance Act and later replaced with the Uniform Fraudulent Transfer Action.

4 Re: Butterworth, 1882, 19 Ch D 588.

8

Offshore Banks and Related Banking Services

So OFTEN PEOPLE with offshore accounts are viewed with suspicion. Many people, even U.S. citizens, have established trusts and hold some of their investments overseas for the sake of tax deferral, greed, protection against future heirs, or fear of confiscation due to litigation. The information contained in this chapter will help us understand why we need offshore financial centers for legitimate business reasons.

The leading offshore centers vary widely in business volume, sophistication, market penetration, and breadth of services. The Cayman Islands is perhaps the most advanced, having edged past the Bahamas in recent years. Panama is one of the oldest, but has fallen victim to political instability and the wrath of the United States. The Netherlands Antilles is another veteran, and another casualty of U.S. displeasure. Its upstart neighbor, Aruba, is now vying for the same business. Barbados and the British Virgin Islands have recently scored notable successes. Anguilla and the Turks and Caicos Islands hope to emulate their successful British neighbors.

Most of these places are small, rather isolated tropical islands where the pace of life is, as the tourist brochures say, unhurried—they walk to the Caribbean clock. While no doubt an admirable quality, leisure is not always conducive to success in business. Nevertheless, these nine jurisdictions account for bank deposits totaling well over $500 billion—roughly half of all the world's merchant shipping registrations and hundreds of thousands of offshore companies.

The Cayman Islands and the Bahamas rank among the world's leading international banking centers in terms of size, ahead of countries such as Switzerland and Germany. The Cayman Islands and Barbados are two of the world's leading offshore insurance centers. Panama hopes to become the world's largest center for ship registration this year, and the Bahamas ship registry is larger than those of India, Brazil, and South Korea.

It should be remembered that most of the financial business exists on paper only. Transactions and decisions are usually made in the great cities of the world and instructions are relayed offshore, where lawyers, accountants, bankers, and bureaucrats take care of the paperwork and occasionally act as hosts to visiting clients. Most new business comes in the form of referrals. These activities have brought an avalanche of fees to offshore professionals and governments in these regions, and there is no sign of a decrease in demand for their services.

Small wonder that there is keen competition. Apart from tourism and financial services, most of these territories have no visible means of support. Lacking natural resources, capital, and manpower, they generally have no significant agricultural or industrial base and are therefore dependent on the outside world for most supplies. (There are exceptions—St. Kitts has its sugar fields and Barbados has its hydrocarbons.)

Offshore businesses generate foreign exchange, tax revenues, and employment, as well as indirect benefits such as tourism. Offshore businesses offer the opportunity of economic diversification and are far more profitable than tourism, once the necessary infrastructure is in place, because they require less manpower and foreign exchange spending. Moreover, even a moderate degree of success can have a large economic impact on the smaller islands.

The need for offshore financial services arises for many reasons. For example:

1. An individual wishes to escape from onerous or capricious restrictions imposed by his or her government.

2. Business owners want to allow corporate diversification into activities not permitted within their countries.

3. Companies or individuals wish to avoid foreign exchange controls.

4. Companies and individuals want to avoid restrictions on foreign investments.

5. Moslem countries prohibit the payment of interest for religious reasons, thereby requiring unique structuring only available offshore.

6. Financial asset holders wish to guard against high inflation in other countries.

7. Owners of wealth desire a stable mechanism to transfer their wealth to heirs without taxation and to be free of the constant rule and tax changes in certain high-tax and high-regulation jurisdictions.

8. Asset owners need a safe haven against political upheaval and wars.

9. Companies or individual citizens may need a properly established contractual intermediary for profit capture away from high-tax and high-regulation jurisdictions.

The desire for these types of services is empirically evident by the phenomenal growth rate of the offshore institutions in the last ten years.

Industry Trends

Since World War II, the demand for offshore financial services has grown rapidly as a result of higher taxation and expanding regulations in many of the industrialized nations, as well as political instability in some of the emerging nations. The rise of multinational companies, whose primary allegiance is to shareholders rather than to any particular country; the expansion of world trade and cross-border investment; and the increase in both personal and corporate wealth also helped to stimulate this growth. Revolutionary advances in technology and communications have also assisted the growth in offshore financial services, erasing the barriers of time and location for even the most remote parts of the world.

Until recently, offshore financial centers were commonly described as *tax havens*, a term that many offshore depositors disliked because it suggested they helped people to circumvent the laws of high-tax countries. But the term accurately reflects the genesis of the business, and remains a condition of its continued existence. No offshore financial center could hope to survive if it imposed any significant levels of taxation.

Tax evasion is probably one of the oldest pastimes, and there is no doubt that offshore financial centers are sometimes used for this purpose. But many offshore activities could more accurately be described as tax *planning*—using legal mechanisms to reduce or eliminate taxes on income, wealth, profits, and inheritance, or to accumulate tax-free income offshore, pending repatriation to a taxable jurisdiction.

Such arrangements are often used when the income or assets in question are international in nature. For example, an author or inventor who receives royalties from many countries may have them paid into an offshore account until the funds are needed at home. International mutual funds may be registered offshore to minimize regulation and boost investor returns. Some of the more popular countries for mutual fund registrations, and their percentage of the market (as of late 1997), are

- Luxembourg (63%)
- Switzerland (10%)
- Ireland (6%)
- Netherlands Antilles (5%)
- Cayman Islands (4%)
- Bvi (3%)
- Jersey (3%)

- Bermuda (2%)
- Isle of Man (0.5%)
- Bahamas (0.4%)
- Singapore (0.3%)

International traders may operate through offshore businesses to increase trading profits, and owners of foreign capital assets may incorporate offshore to avoid capital gains tax when the assets are sold. In many cases, some tax is ultimately paid in the home country, but offshore strategies can help minimize the tax burden or permit repatriation at an economically more favorable time.

Tax minimization is not the only reason for using an offshore financial center. Freedom from regulation is another major attraction as individuals and businesses seek to escape what they regard as onerous, unreasonable, or capricious restrictions imposed by politicians. It is no coincidence that banking, insurance, and ship registration are three of the main pillars of offshore business. They are among the most heavily regulated industries in developed countries. Again, offshore financial centers provide legal mechanisms through which these businesses can avoid very costly and time-consuming regulations in certain circumstances.

Sometimes establishing offshore operations can also allow diversification into activities not permitted at home, or provide a more level playing field, if a company is subject to heavy regulation in its own country while its foreign competitors are not. A prime example is the use of foreign jurisdictions by U.S. and Japanese banks to engage in securities and insurance businesses, which are prohibited at home.

More generally, offshore financial centers are often used to avoid foreign exchange and capital controls, restrictions on foreign investment, and other domestic constraints, such as the prohibition against interest payments in some Moslem countries. In the past, capital controls in the U.S. were a major factor behind the initial growth of the enormous Eurodollar market and its offshore tributaries. Similar restraints are still a fact of life in many countries that attempt to limit the inflow of foreign exchange and the outflow of capital for domestic political reasons, even if such limitations undermine the operations of local businesses. The result is usually a flourishing black market and increased reliance on offshore financial centers. Worldwide experience has shown that capital controls don't work. They have the effect of deterring foreign investments and delaying the introduction of new technology and better marketing strategies.

Another source of demand for offshore services has been the need for a safe haven. Upheavals in Europe before World War I and II stimulated the movement of assets and holding companies to neutral and offshore locations. Political crises and economic realignments have also made wealthy Europeans nervous at times. For example, one well-known European company transferred a substantial amount of assets offshore a few years ago, fearing that its union would make unacceptable demands after a swing to the left in local elections.

Today, the greatest need for a safe haven is probably felt by the more affluent citizens of many countries. Having accumulated some liquid capital, their principal investment goal is to preserve and protect their savings from rampant inflation, corruption, and government incompetence at home. Investing the funds abroad through offshore financial centers accomplishes their investment objectives. This phenomenon, usually known as capital flight, stems from the collapse of confidence in governments, institutions, and currencies due to political instability and economic disarray or uncertainty. By all accounts, the amount of capital flight from foreign persons held in offshore banks is vast.

Offshore banks are improving their image by:

- Locating in countries with a good or improving reputation as offshore financial centers with viable legal and regulatory systems (for example, British, Swiss, Dutch)
- Engaging in legitimate local and international transactions with individuals and firms of good reputation
- Assisting in local and international development projects and small business loans
- Assisting in skills training and education of local personnel and civic-minded persons

- Engaging in image-building advertising in local and international financial publications
- Offering courteous and competent services to customers and regulatory authorities
- Having shareholders, advisors, employees, and individuals of competence with good reputations
- Maintaining a very strong and conservative financial structure

Adam Smith's economic theory of jurisdictions with a competitive advantage holds true: the offshore financial centers exist because capital flows from where it is heavily taxed, controlled, or constrained to areas where it can work for its owners.

The Swiss Banking System

The modern Swiss banking industry got its start when the Huguenots fled France in fear of their lives and took their money with them. This first large influx of immigrants and money into the sleepy cantons that compose the Swiss federation laid the foundation for its identity as being both politically neutral and a financial center. Since then, as war after war has been waged over Europe, the Swiss have benefited from the capital flight of all the nations at war—victor or vanquished. In modern times, with the improvements in travel and communications, wars, political instability, high taxes, and anything else that drives capital flight, the flight capital can be found landing in Switzerland or any one of the other modern offshore financial centers.

Historical Banking Secrecy

The right to banking secrecy in Switzerland was real and not a legend. The right to privacy is expressly protected pursuant to Article 28 of the Swiss Civil Code, and there is a duty to observe the confidentiality traditionally inherent in the contractual relationship between a bank and its customers.

This obligation to secrecy is based on civil law, the breach of which can lead to the bank having to pay damages. According to Article 47 of the Federal Law on Banks and Savings Banks (Bank Act), a violation of banking secrecy is a criminal offense punishable by imprisonment for up to six months (if committed intentionally) or by fine (if committed by negligence). Furthermore, a bank violating banking secrecy may be subject to administrative sanctions imposed by the Federal Banking Commission, which may, in very serious cases, lead to the bank's license being withdrawn and the bank being liquidated.

Breaches of Banking Secrecy

A bank must not disclose to third parties—whether private persons, companies, or governments—information subject to banking secrecy, unless authorized to do so by statutory provisions of Swiss law or by Swiss court orders.

There are key exceptions to the veil of secrecy. Contrary to opinion often held abroad, Swiss banking secrecy is in no way absolute; it can be overridden by statutory provisions that compel the bank to divulge information. Such rules for disclosure of information—usually in a limited scope—can be found in Swiss inheritance law, in procedural laws dealing with debt collection, and in bankruptcy law. The most widely known restrictions of banking secrecy are in bilateral treaties and the laws and regulations dealing with legal assistance in criminal matters. In criminal investigation, banking secrecy can be lifted by court order, for either domestic cases or international cases. Legal assistance in criminal matters is only granted if the country requesting legal assistance grants some form of reciprocity for the Swiss. In tax matters, legal assistance is available to foreign public prosecutors only if the investigated violation of foreign tax laws would be qualified under Swiss law as tax fraud—not just tax evasion. Tax evasion is simply the failure to declare income or assets for taxation; tax fraud is distinguished by alleged fraudulent conduct.

Recently the IRS has begun shifting its special task force to tax fraud and conducting some major-scale audits. (This is the same group of IRS agents who were hired to break tax shelters. Once that task was done, they moved to 941 taxes, then to Schedule C deductions, and are now focusing on overseas tax fraud.) The IRS has a nasty habit of declaring that the individual or entity in question has absolutely no deductions and more income than they actually had for the period under investigation. It is then up to the individual to prove otherwise.

Based upon a special provision of the Swiss-American Treaty on Mutual Assistance in Criminal Matters, legal assistance is available to U.S. prosecutors even in tax evasion cases or if they are conducting a case investigating organized crime or racketeering. If you are accused by the IRS of tax fraud and the accusations contain more than three fraudulent transactions or representations (this puts the investigation under both criminal and civil racketeering statutes— RICO), then the IRS or any other government investigative body may acquire access to any financial information or account records you may have in Switzerland.

The threats have not changed, but the interpretation and the body of law now available to both criminal and civil litigants has grown exponentially. Enforcement of new forfeiture laws has placed the desire for raising money by government agencies ahead of fairness of law enforcement. More and more events are deemed money laundering, racketeering, and fraudulent use of U.S. mail. The reasons behind this growth are simple. In the United States, in our understandable rush to wipe out organized crime and the drug trade, we have adopted a body of law that severely abrogates our rights under the Constitution and changes the rules with respect to privacy and the interpretation under preexisting international treaties.

In a recent conversation I had with a federal law enforcement officer specializing in white-collar crime investigations, he indicated that he was not worried about gaining access to information in Swiss accounts. If fact, the trend to request financial information from the Swiss has been so prevalent in recent years that federal law enforcement has set up an interagency group to do nothing but work with the Swiss. So if you're looking for bank secrecy, it is not going to be found in Switzerland.

The Caribbean and Neighboring Nations

These offshore financial centers (OFCs) include the Bahamas, Bermuda, Antigua, Anguilla, Turks and Caicos Islands, Aruba, Cayman Islands, St. Kitts and Nevis, British Virgin Islands, and Belize. These countries, in most cases, have been nation-states longer than the U.S. In fact, it is on St. Christopher Island in the Bahamas (don't confuse this with the island of Saint Christopher, or St. Kitts, of St. Kitts and Nevis) that Columbus is thought to have first landed in the New World. (Curiously, they don't make a big deal about the event. Need a better PR department, I would think.)

These countries have been experiencing a long-term boom in the operation of offshore financial centers. Some are newcomers to the game, such as Belize and Anguilla, and others are old-time hands such as Bermuda, Bahamas, and the Cayman Islands. These nation-states offer a great deal to the U.S. citizen—financial security, political stability, and a nice place to visit.

The newcomers have much to offer. Their laws are very similar to the laws in the Cayman Islands and Bahamas, with the added benefit of not having an entrenched, expensive bureaucracy to support. These countries offer the maximum flexibility allowed and all of the opportunity at less cost than one would find in London or New York. Belize, however, has the edge. It is a stable country, possesses industry other than tourism and finance, and is readily accessible from all of North and South America.

The pressure being exerted from the United States (the world's largest offshore financial center, if you don't live here) and Great Britain on the OFCs around the world to curb the granting of charters to banks in these locations has had an effect. The application for a bank charter in any British protectorate requires the possession of a banking license from another location and at least two years of operational history.

If you are offered bank shares in an offshore financial center, always proceed with caution as with any investment. But seriously consider the purchase of shares in an institution you may never be able to purchase shares in again. Bahamian and Caymanian bank stocks have been growing at an exceptional rate for the last four years.

Other Offshore Financial Centers

Most of the successful offshore financial centers are located near strong financial centers. Hence, most are located in and around Europe and around the U.S. Here is a list of most of the offshore financial centers.

- Albania
- Alderney
- Aruba
- Austria
- Bahamas
- Barbados
- Belize
- Bermuda
- British Virgin Islands
- Cayman Islands
- Channel Islands
- Cook Islands
- Costa Rica
- Cyprus
- Dominica
- Gibraltar
- Grenada
- Guernsey
- Herm
- Hong Kong
- Ireland (Dublin's offshore financial center)
- Jersey
- Liechtenstein
- Luxembourg
- Malaysia
- Malta
- Mauritius
- Monaco
- Netherlands
- Netherlands Antilles
- Niue
- Panama
- Sark
- Singapore
- St. Kitts and Nevis
- Switzerland
- Turks and Caicos Islands
- Vanuatu
- Western Samoa
- Virgin Islands (United States, for non–U.S. citizens)

For more information, read the *Market Advisors, Inc. Journal*, available by subscription ($75 per year). This publication is owned and published by Market Advisors, Inc. Contact them at:

Market Advisors, Inc.
650 J. Street, #400
Lincoln, Nebraska 68508
(402) 476-3404

Offshore Credit and Debit Cards

Offshore bankers are competing with American bankers for your profitable credit card business, and I believe the offshore credit card, having the advantage of greater privacy of transactions, is the winner. There is nothing illegal about possessing and using an offshore credit card, as long as it is not being used for tax evasion purposes, to use offshore income for personal purposes.

If you truly crave privacy, avoid using your onshore credit cards. They provide an ongoing permanent electronic diary of where you go, what you buy, how much you spend, where you shop, whom you telephone, what telephone companies you use, where you entertain and vacation, which travel agents and airlines you use, and on and on. Charge your discreet expenses offshore! Those involved in major mergers and acquisitions may use their companies' offshore credit cards to disguise their traveling.

U.S. credit card companies (card issuers) analyze credit card data and market it for profit to any firm interested in demographics, consumer profiles, and psychographics. How do you think all those credit card offers with the introductory teaser rates get mailed to you? Buyers for this data also include telemarketing firms, insurance salespeople, mail order houses, the IRS, private detectives, and even competitors of your credit card issuer. I am not aware of any laws prohibiting selling this data at this time. Any assumption of the privacy of domestic credit card transactions is a fallacy.

Recognizing this trend, more and more people are acquiring offshore credit cards for private needs, not for everyday shopping. Be certain that the OS issuing bank is strong and in a jurisdiction that has strong banking privacy laws; not all OS credit cards are equal in this respect. Onshore credit reporting bureaus do not legally have access to the OS card system.

Most offshore credit cards are in reality *secured credit cards* or *debit cards*. This is because you don't have credit established offshore yet. Your card line of credit is generally between 50 percent and 66.66 percent of the amount on deposit in a low-interest–bearing savings account with the offshore bank. The credit charges are usually charged against the bank account. It is wise from the privacy standpoint to use banks that do not have a branch office in the United States. This prevents a subpoena or a *subpoena duces tecum* (an order to provide records without the necessity of a personal appearance) from being served upon the U.S. branch to provide credit card sales records, or, for that matter, any kind of onshore court order from being effective.

General Banking Rules

The rule that one should use an offshore bank that has no U.S. branches applies to your other offshore banking needs. An affiliate bank, even if it does not have a branch in New York City, is required to access the Federal Reserve Bank's wire transfer system for U.S. dollar transfers. Using a correspondent U.S. bank does not give the os bank a legal presence in the United States.

Unless you are suspected of being involved in money laundering or drug trafficking, offshore banks will not honor a request for information or an order from a court that is outside of their jurisdiction. There is much more banking privacy offshore in the tax havens than in the United States. This privacy is slowly being eroded in the British overseas territories and the Channel Islands centers.

In the United States, if you can afford the price, you can do an asset search and identify the banks that a person uses as well as the account numbers and balances. Legal? I reserve comment, but it is done regularly by commercial asset locators—for a fee, of course. Every month the official state bar of California magazine carries advertisements of this nature, and no one seems to be concerned about the privacy issues. I have yet to see or hear of banking privacy being so easily invaded in the tax havens. Such an action would cause a rapid flight of capital to another jurisdiction, and that country would be put out of the tax haven business. We have seen some of side effects occurring with Switzerland as it becomes less popular because of privacy erosion and the Holocaust scandal, where pressure from the world community and the risk of future financial losses opened the door to settlements to Holocaust survivors for claims of unpaid life insurance policies and forced labor. The worldwide Jewish community and others have been affected by the magnitude and severity of the disclosures, and it has had some causal results with regard to Swiss banking. There is an excess of cooperation between Switzerland and the United States in which Switzerland frequently initiates the inquiry with the United States so that it can share the spoils 50-50 with the United States. I still believe that Switzerland has one of the best banking systems in the world, but it is no longer private!

If you appreciate that in many jurisdictions the income generated by the financial community exceeds the income from tourism, you can appreciate why banking privacy is so preciously guarded. The reputation for banking privacy is ultimate, and once lost it can never be fully regained. Those of us in the offshore industry still speak of scandals that occurred many years ago as if they were only yesterday.

Private and Numbered Accounts

The days of private Swiss banking are past. There is no longer such a thing as a secret Swiss numbered bank account. I do not characterize Switzerland as a banking haven for privacy because the Swiss have "sharing arrangements" with other countries, including Germany; if Swiss deposits are found to be of a "criminal nature," the Swiss will share them with the country demanding their return.

Swiss banking records are now too open to outsiders. Furthermore, because of recent banking scandals, responsible offshore banks now are mandated to follow the philosophy of knowing their customers. Western European banks take accounts from people and companies from the former Soviet Union with guarded reluctance. Caribbean banks generally require from new customers a passport or other photo ID, Social Security number or driver's license number (always give the latter), a personal visit, a reference letter from one's present bank, and perhaps even sponsors. Some even correspond with the bank issuing the reference letter to verify it. Unfortunately, this erodes your privacy, as the inquiry letter from the offshore bank becomes a permanent part of your file with your onshore bank. See Figure 8.1 for a sample of a minimally acceptable reference letter by Barclays Bank, Nassau. A more detailed letter is shown in Figure 8.2.

Figure 8.1: A Minimally Acceptable Bank Reference Letter

Your bank's letterhead

January 12, 2000

Barclays Bank
Bay Street Branch
P. O. Box N8350
Nassau, Bahamas

Attention: Bank Manager
Reference: John Q. Public

To Whom It May Concern:

This letter is to verify that our banking customer, John Q. Public, has had an account with our bank since February 14, 1992. Mr. Public has handled his account in a satisfactory manner.

Yours truly,

Alice Banker
Vice President

Many offshore banks now require their foreign customers to execute a consent form (see Figure 8.3 for a sample from Canadian Imperial Bank of Commerce in Nassau). Royal Bank of Canada requires the disclosure of the beneficial owners on any corporate bank account. The release enables the bank to provide banking information to the governments (read: IRS, Revenue Canada, or Inland Revenue) of other jurisdictions. This overrides the banking privacy laws and obligations of confidentiality of the Bahamas.

Figure 8.2: A More Detailed Bank Reference Letter

The XYZ Bank

January 12, 2000
Lloyd's of London
Box 114GT
Grand Cayman
Cayman Islands

To Whom It May Concern:

I have had the privilege of knowing _____ personally and professionally for over ____ years. Mr. _____ has been involved in a business banking relationship with our bank since _____. I have personally advised him, and our bank has represented him and financed many of his business dealings.

My personal experience with him indicates that he is capable, professional, and of good moral character. I have the highest regard for Mr. _____ and recommend him highly. Should the need arise, I would be happy to discuss further and confidentially the specifics of my relationship with Mr. _____.

If you have any questions, do not hesitate to call me at _____.

Sincerely,

Joe Banker
Vice President

The European Commission (EC) would like to standardize banking among its member countries, and numbered banking is not compatible with its agenda. Even though the glamour of the *chop block account*, the Austrian *Sparbuch account*, and the *numbered account* are disappearing, I suggest that we take a moment to discuss them for historical purposes.

The Chop Block Account

In an effort to provide banking services to their wealthy but illiterate customers, Hong Kong's British banks developed and accepted (some still do to a limited degree) a hand-printing device called the *chop block*. They were used just as one uses the rubber stamp. The adult population was largely illiterate, so this was essential to conduct commerce. As an alternative to the signature, Chinese would "chop" instructions to their bank. The chop originally was carved from ivory, but now is carved on wood or stone or cast in metal. Because it was hand-carved, each stamp was unique. The chop seal was fully accepted by the bank. The chop was like a bearer instrument; whoever had possession of the chop effectively controlled the assets. If some foreign national would open a chop account for you and then turn over the chop to you, you would have an anonymous account. Currently, fewer and fewer Hong Kong banks accept the block, some limiting its use only to passbook savings accounts.

The Sparbuch Account

Carrying the full name of the Austrian Ueberbringer Sparbuch, this private numbered savings bank account is exclusively Austrian. It is a bearer savings account book. The European Commission, under the "Doctrine of Euro-compatible" (author's language), had initially appeared to compel Austria to discontinue issuing this type of account effective July 1, 1996. But it has apparently survived. At this time, it appears that existing accounts will remain private under Austrian banking secrecy laws, but new trading and activities will be curtailed. The Sparbuch is intended to be a means of creating an anonymous bearer account for complete personal privacy. Although appearing suspicious to the outside world, it is completely legal in Austria. One could open the Sparbuch account in any name, so long as it isn't obscene. They are usually opened through "agents" who charge an administrative fee (from $50 to $280) for doing so. The account is further protected by

Figure 8.3: Consent Form—An Example

From:_____   _____

      Name   Social Security Number

            _____   (hereinafter referred to as "the Customer")

      Address

      _____

      _____

To: Canadian Bank of Commerce (hereinafter referred to as "the Bank")

1. The Customer, being neither a citizen nor a resident of the Bahamas, acknowledges that the governments of other jurisdictions may have valid powers under their laws to require the Bank, under certain circumstances and after specified procedures have been accomplished, to produce information and records of the Bank to the specified governmental and/or judicial authorities of those jurisdictions.

2. The Customer has been advised and so acknowledges that the Bank's operations in the Bahamas and its obligations of confidentiality are governed by laws of the Bahamas, which may not permit the production of information and records referred to in Paragraph 1 above, unless the Customer has specifically authorized the Bank to do so.

3. The Customer hereby instructs the Bank upon the happening of an event in Paragraph 1 hereof to give information and to produce records pertaining to all transactions of the nature referred to in Paragraph 4 hereof where and to the extent the Bank is of the opinion that the law of those other jurisdictions requires the Bank to do so, to those governmental and judicial authorities of those other jurisdictions.

4. These instructions extend to information and records relating to transactions between the Customer and the Bank and to all accounts of the company and/or its principals.

_____   _____

      Place   Date

_____

      Signature of Customer

a personal password. Walk in with the passbook and the password, and all the money is yours. Forget the password, and say good-bye to your money.

The *Wertpapierbuch account*, a securities book account, was similar in certain respects to the Sparbuch. It previously allowed you to purchase and sell stocks and bonds with comparable privacy. Effective July 1, 1996, Austria banned this form of anonymous security trading account to comply with EC initiatives. Only new trading will be prohibited; standing accounts will be permitted so long as there is no new trading.

The Numbered Account

Older novels and movies often portrayed the intrigue of transferring huge sums of money merely by providing an instruction on a numbered account. Those days are long gone. Strict rules imposed in all industrialized countries require banks to know their customers.

Monetary Policies and Exchange Controls

Monetary policies and exchange controls can be formal and expressed or de facto. Many countries have laws regarding exchange controls that generally limit the amount of money one may move outside of that country without a license to do so. Exchange controls are meant to limit flight capital, which, since it rarely returns to that country, results in permanent economic damage to the economy as well as a local black market in currencies.

Swiss Postfinance Services

The state-owned financial institutions called Swiss Postfinance operate more than 3,000 "ordinary post offices" within Switzerland that also process financial transactions such as their fund transfer operations for private and corporate accounts to Swiss residents as well as foreigners (individuals and/or companies) in eighteen currencies with alternative services through the Internet to anywhere in the world.

Offshore Foreign Currency Accounts

A typical offshore foreign currency account is the type found in the Channel Islands banks. Since they deal with most of the Western European countries, they accept deposits in most major currencies, including Spanish pesetas, Swiss francs, and Euros. Debit cards, investment services, and interest-bearing checking accounts may also be available. Terms vary from a two-day notice account to fixed terms of one, two, three, six, and twelve months.

Private Banking

Private banking has at least two definitions. One (the original meaning) is the use of a private bank to assist high net worth (HNW) people in their investing and asset management. The second, newer meaning is the formation of your own personal private bank to handle banking needs, including your own. Private banking is not merely banking in privacy: it is the utilization of an offshore private bank for your onshore and international personal and/or business needs, providing asset protection and tax deferral, where structured properly. If you can justify the economics, an OS private bank can be created just for you, issuing Visa cards carrying your portrait. Process that thought for a moment!

In its original context, a private bank offers its services only to HNW individuals. It is estimated are that such private banks currently manage more than $2.5 trillion in OS funds, comprising significant flight capital. An international OS bank may create a private banking department for its HNW customers. The definition of an HNW customer is one who has *liquid assets* to manage in excess of half a million dollars. HNW individuals seek protection, total service, and flexibility; they need their personal wealth to fund business ventures as required without undue complications. While the funds are awaiting utilization, the private bankers are expected to provide fund or asset management, and they are more than happy to do so because they generate management fees of about 0.5 to 1.5 percent per year on the assets under management. Asset management services can range from a fully discretionary account to a customer-directed one. Switzerland continues to be the global kingpin of private banking with approximately a 40 percent market share.

Your Personal Private Bank

Weekly, I see promotional advertisements in the *Wall Street Journal* offering to sell private os Class B banks. The advertisers don't indicate what they are selling, but they are the less prestigious Class B bank licenses. Os banks are generally licensed as either a Class A (+) or Class B (–) bank. The Class A bank is a retail bank with the ability to have a storefront operation in the country granting the bank license (country of formation). It is what you are accustomed to seeing in the U.S. The Class B bank is a private bank not licensed to provide banking services to the residents of the license-granting country. Class A bank licenses are very difficult to obtain, even in the second-tier jurisdictions. First-tier countries are granting Class A licenses only to existing Class A banks from other jurisdictions that have high capitalization and long-term successful track records. Class B bank promoters charge whatever the traffic will bear. I have heard reports of fees between $40,000 and $120,000 for Class B formation costs. Some promoters are telling their suckers that os banks are not subject to U.S. taxation—but don't you believe it. Offshore banking licenses are being marketed over the Internet without regulatory control. I received the following E-mail offering "World–U.S. Financial Services" of Ridgewood, New Jersey:

> I have available for immediate sale four offshore banking licenses:
>
> 1. Bank Licensed in Nauru in 1998—asking $150,000
>
> 2. Bank Licensed in Kuiu Thlingit Nation in 1998 "A" License—asking $50,000
>
> 3. Bank Licensed in DOM in 1998 "A" License—asking $10,000
>
> 4. Bank Licensed in Antigua and Barbuda in 1993 (new ownership is a must—old owners were on the wrong side of the

political fence) immediate closing. Bank comes with complete website, two web addresses, two correspondent accounts, telex, swift address, and other. Can be delivered with or without account holders—asking US$100,000.

My associate, Jay Adkisson, Esq., helped me dissect this E-mail's claims.

The Antiguan bank was in the nefarious Caribbean Bank of Commerce, Ltd., which has come to be known as "Caribbean Bank of Crooks," and has been implicated in misconduct accounting.

"DOM" refers to the nonexistent Dominion of Melchizedek, a fictitious nation.

We had a hard time trying to figure out just what the "Kuiu Thlingit Nation" was, but a source has since told us that it is a purported Native American tribe that is used as a backdrop by scam artists to concoct phony bank licenses. Native American banks are the latest craze by scam artists, who promise that these banks have absolute secrecy and are not subject to the U.S. jurisdiction or taxation—but recent convictions of promoters by the U.S. Attorney's Office has proved otherwise.

The reference to the Nauru bank is mostly pathetic—probably hundreds of worthless sham banks have been created on that reef in the last couple of years, and the ownership of a Nauru bank is only worth the identity of the owner as a true sucker.

Before rushing off to create your own bank, consider some of the following questions that need to be analyzed and answered:

1. Why bother? A custom-created IBC can perform most of the same functions.

2. Who will do a feasibility study for you?

3. Where should you establish it?

4. What can it do and not do?

5. What should you expect of it?

6. What will it cost to operate and to produce satisfactory audited balance sheets?

7. How long will it take?

8. Who can use it?

9. Who will manage it?

10. Who will be the fund or asset manager?

11. Who should create it?

Personal Private Bank Requirements

Abuses in personal banking abound. Marginal banking licenses from cash-strapped minor tax havens are being used to claim exemptions on income tax by U.S. persons. I see frequent advertisements hawking private banks and their benefits. It is only a matter of time before the offshore banking abuses will be under IRS scrutiny. The bank must be a qualified business unit under a facts and circumstances analysis, engaged in the active conduct of the business of banking. To achieve tax deferral, complex structuring is required to avoid the IRC rules with respect to passive foreign investment companies (PFIC) or foreign personal holding companies (FPHC).

Some of the factors that are considered to determine a banks's bona fides include:

- Provides financial and technical advice to customers.
- Advises customers on financial needs, including funding and financial products.
- Makes loans, enters into leases, extends credit, or enters into other transactions with customers that generate income that would be considered *derived in the active conduct of banking*, financing, or similar business.
- Solicits customers and vendors. Accepts deposits from local citizenry, bona fide residents, on a regular basis. The level of such deposits must be substantial (not just one or two depositors).
- Designs and tailors financial products to customers' needs.
- Negotiates terms with customers.

- Performs credit analysis on customers and evaluates noncredit risks.
- Holds collateral for transactions with customers.
- Responds to customers' failure to satisfy their obligations.
- Performs remarketing activities following termination of transactions with customers.

If your private bank is not complying with these indicia of banking, it might not be qualified as a business unit eligible for the income tax retained earnings exemption. You may be running a sham banking operation.

Sicherheit und Privat Bank

At the time of drafting this book, the Sicherheit und Privat (Security and Privacy) Bank was chartered as an Austrian bank and attempted to initiate a high-tech Internet private bank. (See *TIME Digital* for February 23, 1999.) With no storefront operation, this Internet bank used the virtual doors of the Internet. For client privacy, transactions were to be encrypted. They are attempting to use new concepts of digital cash, digital letters of credit, and a special credit card issued by MasterCard which they claim has privacy protection. Anonymous accounts are allowed. (Don't think the EU will like that!) For stock trading, they have developed a secure passphase program called "Pilot," using a string of encoded numbers unique for each transaction. They can be contacted in Switzerland at ++ 604-913-2180 or by E-mail at:

Spbank@schloss.li

Privacy

As the Internet becomes more ubiquitous, more and more financial and encrypted transactions will occur by secure electronics. Many banks are seeking a proprietary global position by their affiliations. There is finally an acceptance of the security of credit card transactions over the Internet.

9

Annuities

THE *ANNUITY* APPEARS to be one of the fastest-growing products offered by the U.S. insurance industry, and now banks. Banks have discovered a new profit center in annuity products, and banks now account for approximately 25 percent of the annuity sales in the United States. In a deferred annuity, all income taxes are deferred until the annuity matures. Capital gains and income accumulate tax deferred. This results in a stream of payments made to the annuitant during his or her lifetime under the annuity agreement. Taxes are paid on the income, interest earned, and the capital gains, but only at the tax rates in effect when received. Currently, there is no annual limit on purchases, but there is no tax credit for purchases. An annuity is not an insurance policy. Annuities are written in various manners and include the following: *contingent annuity, deferred annuity, fixed annuity, refund annuity,* and *variable annuity.* An *annuity certain contract* makes payments over a specific period of time that continue upon the death of the annuitant. Annuities are popular because of tax deferral; and, because they encourage savings, they are endorsed by the U.S. government. American insurance companies finally noticed what the Swiss were doing and wanted a piece of the action.

It is obvious why annuities have become so popular by providing tax deferral on earnings. They can also be used to supplement an IRA or 401(k) without any annual limit upon purchase dollar amount. Annuities are intended to provide for long-term tax deferral, although the immediate-pay annuity is also available. The annuity affords an opportunity to let capital grow and compound with an accumulation of interest and dividends, free of ongoing annual taxes. There are no taxes until distribution to the *annuitant* (except for the Swiss annuity, a decided disadvantage). As a caveat, for an annuity purchased for cash, the distributions are taxed at the ordinary income tax rates, not at the long-term capital gains rates. No federal, state, or local taxes are assessed during the compounding period. It affords an excellent opportunity to provide for your retirement years, when you'll appreciate the security of receiving regular monthly or quarterly payments.

Much has been written about the various types of annuities, and I will leave that subject to other writers. Study the new, strange vocabulary and the cost factors for the initial purchase and ongoing expenses. For instance, can you define *immediate annuity, deferred annuity, variable annuity, fixed annuity, single premium, lump-sum* or *periodic fixed premiums*, and *two-life gift annuity*? Your annuity is burdened with annual administrative expenses (and profits). Reasonable annual costs can vary from 1.4 to 2.25 percent. I highly recommend some background reading at your library before proceeding with the remainder of this chapter. For an excellent overview of OS annuities, go to http://www.protectyou.com/apn8-1-fr.html.

Going Offshore—the Swiss Annuity

Many annuities offered to the consumer come directly from and are actively solicited by offshore annuity companies. The Swiss are famous in this industry. I will use the term "company" hereafter for simplicity. Curiously, the annuity is not considered by the U.S. Supreme Court to be an insurance policy, but rather a written unsecured contract (a promise) to pay the annuitant (that's you) at a certain rate by the company, commencing upon the effective date you have selected, on an immediate-pay basis or deferred, until your death. After your death, the remaining balance may be part of your U.S. estate. The terms of the annuity depend upon your age, health, type of investment selected, last-to-die provisions, and other factors. *Last-to-die annuities* are also referred to as *second-to-die* or *joint survivor annuities*. The annuity may be treated as an offering of an investment in some dividend formats under many jurisdictions. The annuity may or may not have residual value that flows into your estate upon your death—for example, in a last-to-die, life-only annuity.

Upon receipt of annuity distributions, certain tax rules apply. Where the private annuity was funded with stock, the return of your own funds (the basis) is not a taxable event. Only the capital gains and interest (dividends) paid by the company are taxable in the tax year earned, *not* the year distributed. Few offshore companies issue a U.S. form 1099R at year-end, so it is important for you to keep good tax records.

A Swiss annuity offers excellent asset protection, but with the recent tax law changes in the United States, that is its principal purpose. It is best used as an immediate annuity with full distributions of any earnings. Under Swiss law, an annuity cannot be seized by any court-ordered collection procedure instigated by creditors. Thus, even though you might become the victim of a frivolous lawsuit, the judgment could not be enforced in Switzerland. Swiss annuities are exempt from reporting to the IRS, even though the amount may be over $10,000. Most Swiss annuities allow you to designate a choice of several currencies or gold—for example, the Swiss franc, the deutsche mark, or the Euro. In many years, the Swiss franc has outperformed the U.S. dollar. The profits earned by the annuity are free of Swiss taxes. Interest rates paid are quite low by American standards. In 1999, the long-term rate paid was 3.5 percent, with talk of lowering it to a mere 2.5 percent. But they were starting to copy their American competitors in offering higher returns by participation in profit-related structures. Swiss insurance companies are extremely stable, giving the Swiss annuitant risk-free protection of the principal, but they are intended for very long-term investing. In

135 years, no Swiss insurance company has failed to meet its financial obligations or ceased operations. They provide trust, stability, discretion, and reliability.

The Private Annuity

The offshore private annuity is a derivation of the onshore scenario in which an elderly person transfers a highly appreciated business interest to a child or younger heir apparent, neither having the money to purchase the business outright. This results in a stream of payments that substitutes for insurance. The value of the private annuity must be at least the value of the asset transferred.

An offshore private annuity is a further refinement. A private annuity is defined as an *unsecured contract* between the issuing company (the offshore IBC) and the annuitant and is based upon the age and health of the annuitant at the time of contracting (life expectancy), the maturity date, and the stream of payments. The life expectancy tables can't be used where the death of the annuitant is certain within twelve months.

Under one of the last Internal Revenue Code's more popular loopholes, intended to encourage the future financial security of the RA and reduce the need for government old-age assistance, we find a variation of the traditional annuity. The *offshore private annuity contract* is becoming a more popular variation of the basic annuity as an advanced international tax planning and asset protection strategy. The private annuity (PA) is generally issued by or through an OS IBC created specifically for that purpose. The PA issued offshore can afford better asset protection to the annuitants in that the principal cannot be reached by an onshore creditor. If the PA is irrevocable and issued from offshore, no creditor or domestic court order can affect its OS sanctity. The exception would be for the income stream received by the annuitant, which could be attached by creditors, but only as it is received.

Continuing with the scenario, the RA, as the annuitant, purchases a lump-sum private annuity from the IBC. The annuitant pays money or transfers assets (for example, some highly appreciated stock) as the consideration for the PA, or perhaps that money that was borrowed under an equity stripping arrangement. Alternatively, he or she can transfer highly appreciated liquid assets at current market value for the PA. The IBC takes and gives equal value for value and neither has a capital gains obligation upon the transfer; it is not a sale if structured correctly. The capital gains tax problem has been shifted to the offshore IBC. The annuitant pays capital gains and income taxes later as the annuity payment stream begins. After the death of the annuitant, the private annuity may be part of the decedent's estate unless other provisions are made in structuring the PA. The market value of the asset has been frozen in return for the face value of the PA. The capital gains and income taxes are deferred until receipt.

The IBC usually obtains the annuity contract from another entity, usually another OS IBC. Upon maturity of the PA, the IBC acts as the fulfillment organization and makes the appropriate payments.

10

Other Structures and Strategies

Offshore Exempt Companies

In those jurisdictions that don't approve of the Caribbean-style company act (most of the European jurisdictions don't) but do want to attract and encourage international company business, we find local variations of exempt company acts. Some jurisdictions may believe that the IBC is a tainted form of company structure used by some for tax evasion or at least for "sharp practices."

Some legal scholars even go so far as to postulate that the IBC may create a unique, untested legal problem: actual recognition of the IBC in the international courts. The interesting legal issue is that if a jurisdiction has two types of companies—one for locals that requires complete disclosure, and a second type of company (the IBC), to be used only by foreigners that requires no disclosure and provides complete privacy—should the latter be given international recognition? There has not yet been a case addressing this issue.

OS Company Limited by Guaranty

This form of company (corporation) has different characteristics than in America. It is comparable to the limited liability company. The financial exposure of the principals is limited by law to their capitalization in the company and any further guaranty of a call for additional funds. It is generally authorized under the English type of company laws, as found in the Bahamas, the British Virgin Islands, Hong Kong, Gibraltar, Cyprus, Ireland, and the Isle of Man, among others. With drafting skills, for example, a company can be formed with the characteristics of a partnership.

Limited-Lifetime Company

Under traditional U.S. corporate laws, a corporation has an infinite lifetime. Limiting the lifetime of the company provides for automatic liquidation of the company upon the expiration of its established lifetime or a resignation of a member. Further provisions could also be made that would restrict the transferability of interests in the company, which is more difficult to do with an IBC.

Contract Hybrid Company

This is a special form of exempt company originally developed in the Isle of Man. Some authorities believe it is not a company and is actually a trust. It was first presented at the American Bar Association meeting in London in 1996. The contract hybrid company (CHC) was developed in anticipation of the ultimate passage of the Revenue Reconciliation Bill of 1995. The CHC provides for U.S. persons to take and hold assets offshore without giving rise to any tax liability to the United States or any U.S. reporting requirements. A U.S. tax will arise when the assets are repatriated to the United States, but so long as assets remain in the contract hybrid company, taxes are indefinitely deferred. Because CHCs are proprietary and without mass competition, they are quite dearly priced, starting at a minimum of $16,000 to set up and $8,000 to maintain annually. The principle issue remains as to whether the IRS will treat it as a corporation or as a trust.

Demystifying Residence: Domicile, Citizenship, and Passports

For a number of decades, Europeans have been using the elements of residence, domicile, citizenship, and passports to implement very successful tax-avoidance and asset protection strategies. In recent years, a number of reluctant Americans have also been following this strategy.

People interested in the question of residence have various personal agendas and may be motivated by a combination of any of the following:

- Fear that holding a specific nationality's passport puts one in high peril from terrorists. For example, Americans are very popular with terrorists who take hostages for ransom.
- Fears of eventual political instability in the United States, government overregulation, or policies and taxes construed as confiscatory; concerns over lack of personal privacy or perceived weaknesses in the American banking system; preparation for an os retirement; a quest for financial security.
- Concern that certain countries may unexpectedly confiscate one's principal passport because it contains a visa or entry stamp from a prohibited country, or a concern that while one is visiting offshore, civil disobedience or war may prompt confiscation of one's passport.
- Need to open an offshore bank account or brokerage account more privately.
- Limitation of some real estate acquisitions, employment opportunities, or business ventures to only those with passports.
- Need to legally preserve or salvage some assets if one is a party to a hostile divorce or partnership dissolution. One can legally open an os bank account using tax-neutral money with the second passport in a second name as an a.k.a. (also known as), so long as it is not for any fraudulent intent.

- Need for a temporary refuge after a bankruptcy or if one is a victim of a runaway jury verdict.
- Ability to travel without creating a permanent record of where one has been on one's U.S. passport.

To begin to develop strategies in this area, you must first understand the vocabulary.

Residency

Residency generally has both a tax and an immigration element. Tax residency is usually based upon the number of days one resides in a jurisdiction or a review of various indicia of residency indicating centralization of living in the jurisdiction. Immigration residency is usually granted on a temporary or permanent basis by a country. It may allow physical presence, reentry, employment or study rights, and/or land ownership.

Domicile

Domicile is an estate tax concept that looks at a person's "ultimate home." All persons, even "perpetual tourists," are deemed under law to have a domicile. A person acquires a *domicile of origin* at birth. He or she may then acquire a *domicile of choice* by changing residence and acquiring long-term indicia of domicile, such as gravesites and new wills. One then can acquire a subsequent domicile of choice by severing these ties and reacquiring the same in a new jurisdiction. If a person abandons his or her last domicile of choice without acquiring a new one, then his or her domicile either reverts back to the last domicile under the U.S. rule or the domicile of origin under the British rule.

The late violinist Sir Yehudi Menuhin was an American by birth but lived most of his life in Europe. In a 1950 interview, he called himself an "internationalist," a term I prefer over "perpetual tourist." After he received honorary Swiss citizenship in 1970 for his civic service to that country, the U.S. State Department threatened to revoke Menuhin's U.S. citizenship but later relented, setting the stage for further reflection on dual citizenship of Americans and, ultimately, clearly allowing such for Americans.

Citizenship

Citizenship is a status granted by a country and may include various rights, such as travel documents (passports), voting, land ownership, and the ability to hold public office. A country may choose to grant citizenship through various methods, including:

- Birth in the jurisdiction
- Lineage (through parents or grandparents)
- Marriage
- Naturalization
- Religious affiliation (for example, the law of return to Israel)
- Meritorious service
- Economic benefit to the country

Passports

Passports are generally thought of as travel documents issued by a country to its citizens. However, entrepreneurs have created new passport-like documents that have values ranging from minimal to worthless and even dangerous. This genre includes the following variations:

Camouflage Passports   The so-called *camouflage passport* is a nonofficial document of a nonexistent country. It can be of extremely high quality and have a genuine appearance. It is generally created using the name of a former country—for example, the Republic of Ceylon (now called Sri Lanka) or British Honduras (now called Belize). It is a novelty item not issued by any government, and is legal to possess in most countries if not utilized for fraudulent purposes. It is never to be used for entry into a country or for any custom purposes. To do so would be fraudulent and generally carries a heavy criminal sentence.

Further supportive evidence of your purported citizenship is also provided in the form of a driver's license and supplementary identification. Camouflage passports are relatively inexpensive to acquire. They may be useful to those persons who believe they offer protection against terrorists or hijackers, angry foreign mobs, surly hotel clerks, or those opposed to the "wealthy American." The user hopes that the passport will protect him or her against acts of terrorism directed toward Americans by presenting the passport in lieu of his or her true American passport.

Bogus Passports   Beware of bogus or fraudulent passports, which can be either fakes or real documents illegally obtained. For example, Venezuelan passports were being sold on the black market. Apparently, disgruntled displaced government employees took official documents when they left or were discharged. They in turn sold these genuine but illegal documents underground to obtain additional income.

Avoid passports that are fraudulently obtained. I have heard of "love child" passports obtained from Italy and Brazil claiming that the bearer is the illegitimate child of one of their citizens.

Noncitizenship Passports   Several countries (notably Panama and Uruguay) issue passports for noncitizens. Typically, a five-year residency is required to receive this passport.

Obtain a passport through *legal* means, not by answering a dubious advertisement. Be certain it is being issued by the *current* government to avoid wasting your money, being embarrassed, or being arrested. (Canada may sentence you up to seven years for obtaining a passport illegally.)

Renouncing U.S. Citizenship

Now that you are familiar with the terminology, let's discuss the strategy for the reluctant American to locate and obtain a new residence, domicile, and/or citizenship to reduce or eliminate U.S. tax liability. You may immediately recoil at the suggestion that you renounce your U.S. citizenship. However, only two other countries (the Philippines and Eritrea) are income tax–based on citizenship, which results in being taxed upon worldwide income. Compare this with British citizens, who are only taxed based on the tax rate where they reside. For example, an American working in the Cayman Islands—where there is no income tax—would pay income tax to the United States, but a British citizen working there would pay no taxes. Millions of Brits, Canadians, Aussies, and other nationals seem to get along quite nicely without U.S. citizenship; Americans who stop and think might begin to warm up to the concept.

It could make sense for you if it would *also* result in substantial tax savings. This political agenda of soaking the rich businessperson who is "running" offshore and "hiding" with his or her millions has resulted in many proposed changes to our tax code. If you are entertaining the thought of renunciation, your personal plan may take years to mature fully. For example, obtaining a Canadian citizenship requires a three-year residency.

The U.S. and Canada no longer let you just move offshore and disappear with your assets. Recent legislation in the U.S. imposes "reporting requirements" upon you for transfers to an offshore trust. Under current tax law the report is made using Form 3520, which is filed with your 1040 form the following year on April 15. (See discussion of Forms 3520 and 3520-A in Chapter 11, page 179 and 180) If you then die offshore, the assets in your offshore trust are part of your U.S. estate. These events are called *reportable transfers*.

For guidance, I refer you to an expert citizenship and residence attorney specializing in this field, David Lesperance (see Appendix C). For U.S. tax advice on the ramifications of renunciation, I refer you to CPA Vernon Jacobs (also Appendix C). For general information on the different tax havens, see the list of websites in Appendix C. For information on some of the tax ramifications of second citizenships and renunciation of U.S. citizenship, see Chapter 11, page 174.

Implementing an exit strategy involves careful planning. It may be necessary to avoid the ten-year attribution rule[1] on U.S. source income upon expatriation. It is also necessary to avoid unwanted tax liabilities in the jurisdiction of your new citizenship, domicile, and residence. Note that all three elements may be in the same country or may be in three different countries. By now you should realize that this is clearly a complicated process. Your advisor should address the following issues:

- An American may legally acquire a second passport or citizenship without the risk of automatically losing U.S. citizenship. In fact, the renunciation of one's U.S. citizenship is quite a formal, complex, and lengthy process and does not include, as a basis, the mere acquisition of a second passport by a U.S. person.

- One must also distinguish between the acquisition of a passport and the acquisition of citizenship in a second country. One can obtain an "economic" passport without ever becoming a citizen. Many tax havens are seeking capital for development; as an incentive for economic participation, these countries may reward the investor with a passport but not necessarily citizenship. Typical programs require placing funds in a "local" bank for a specified term, establishing a new business enterprise, and/or purchasing real estate in a government-approved development. However, the programs are not useful since the expatriating American must secure a new citizenship. Real citizenship programs also issue a citizen's travel document, a passport.

- Secure a second passport that is functional. An example would be one from the Caribbean nation of Grenada. This citizenship allows extensive visa-free traveling including the United States if one is also holding a Canadian or Bermuda residence. This may be particularly beneficial for an expatriating American. But be warned that political instability in a country can result in rapid, major changes in passport and citizenship requirements, possibly nullifying your status.

The analytical process described in Chapter 4 applies here, as well. How do you select the best jurisdiction for you or for you and your family? Some of the factors to consider in selecting the best jurisdiction for a second passport or citizenship follow:

- Political stability of the country. Would you want to live or retire there? Can you still visit the United States?
- Proximity to the United States, to family or friends, and perhaps to the business interest that you turned over to your child or younger partner.
- Your association with the jurisdiction, its principal language and culture, your ancestors, its principal religion, and so on. Are you prepared to take a two- to three-year period to learn a new language so that you can enjoy the new country, speak with the locals, make new friends, and enjoy the cultural aspects in the native tongue?
- Banking stability and privacy. The security of the U.S. banking system is provided by the Federal Deposit Insurance Corporation (FDIC). Only the United States and Canada have government account insurance; there is no counterpart in the entire world. Consequently, the choice of your bank requires a new factor not generally considered by the reluctant American: that is, How strong is the bank and how safe are my funds on deposit? Lest you forget, the strongest banks in the world are not U.S. banks!
- Visa-free traveling. The ability to travel free of the need for a visa to as many countries as possible, especially the European countries, should be an essential requirement.
- Duration (lifetime) and renewability.
- Initial and future costs.

The Living Trust

This form of "non-APT" trust was discussed in Chapter 7 (page 74). Of principal importance here is that you recognize that it is not intended as an asset protection tool. The living trust is tax neutral.

Typical Second Citizenship Acquisition Programs

Belize offers "economic citizenships." Each year, up to 500 Belize citizenships may be sold under the Belize Economic Citizenship Program for a minimum fee of $25,000 (U.S.).

The Caribbean jurisdiction of Grenada affords a good example of the second citizenship mechanism. Presently, Grenada is characterized as a socially stable country. Its population is primarily of African descent, friendly toward other races, and respectful of the law. Grenada, a British Commonwealth country, needs foreign investment to bolster its economy, elevate its banking system, and become recognized as a leading tax haven. Grenada rewards participants with a citizenship and a passport: you pay the required government and professional fees of $45,000 (U.S.) to qualify. For an additional fee, your family members may be added to the program as well.

With your new citizenship, you can reside on an exceptionally beautiful Caribbean island. When bored, you can use your new passport and visit over ninety countries without the need for a visa, including the British Commonwealth and many European countries.

Here is a list of some second passport jurisdictions. But please note the following ratings:

1. (+) Useful and functional

2. (−) Avoid unless you have family or cultural ties with these countries.

3. (− −) Avoid because of bogus, illegal passports on the black market or fraudulent passports.

- African countries (− −)
- Argentina (−)
- Banking passports (−)
- Belize (−)
- Brazil (− −)
- Chad (−)

- Chile (– –)
- Diplomatic passports (+ or –) When purchased, use with caution
- Dominica (+)
- Dominican Republic (– –)
- Grenada (+)
- Guatemala (– –)
- Honduras (– –)
- Israel (+ or –) Available for Jews only; may be dangerous to possess in a terrorist hijacking situation or with children of military age
- Mexico (– –)
- Nigeria (– –) Not generally honored in the diplomatic community
- Non–United Nations countries (– –)
- Panama (–)
- Paraguay (– –)
- Peru (+) Economic residence granted for financial participation in the country, not a passport program
- Portugal (–)
- Sierra Leone (–)
- Spain (–)
- St. Kitts and Nevis (+)
- Uruguay (–) Limited in scope to non-nationals; not a citizenship program
- Venezuela (– –)
- World citizenships (– –) Bogus

Its primary purpose is to serve as an estate planning tool created for its inherent expediency in the disposition of assets upon death or disability of the settlor, for avoiding some types of probate delays, and for reducing overall probate costs. Since it is a revocable trust, it easily fails when under attack by a judgment creditor.

The Family Limited Partnership

The parties to the family limited partnership (FLP) are the same as in a traditional limited partnership; that is, the general partners (GPs) and the limited partners (LPs). The primary difference is that the LPs are generally family members (usually children) to whom the GPs (usually parents) are conveying their interest in an asset to the FLP.

Initially, the FLP was thought to have many favorable attributes, including asset protection of real property, a stock portfolio, or the family business. However, the fragmenting of the ownership interest among many LPs resulted in a valuation discounting of the fair market value (over a range of 20 to 40 percent)[2] of the property. One needs an expert appraiser, though, to support the discounted value. Costs for a competent appraisal may be in the thousands of dollars. I have seen legal fees for the FLP run between $5,000 and $50,000.

I often see FLPs being used by practitioners principally because of the reluctance of their clients to go directly offshore with their personal property assets. FLP asset protection was thought to be achieved by the following rationale and sequence:

1. The claimant would first sue a limited partner and get a judgment.

2. He or she would then seek a charging order from that court against the limited partner's respective interest in the partnership. Although the judgment creditor would prefer to dissolve the LP, he or she is limited to this remedy.

3. Although the judgment creditor could obtain a lien against the LP's interest, it would be relatively useless because LPs have no power to get to the assets of the FLP without the consent of the GP, they can only reach the distributions from the LP.

4. The effect would be to create a taxable event in the eyes of the IRS—this so-called *phantom income*[3] is subject to

taxes by the judgment creditor, although never actually receiving money.

5. The further effect then should be to discourage litigation against the limited partner, even more so if the LP were an offshore company or person.

6. The judgment creditor could also foreclose on the charging order if permitted under state laws.[4]

Well, it hasn't necessarily worked out exactly that way. Some believe that the FLP is shaky as an asset protection tool—I'll explain why in just a bit, but let's first discuss some advantages.

On the positive side, the FLP continues to be an excellent estate planning tool for conservatively reducing the value of an estate but only in the correct factual situation (i.e., there should be a business purpose and the discount should not be ludicrous). Where there is a highly appreciated asset—for example, real property or the family business—the owner can transfer the asset to the FLP and remain in control as the general partner with a 1 to 2 percent interest. Since the remaining interest has been divided among many LPs and the owner has no control, the LP interest now has a discounted value, a reduced fair market value.[5] The sum of the LP interests is highly discounted from the original fair market value, reducing the exposure to estate taxes. See a qualified appraiser about obtaining the necessary appraisal or discount valuation for the new FLP partnership interests. It should be documented at the time of the transaction for possible later use in an IRS audit. The lower the valuation discount, the less likely it will precipitate an IRS audit, so don't be overly aggressive! If you are, the IRS may assess a penalty tax as high as 40 percent.

A further advantage of the FLP is the ability to shift income to family members who may be in a lower income tax bracket than the GP.

The Weakness of the FLP as an AP Tool

The first problem for the judgment creditor arises when the general partner elects to withhold distributions to the limited partners. Does the creditor with the charging order have any recourse? What if the

general partner selectively withholds dividends from the limited partner who has the charging order by complying with the limiting language in the partnership agreement that distributions may be made
only to family members? This is similar to the so-called spendthrift
provisions in a trust. Would this be characterized as a fraud on the
future creditor or a preference problem under bankruptcy law in a
later bankruptcy? Could the creditor outwait the partnership? Could
this force a settlement between the creditor and the limited partner
for an earlier resolution? What if the creditor is successful in placing the partnership into an involuntary bankruptcy? Are the bankruptcy trustee's interests the same as the judgment creditor with the
charging order? Not very likely. All of these are interesting complications of the FLP. I have more questions than answers.

Onshore real estate creates further problems. If the FLP involves
real property as the principal asset, you can't move it offshore. No
matter what you do on paper, the court of the country in which the
real property is located continues to have exclusive jurisdiction over
the real estate. If the judge doesn't like the factual situation sur-
rounding the FLP, he or she can make an order affecting the real
property. If the offshore LP is unhappy about what the U.S. court has
done, he or she can always submit to the jurisdiction of that court
and try to oppose the court's action—but that would be counter-
productive to maintaining the privacy of the offshore LP.

Liquid assets and mobile personal property are best suited for
asset protection treatment, as they can actually be moved offshore.

The FLP is not a structure that you create and forget. It requires
that you follow the formalities of being an ongoing limited partnership.
You need to function as an FLP and not revert to the casual, informal
ways of operating as commonly practiced among family members.

A partnership is traditionally business motivated and oriented.
It must have a stated business purpose and, as such, it uses a business checking account, pays real and personal taxes, charges family
members the going market rate for use of the FLP's assets, files the
necessary tax returns, acquires the necessary insurance at reasonable
levels, and uses the partnership bank account for partnership transactions. Paying the LPs personally and then seeking reimbursement
from the partnership is not encouraged.

Each time the partners fail to operate as a true partnership, it weakens the protection claimed by the FLP. Where the LP agreement provides that, upon a creditor demand being made upon an LP, the partnership will be dissolved, then the security of the FLP begins to unravel.

The attack upon the FLP to avoid the charging order problem is brought under a suspicion of fraud, and, further, seeks a dissolution of the partnership and a disposition of its assets. The legal argument is raised that since the FLP *was created primarily for asset protection*, as demonstrated by the lack of compliance with the formalities of operating as a true business partnership and the lack of a primary for-profit business, it is a fraud upon the judgment creditor of a limited partner. Further support to the creditor's attack on the FLP comes from the type of professionals that formed the FLP. If they were an "asset protection" company, a judge would likely side with the judgment creditor. In two cases where partners took steps to frustrate a charging order, the courts *allowed foreclosure on the real property*.

A conservative position would be that if all of the potential problems were sufficiently addressed, the FLP could provide some degree of asset protection. However, never let the legal problems of one limited partner destroy the entire FLP structure and cause the loss of the property to foreclosure.

An FLP Checklist

1. The FLP should be a *limited* partnership. The asset being transferred should have a value not less than $1 million. Don't mix different types of assets.

2. Provide for successor general partners.

3. Restrict dissolution of the FLP by using antiliquidation clauses.

4. Provide restrictive language in the FLP agreement to the effect that a creditor who acquires a limited partnership interest does not become a partner.

5. Provide for assessment powers on all parties holding an interest in the FLP, whether or not they are partners.

6. Consider including optional language allowing buyout by other partners with extended provisions for payments.

7. Provide in the agreement for assessment powers over the judgment creditor for the cost of becoming an owner.

8. Have guaranteed payments to partners, which devalue the FLP market value because they are an encumbrance.

9. Provide for full indemnification of the general partner for legal exposure—for example, costs of toxic contamination removal, underinsured court judgment, underinsured acts of God, and so on.

10. Creating an FLP and transferring assets for asset protection must be done *before* a liability arises.

For detailed information about FLPs, go to:

www.haledorf.com/trust_news.html

Real Property Equity Stripping: An Asset Protection Tool

The high-profile person attracts litigation as the candle flame the moth. Jealousy and greed are factors, as well as a surplus of attorneys. Accept it as a fact of life in our highly litigious society. Very few contingent-fee attorneys would pursue an expensive case and advance extraordinary costs for investigators, depositions, and experts without there being a perceived pot of gold at the end of the rainbow. Logically then, they are pursuing the malpractice insurance policy limit, a regulatory or licensing agency's recovery fund, or the defendant's deep pockets (your hard-earned assets).

Determining whether an individual has deep pockets is relatively easy, since tradition, naivete, ego, and the need for a favorable financial statement keep major assets such as real property highly visible. And an asset search is relatively inexpensive and easy to obtain from the public records, so plaintiff's counsel can make this determination fairly cheaply.

The obvious answer is balance, moderation, and a change of lifestyle. You can be a litigation target at any time; you needn't be in a high-profile industry (neurosurgery, real estate development, or soliciting funds) to become a victim of an overzealous plaintiff's counsel. As a safeguard, consider following the 70:30, 60:40, or 50:50 rules. Reserve a substantial percentage of your estate as the U.S.-based sacrificial lamb, willingly if begrudgingly given up for litigation reserves, and place the balance (50 to 70 percent) out of the reach of creditors as your nest egg. Placing only one-quarter or one-third of your estate into an APT would be even better from a fraud defense perspective. Remember that people cannot legally totally strip themselves of all assets. To do so would clearly be fraud against future claimants and judgment creditors.

A solution that I advocate for highly appreciated real estate (other than the FLP) has acquired the label *equity stripping*. Through a special arrangement with offshore lenders, significant equity can be stripped from your real property. The residence, for example, can be stripped to the homestead level in order to discourage litigation, encourage earlier and cheaper settlements, and/or fully protect against a runaway jury verdict. The corresponding funds received then would need to be placed in an exempt asset and then be gifted, used to purchase an annuity, and/or be transferred to irrevocable instruments. To survive an attack, this strategy requires a real loan and real mortgages or liens being placed on the real estate in a timely manner. Don't procrastinate—the earlier the better for this strategy.

The Unincorporated Organization or Unincorporated Business Organization

The *unincorporated organization* (UO), or *unincorporated business organization* (UBO) (–), is an archaic form of business structure presumably used for asset protection and miraculous tax avoidance benefits (see Figure 10.1). These were highly touted in the past by promoters in the classified advertisement pages of the *Wall Street Journal*, but now have gone the way of the dodo bird, thankfully. It remains a farce and is a fraud perpetuated on the public. Figure 10.1 remains, however, as a useful teaching tool.

Proprietary Triple-Trust Structure

For several years, until he withdrew from the trust business, Karl Loren proposed and marketed a layered structure consisting of three trusts in series (–) (see Figure 10.2). The first trust was a domestic trust identified as an unincorporated business organization doing business as a trust (UO). The beneficiary of the domestic trust was the first OS trust (FT 1). The beneficiary of FT 1 was the second OS trust, FT 2. Each trust had a trustee and trust protector, and possibly a committee of advisors.

The assets to be protected were transferred to the UO in return for a *certificate of beneficial interest* (CBI) that was alleged to be a tax-free exchange of equal value. The asset then was gone, deleted from the balance sheet and records of the settlor. The certificate was of contingent value and thus not very marketable, so it would not be an attractive asset for attachment by a judgment creditor. (However, nothing I could locate in my research supported the proposition of a tax-free transfer for a CBI.)

It was asserted that money could flow from the UO to FT 1 and then to FT 2 free of U.S. taxes. The tax argument was that since FT 2 received no U.S. source of income and was not doing business effectively connected with the U.S., then FT 2 had no obligation to file a U.S. tax return or to pay U.S. taxes. I never was able to accept that premise comfortably.

Contemporary Three-Tier Structure

Capitalizing on a more modern variation of the proprietary triple-trust structure, current tax savings promoters are marketing a variation of the three-box structure (–) and are still claiming total tax

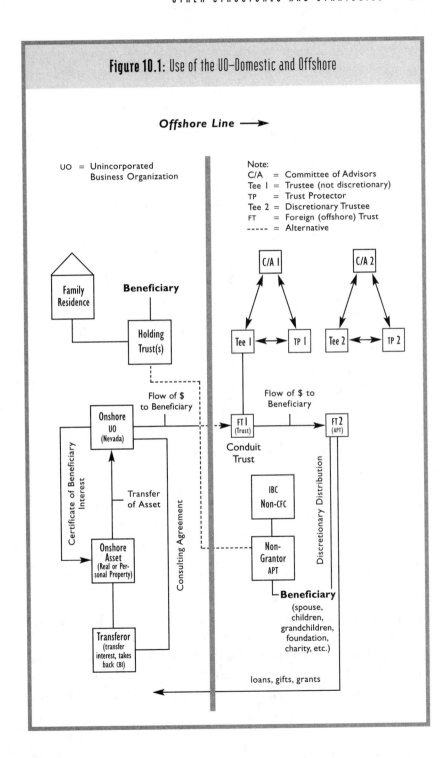

Figure 10.1: Use of the UO–Domestic and Offshore

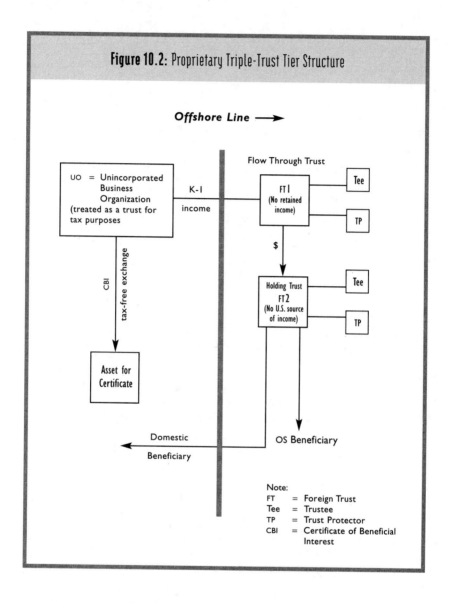

Figure 10.2: Proprietary Triple-Trust Tier Structure

avoidance. A call to me in January 1996 from a Las Vegas chiropractor confirmed that it was indeed true. The first box of the structure was changed to an LLC from a domestic UO filing as a trust (see Figure 10.3). The same tax avoidance claims were now made for this newer, modified structure as were previously postulated by Mr. Loren.

See if you follow this logic. Box 1, the LLC, distributes income to Box 2, the first offshore entity, an APT called FT 1. The LLC issues a form K-1 to FT 1. The sole beneficiary of FT 1 is FT 2, another OS APT. FT 1 distributes all of this income to FT 2, OS APT to OS APT, from one zero-tax jurisdiction to another zero-tax jurisdiction. Now, if you are still with me, follow further: because FT 2 did not receive any U.S. source income or money effectively connected with the United States, it did not need to pay U.S. income taxes on the money received. Is this tax-avoidance scheme U.S. tax compliant, or is it in the gray area—or even the clearly black area? The consensus of my colleagues was that it fell into the black area and was not tax compliant. If you are using this structure, you need to see an international tax expert immediately and implement remedial action (see Appendix C).

The above strategy is presented for historical purposes and is not recommended prospectively. Readers should shy away from promoters who offer such a so-called solution to mitigate U.S. taxes since it does no such thing. Conversely, it would likely cause an IRS audit. Attorney J. Richard Duke of Birmingham, Alabama, offered an unequivocal rejection of the structure:

> This structure will not work, whether funded by the U.S. settlor or a foreigner. If the settlor funds the structure, he is the settlor. The foreign corporation that creates the foreign trust is treated as a domestic corporation under the tax laws; and, if a foreigner funds the structure, Form 3520 requires a complete explanation of how this comes about, the specific code provision that states that a U.S. person is not taxed, and other information. One cannot meet these filing requirements and defer or avoid U.S. taxation under this structure.

The Pure Trust Scam

The pure trust is a member of that genre of abusive trust arrangements consisting of one or more domestic (onshore) trusts ultimately flowing into (followed by) an offshore trust or two, perhaps with several IBCs, with unwarranted claims of U.S. tax avoidance. Their

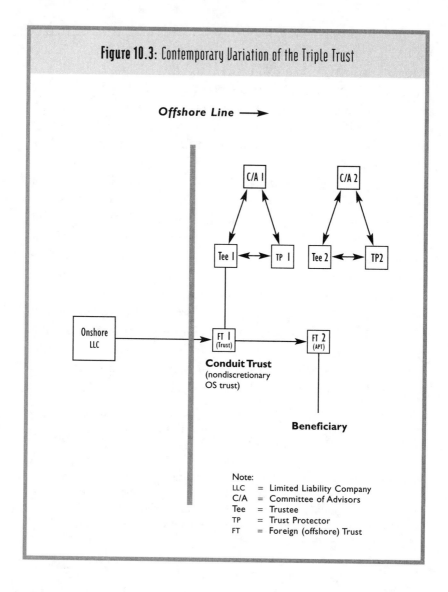

Figure 10.3: Contemporary Variation of the Triple Trust

Offshore Line ⟶

Note:
LLC = Limited Liability Company
C/A = Committee of Advisors
Tee = Trustee
TP = Trust Protector
FT = Foreign (offshore) Trust

method is the same in that titles of assets are transferred away, out of your name—but you maintain full control. You can't do it—it won't work!

The genre of abusive trust scams carries many labels; look out for the following terms or variations of these terms that give them away:

- Business organization common-law trust
- Constitutional trust
- Equity trust
- Family estate trust
- Pure trust
- Unincorporated business trust organization, sometimes marketed as an unincorporated business organization

A pure trust is one in which there are at least three parties: the creator or settlor (never grantor), the trustee, and the beneficiary. Each is a separate entity. A pure trust is claimed to be a lawful, irrevocable, separate legal entity. There *must* be a minimum of three entities (parties).

Its advocates (promoters, in some instances) quote case language supporting this definition, such as, "It is established by legal precedent that pure trusts are lawful, valid business organizations," or " . . . a trust or trust estate is a legal entity for most purposes, as are common-law trusts."

Unfortunately, some promoters advocate the use of trusts in a non–tax-compliant manner. Their pure trust package is a scam structured primarily to evade taxes based on legitimate trust laws. The pure trust has been tested in the courts in a series of cases called the *family trust cases*, which hold that the creator of a pure trust is to be responsible for the taxes that he or she so carefully tried to evade. Not surprisingly, the promoters of the scam have long since disappeared. Due diligence will prevent your getting drawn into this quagmire.

Some promotional literature and advocates state that the procedure for establishing a pure trust is under "contract" law—a common-law contract rather than a statutory law contract. As a consequence, one isolates oneself from being a taxable entity, protecting against exposure to liabilities and government intervention.

A trust is sometimes called a *pure contractual trust*. It is created by an instrument (document) called a *declaration of trust*, which is written under common law with no reference to the jurisdiction of a state or federal statutory law. The pure trust is set up by the settlor and the first trustee for the benefit of the beneficiary. Be aware that if you retain ownership or are still in control of any trust assets, creditors could pierce the protective veil supposedly provided by the pure trust vehicle.

Assets are usually transferred to the pure trust by way of donations or gifting to the trust—for example, from a third party (see Chapter 11, discussion of Form 709, page 178). Promoters claim that if the pure trust has a situs in a state that recognizes its legality (for example, Florida), the trust can function under the control of "U.S. common law," which will recognize and acknowledge the state's laws and statutes. They further claim that if you wish to establish a situs in any other state, province, or country, that you simply change the situs or jurisdiction address by passing appropriate "trust minutes," as would be the case under typical contract law.

There are further refinements to the pure trust. It may be structured as a business trust so it can operate an existing business for profit, or as a management trust. Being an entity—a person under the IRC—the trust must obtain a tax ID to function. It is permitted to operate an existing business that has been transferred to the trust, but only for the purpose of sale or liquidation and subsequent distribution of the assets to the beneficiaries at a later date as defined in the trust or under the discretion of the trustee.

Promoters also market the pure trust as an asset protection device. They claim that using such a trust isolates your personal assets from the separate conduct of the pure trust. They allege that trust assets belong to the trust, not you. If there is a judgment entered against you, your creditor cannot seize what is owned by the pure trust, a separate person. If you had previously transferred title to your assets to the trust, without knowledge of any claim against you, then the assets are protected from your creditors. Conversely, as a person, the trust can be sued or can sue others.

It is further claimed that the creator's filing bankruptcy will not affect the trust, nor will a subsequent divorce. Others have used the pure trust as an alternative to a prenuptial agreement.

At this point, you may be shouting, "If a pure trust is so wonderful, why doesn't everyone use it?" The trust promoters are pretty slick in this regard. The following examples are typical of their approach; see if you can pick up on the psychology being employed to capture you. These examples are provided without endorsement or rejection, though I have already given pure trusts a poor (– – –) rating. You must make your own decision as to suitability for your purposes. Here is an example of the sales pitch:

> Truth is, not everybody can operate a pure trust. It takes a small degree of finesse and business savvy to understand and remain under the protection of a TRUST. The average person will not want to devote the time or the patience to grasp the knowledge and understanding they need in order to work through a TRUST. Sometimes, there are no clear-cut rules concerning trusts. It may involve legal matters and rulings, etc. at times. It's clear, though, that those people who take more chances, end up with more in the end. It's like anything else worth having; the average people won't do it. Now, obviously, you're not average or you wouldn't be reading this information. You've gone through considerable time and research to get this far in your understanding of a pure trust and I know you're serious about wanting to understand all you can.

Were you sold on this product? The hype continues:

> You should be the First Trustee, the one who contracts initially with the Settlor to donate assets to the trust organization for the benefit of the beneficiary(ies). The Settlor should be someone neutral, whether it be a friend, associate or partner. Someone, obviously, you trust considerably. Even though they won't have any day-to-day duties of maintaining the trust, they help with the initial input of naming the beneficiaries. I would set up your children as beneficiaries. If you don't have children, use a brother, sister, niece or nephew, etc. with whom you can work directly to support the credibility of the trust.

Unfortunately, the promoter discourages the use of a will if you have a pure trust, without regard to what happens if a court strikes down a pure trust in total. Read this promotional material with that concern in mind.

> The pure trust is all an estate one needs to direct the proper distribution of present and future assets. You've already transferred ownership of your assets to the trust. Now, it's just a matter of who controls those assets. . . . Upon your death, if your heirs are the beneficiaries of the trust, there are no changes required. The heirs appoint a new First Trustee (if that was your title) and conduct business as usual. If your heirs were not the beneficiaries at the

time of your death, and would like to be afterwards, the present beneficiaries need to relinquish their position and have it cleared by the trustees. If your heirs simply want to control the assets like you did before your death, you need to make sure their names are established as "Successor Trustees" in appropriate minutes. That way, in the event of your death, they automatically take over your position as First Trustee.

The promoters further claim that "everything you need to know" is in their "simple pure trust kit." Just follow the format of the promotional materials and sample formats that are included and you'll do just fine. And finally, they state:

> FINAL NOTE: The procedure of operating a TRUST is always an ongoing learning situation. You will always be learning new ways in which to maneuver yourself or your assets to be most favorable for your tax situation or financial well-being. Although we can't be your legal or tax advisor, we will tell you everything we know about the position of running a TRUST. If you ever need to talk to us or have any questions, we will be glad to talk. Drop us a line or pick up the phone and call. We'll do everything we can to help you.

The Business Trust

The *business trust* (BT) (– – –) remains with us to this date. The IRS recognizes four general classifications of trusts: the ordinary trust, the investment trust, the liquidating trust, and the business trust. You probably are most familiar with the ordinary trust, usually created by a will or an *inter vivos* declaration. This trust is intended for the orderly management and distribution of assets upon death or providing for holding property of minors.

The business trust is either an evolution of the "Massachusetts business trust" or an entity unto itself. Its advocates claim that it is an excellent asset protection tool. Some even claim it results in tax reduction. Well, that depends.

Some structures include two trusts in series: an operating trust held by its beneficiary, the holding trust. Initially, the business or real property is transferred to the operating trust. While the original owner remains on as an asset manager, he or she is receiving Form 1099 income for his or her services. The trust is "insured" in its own name and defends any lawsuits against it and the asset manager. But the original owner of the asset claims no interest in it any longer, and therefore he or she shouldn't be a defendant in any lawsuit against the business trust.

The business trust is not a traditional entity, so few CPAs or business attorneys will recognize or encourage utilizing it. To find out more about it, you need to get with the cult that perpetuates it. The promoters are under heavy fire from the IRS because of their claims of tax avoidance. The BT and its progeny have been characterized by the IRS as being abusive trusts. It is promoted with promises of tax benefits without the taxpayer giving up control of the assets and continuing to derive benefits, as before the BT was put in place. The abusive BTs fall into five areas:

1. **The basic business trust.** The owner of a sole proprietorship transfers ownership of his or her business enterprise to a newly formed BT. Some promoters refer to this entity as an unincorporated business organization (UBO). In some situations, the transferor takes back, on a tax-free exchange basis, a certificate of ownership. These certificates have the appearance of a traditional stock certificate and are referred to as certificates of beneficial interest (CBIS) or units of beneficial interest (UBIS). By imaginative expense payments to the transferor and to other trusts that he or she has created, the BT has no or little taxable income. Promotional claims are also made that this eliminates the need to pay self-employment taxes. Further claims are made that since the CBIS or UBIS can be canceled upon death of the original business owner or transferred to the children for a token payment, you have avoided estate death tax liability.

2. **The family residence trust.** The transferor transfers title to the residence to the trust, as well as all the furnishings. The trust becomes the landlord. Promoters claim that the new trust has a stepped-up basis and when it sells the real

property, it can avoid or reduce capital gains taxes. Usually, the normal indicia of a landlord-tenant relationship is missing in that rent is generally not paid and the transferor pays real property taxes, mortgage payments, and insurance directly instead of the landlord doing so.

3. **The service or equipment trust.** Major items are transferred to the trust, which then charges the other trust exorbitant rental rates. For the transferred equipment, a CBI is given with claims that it is a tax-free exchange. Other trust services are also purchased for inflated fees to reduce the income of the BT.

4. **The charitable trust.** Assets are transferred to a newly created trust. The trust is not exempt from taxation under IRC rules, but that doesn't stop the promoters. They still claim that the donor can deduct the "gifts" made to the trust. The trust takes on such philanthropic and charitable causes as providing college aid to the business owner's children and grandchildren.

5. **The final trust.** This is usually the holding trust or holding entity. It is sited offshore in a tax-free tax haven for further asset protection and claims of tax benefits. This trust may hold (own or possess) the CBIS or UBIS. Further claims are made that when the final trust pays the income to a second offshore trust, that second trust has no U.S. liability since it is an offshore trust and it is not receiving U.S. source income. This is a false assumption in that the original source obligations are not eliminated by transferring money through multiple offshore trusts.

The Pure Equity Trust

The *pure equity trust* (– – –) is marketed by promoters as a specially designed trust claiming attributes consisting of the "greatest possible advantages" for asset protection, tax savings, simplicity of trust management, and flexibility. The creator exchanges assets with the trust, and in return receives a certificate of beneficial interest (CBI) in units of beneficial interest (UBI) in the trust. Generally, one unit equals 1 percent. The beneficiaries hold (own) the CBIs. This promotion is quite similar to the business trust.

The creator is not a beneficiary, but is usually retained by the trustees to "manage" the assets. The trustees are of two types— *independent* and *adverse*. *Independent* is defined as not being related by blood, marriage, adoption, or an employer-employee relationship with the creator. The *adverse trustee* is defined as one who has a substantial beneficial interest in the trust assets as well as the income or benefits derived from the trust.

Providing for a Child in a High-Risk Profession

High net worth parents wanting to give to an adult child working in an industry fraught with the risks of litigation have to be concerned that what they give could be lost to a successful litigant. To satisfy this concern, parents could give to an irrevocable domestic trust, a family limited partnership, or an offshore trust for the benefit of that child and the children of that child (their grandchildren) in a form of an educational trust or a fully discretionary trust, containing spendthrift clauses that would provide for the child's well-being (+++). Such a trust could not be invaded by the child's creditors. In this form of trust, the child is only a discretionary beneficiary and never can be construed as a settlor. Other forms of trust that might also be considered are special needs trusts or purpose trusts.

Offshore Charitable or Private Foundations

The offshore charitable foundation (+ or –, depending upon the jurisdiction and tax reforms) is no longer just for the very wealthy families. The Ford Foundation and the Rockefeller Foundation are clearly the pioneers, but now many foundations may be formed by less wealthy Americans to implement their altruistic and charitable philosophies. Os charitable foundations are less costly to form and

Characteristics of a Fraudulent Trust

- Intuition tells you it is an abusive trust.
- Promoters suggest that the trust is guaranteed to eliminate all taxes.
- Promoters claim that the trust will permit tax-free personal grants for school scholarships, medical expenses, special loans, and so on.
- You become a "caretaker" (maintain full control) of your own residence.
- You receive a *pre-filing notice* from the IRS. By then, it may be too late for remedial action.

administer than their American counterparts. Further, they are free of overly restrictive U.S. laws that limit, overcontrol, and monitor. Some of the advantages of a private foundation are:

- It is a legal entity.
- It is relatively easy to form.
- It is less costly to create than an APT.
- It is easier to replace a board member of the foundation than to replace a trustee of an APT.

The Liechtenstein form of private foundation, the *Stiftung*, can also be found in other countries such as the Netherlands Antilles and Panama. The uses are quite varied and include:

- Religious, charitable, public, or family objectives
- Asset protection
- Preservation of family wealth
- International estate planning
- Isolation of specific assets from the balance of the assets

It is not intended to be profit oriented, so it may not generally engage in commercial activities on a regular basis. It may engage in commercial transactions to the extent necessary to accomplish its charter. For example, if the foundation holds stock in a company, it may exercise its rights as a shareholder of a corporation.

However, one negative aspect is a loss of U.S. tax deductibility for U.S. source gifts or donations to a foreign charity or foundation. Private-interest foundations are used as asset protection vehicles for high net worth persons. Panama has developed the use of the foundation as an asset protection tool.

There are two types of foundations: an *inter vivos foundation*, which may be established during the founder's lifetime, and a *postmortem foundation*, which is established after his or her death. The private-interest foundation, once registered in the public registry, is considered an independent, legal person, apart and separate from the founder.

The founder or third persons may transfer assets to the foundation. The foundation may be used to hold any type of asset, present or future, and may derive its income from any type of legal business, which should be held in an underlying corporation. The assets of the foundation will constitute a separate estate from those of the founder and beneficiaries. They may not be seized, liened, or subjected to any lawsuit in connection with activity of the founder or beneficiary. Under no circumstances shall the assets of the foundation be used to satisfy personal obligations of the founder or of the beneficiaries.

Often, the founder retains control over the foundation through maintaining the power of appointment of the *foundation council*. The founder may serve as a member of the foundation council as a beneficiary or as protector. The founder retains the power to remove all of these powers if so desired or may reassign them to another person in the foundation. The founder can be a natural or legal person. Furthermore, a nominee could be used as the founder, wherefore the individual's name does not need to appear in the *memorandum of constitution*.

The foundation council is similar to the board of directors of a corporation. It makes all the decisions for the benefit of the foundation. The council has the obligation to administer the foundation assets for the benefit of the beneficiaries. In case of mismanagement of the assets of the foundation by the foundation council, the beneficiaries can object to the actions of the council.

The beneficiaries are the persons for whose benefit the foundation is established (often the family members of the founder). They can be natural and/or legal persons. The objectives of the foundation often address the education and health needs of the beneficiaries or grantees, such as the extended family of the founder. The beneficiaries of the foundation need not appear in the memorandum of constitution of the foundation. Only the persons involved in the creation of the foundation know the identities of the beneficiaries, as established in the bylaws. The bylaws are private and are not registered in the public registry. A court order is the only way for a third party to identify the beneficiaries of a foundation.

An additional protection provided by 1995 legislation is that all persons involved in any activities, transactions, or operations related to the foundation are required to maintain full secrecy and confidentiality at all times. The punishment for breach of this duty is six months of imprisonment and a $50,000 fine, with the potential for further civil liability. This applies to persons involved in any transaction (such as constitution, amendments, and bylaws) of the foundation, irrespective of whether they work in the private or public sector.

With the proper personal planning, a private foundation can be used as an integral part of estate planning. It is useful to keep in mind that foundations have been established with the intent to attract capital from foreign investors, and in exchange the investor will receive secrecy on the operations made, asset protection, and tax exemptions.

Bankruptcy with an Asset Preservation Plan

You should try to avoid personal bankruptcy. Federal bankruptcy judges have tremendous powers and are not reluctant to use them. If, regrettably, as the last recourse, one must file a bankruptcy, one should consider the following:

- Make a complete disclosure of your offshore transfers and interests on the schedules that accompany your petition, as filed with the bankruptcy court. In a 1992 case in Virginia, the court denied a bankruptcy discharge because the petitioner failed to schedule his Bermuda APT. The court found that the debtor knew he had a reversionary interest in the APT and chose to conceal that interest with the intent to at least "hinder and delay his creditors." On the more positive side, the creditor could not get assets from the Bermuda trust and ultimately settled with the trustee of the APT in a private settlement at a substantial discount.

- Assume that disgruntled former employees, a vexatious former spouse, dissatisfied partners, parasitic relatives, or others in your personal and/or business life are now adversarial toward you because of the losses they sustained in the filing of your bankruptcy. They are likely to inform the trustee.

- If the bankruptcy trustee for your case detects a fraud upon the court, omissions in the schedules filed with the court, or evidence that you're concealing assets and lying, he or she is compelled to pursue you and your former assets, wherever situated. A U.S. bankruptcy trustee has been known to go to the Isle of Man seeking recovery of concealed assets, and as he was able to make a case for fraud, the Isle of Man courts took jurisdiction over the funds hidden there. Many offshore jurisdictions are entering into treaties which require cooperation in transnational bankruptcy proceedings.

- The trustee specializes in locating and detecting concealed assets and does so on an ongoing basis. It is a full-time occupation, and he or she has the expertise and experience to locate them. The trustee earns fees based on the recovery of assets. This is a very motivating factor. The trustee's attorneys work on a form of contingent fee—if they recover assets, they

are paid for their services at a court-approved hourly
rate plus all reasonable costs. No recovery, no attorney
fees.

- A failure to list one's interest in an APT may be the
  basis for a bankruptcy judge denying your bankruptcy
  discharge *and* prohibiting you from filing bankruptcy
  again for six years.
- If your conduct is found abusive enough to be
  characterized as having made fraudulent transfers and
  your conduct violates the bankruptcy code, you may be
  referred by the court to the U.S. Attorney for
  investigation and prosecution for bankruptcy crimes.
  You could go to jail!
- The "look back" period for examining the fraudulent
  transfers of assets depends upon several factors:

  - The relationship of the transferee to you
  - Whether the transfer occurred during the ninety
    days prior to filing the bankruptcy petition (the so-
    called *preference transfer*)
  - Whether the transfer was to an insider during the
    one-year period preceding the filing
  - The statute of limitations for fraud under your state
    laws

- Don't forget that it is legal to convert nonexempt
  assets to exempt assets (called *transmogrifying*)
  before you file your bankruptcy. Your bankruptcy
  attorney, being an officer of the court, is limited as
  to how far he or she may go in advising you to
  transmogrify, but can certainly tell you what the
  legal exemptions are in each of the states of the
  United States. If a relocation is viable, ask about the
  preferred states. If your bankruptcy attorney doesn't
  know, get a better attorney. Texas and Florida, for
  example, are most generous with their homestead
  allowance.

- The U.S. bankruptcy code has not abrogated the Statute of Elizabeth with respect to future known and unknown claimants (creditors).

Foreign Income Exclusion

Those who live outside the United States for 330 days per year may have an IRS income tax opportunity. There is an annual exemption of foreign earned income that is scheduled according to the following scale:

Calendar year	Amount allowed as exempt
1999	$74,000
2000	$76,000
2001	$78,000
2002	$80,000
2003	Under present law, the same as for 2002 and for the later years

See IRS Form 2555 for further details. To obtain this exemption, the taxpayer must be a bona fide resident of a foreign country or meet the alternative physical presence test on a calendar year basis. Physical presence is defined as being outside of the U.S. for 330 full days in the calendar year. Also, the compensation must be for personal services, not investment income. The terms *bona fide* and *presence test* are clarified in the IRC at §911. There also are special provisions for the situation of a husband and wife both working offshore. This is a more complicated section than it appears to be at first blush. Get competent tax advice to do it correctly, and save a lot of income taxes and avoid hassles with the IRS.

So there must be *foreign earned income* for services rendered in a foreign country, and you must pass the *bona fide residence test* or the *physical presence test*. Meeting the foreign residency requirements is the major problem. The two tests are:

1. **Bona fide residence test.** To satisfy this test, the taxpayer must demonstrate that he or she has been a bona fide resident of a foreign country or combination of foreign countries for an uninterrupted period that includes an entire taxable year.

2. **Presence test.** The taxpayer must meet the burden of proving that during any period of twelve consecutive months, he or she was "present" in a foreign country or countries during at least 330 full days.

Determining Where Your Tax Abode Is Located

The courts and the IRS use some of the following parameters as a test to determine whether you are an offshore resident:

1. The physical location of your permanent home, regardless of whether it is now rental property

2. If you are married, the location of your family while working offshore

3. An analysis of the total time spent in the U.S. as compared to offshore, especially during your vacation or time-off periods

4. The locations of your reported bank accounts

5. The jurisdiction of the driver's license you are using

6. The jurisdiction where your vehicles are registered

7. The location where you are legally entitled and registered to vote

8. The place where you receive your personal mail in the normal course of everyday events

9. The location of your primary social, cultural, and political relationships and religious affiliations outside of the U.S.

10. The locations of any real property or businesses in which you have an interest

11. Whether income tax or other taxes are paid to a foreign country

12. Whether you speak the native language of the country in which you are working

13. The location of the issuer of any credit cards you are using

14. Whether you are being paid in U.S. dollars

15. Whether you are paying for offshore lodging, food, and other necessities of life

Viatical Settlements (—)

Viatical settlements are not an investment in debt instruments, but purchasing the death benefits from insurance policies of people who are terminally ill. The mutual benefit is to give money to terminally ill people before death so that they may perhaps more fully enjoy their last moments on Earth. I must caution you about the solvency of the insurance company issuing the policy. What happens if it fails after you have paid the ill party? As to the tax ramifications, see IRS Publication 525, "Taxable and Nontaxable Income," for more information. It states: "Life insurance proceeds paid to you because of the death of the insured person are not taxable unless the policy was turned over to you for a price."

Foreign Sales Corporations

The IRC has provided tax incentives to exporting companies with sales that qualify as *foreign sales corporations* (FSC). This is a complex topic requiring the services of an expert in the field. More than 3,600 FSCs have been formed, clearly a testimony of their benefits to

U.S. companies. They usually have offshore management companies providing the physical presence that meets the FSC foreign presence test and performing some of the administrative tasks necessary to qualify as an FSC. St. Thomas, the U.S. Virgin Islands, and Barbados have been used for these services. The FSC is currently under attack—the European Union has argued that the FSC regime violates some World Trade Organization policies.

Offshore Betting and Gaming Licenses

We are seeing a phenomenal growth of gaming on the Internet, which is illegal for U.S. residents. It is likely that the United States casinos will put more and more pressure on Congress to limit this growth industry and to enforce the prohibitions against Americans gambling in this manner. However, this is the procedure that non-American persons use to create their virtual casinos. For example, if a U.K. bookmaker moves his casino to an OS site, he can take tax-free bets from his U.K. customers. Tax-free competition from OS casinos is growing.

Pre-licensing activities:

- An offshore corporation must be formed upon the granting of the gaming license; this is not an IBC but a true local corporation.
- The use of the word *casino* in the company's name is prohibited in many jurisdictions.
- A business plan, including an outline of business operations, must be submitted for approval to the appropriate government office.
- Beneficial owners of the corporation, officers, and directors must submit character, bank, and professional references (verified either by the local government or through outcontracting with international companies that perform such services), police records, and passport copies.
- You must pay a processing fee per person.

- You must provide appropriate safeguards to prevent local citizens from placing bets.
- Banking transactions must clear through a local bank.

Upon approval and the granting of the license:
- Work permits are required for all non-nationals.
- Payment of the registration fee, between $80,000 and $100,000 in the jurisdictions that I have investigated.
- Expect an annual renewal fee in the order of $40,000.
- Report any changes in the directors or beneficial owners within a specified reporting period.
- Any advertising must be first cleared by the local government.

Endnotes

1 If your principal purpose of renouncing your citizenship is for tax purposes, you will still owe them for a period of up to ten years, as far as the IRS is concerned.

2 The greater the discount taken, the more IRS "chokes" on it. While a 20 percent discount is generally IRS acceptable, 30 percent pushes the IRS envelope of tolerance, 40 percent will most assuredly involve a dispute.

3 While this book was being drafted, federal legislation was pending that gave judgment creditors relief from the phenomena of phantom income tax recapture. Consult with your tax advisor for the current status and proper treatment of this tax relief measure.

4 The Georgia Uniform Partnership Act (UPA) does not provide for foreclosures of limited partnership interests. Many planners thus make Georgia the state of choice for FLPs.

5 The valuation discount is based on two factors: 1. a lack of transferability due to those restrictions contained in the FLP agreement; and 2. the creation of minority ownership (even where the LPs own 98 percent) of the FLP. Minority ownership means a lack of control.

11

Tax Treatment, Ramifications, and Deferral

No man in this country is under the smallest obligation, moral or otherwise, to arrange his legal relation to his business or to his property as to enable the Inland Revenue to put the largest possible shovel into his stores.

BRITISH JUDGE LORD CLYDE

You can have a lord, you can have a king, but the man to fear is the tax collector.

FOUND IN THE TIGRIS AND
EUPHRATES VALLEY,
CIRCA 4000 B.C.

. . . in the last twelve years, there have been about 9,500 tax code changes.

COMMISSIONER OF INTERNAL
REVENUE CHARLES O. ROSSOTTI,
MAY 1999

THE PROBLEM WITH writing about taxes is that the information here may quickly become outdated[1] by new legislation. Further, the quantity of incorrect information and the promulgation of misinformation by tax-scheme hucksters are staggering. Your offshore planner needs to update you and do remedial work before you can proceed.

If you don't use offshore planners who understand the relevant U.S. tax laws, you will very likely be in noncompliance with those tax laws.

I use the word *foreign* in this chapter to be consistent with the IRC. The U.S. Congress has become notorious for changing the tax code without "grandfathering" existing structures, making OS tax planning extremely difficult. Accordingly, the appropriate disclaimer would be that you should treat this section as reference and historic material for academic discussions. Review any of the materials, especially the tax materials in this book, with your informed consultant before proceeding.

Your possible participation in foreign accounts and foreign trusts is required to be disclosed to the IRS on Schedule B of the 1040 tax form.

Offshore jurisdictions, with their low tax rates, tax exemptions, and, in some cases, lack of taxes, occupy a vital and growing role in international tax deferral or possible avoidance. The tax regimen of the jurisdiction being considered is a most important consideration.

For privacy, it should be axiomatic that offshore funds remain offshore, out of the U.S. banking system, which lacks privacy.

As a general proposition, no U.S. tax savings should be anticipated unless one uses tax-deferral devices such as offshore annuities or insurance products or invests in specific stocks for future capital gains rather than current dividends[2] or income.

The United States is unusual with respect to other major industrialized nations in that it taxes its citizens and foreign residents on the basis of their worldwide income; only citizens from the Philippines, Romania, and Eritrea suffer from this same problem. If a U.K. citizen works in the Cayman Islands, he or she pays no income tax, since the Caymans have none and the United Kingdom doesn't tax offshore income. But a U.S. person working in the Caymans would, after an initial offshore exemption, pay taxes to the United States. The price for the privilege of U.S. citizenship is high—maybe even inequitable!

Paradoxically, the United States is a safe tax haven for around 90 percent of the world's population and foreign central banks. To encourage foreign investment in the U.S. stock market, the offshore investor pays no capital gains on U.S. security transactions. To encourage deposits in the U.S. banking system, there are no U.S. taxes on interest earned.

Tax Implications for U.S. Persons

The IRS presumes that most American-owned OS entities are tax-neutral flow-through vehicles where the tax liabilities are attributed to U.S. persons. When using an offshore IBC, great care must be used to not trigger the U.S. controlled foreign corporation (CFC) rules limiting ownership.

The primary factor is the threshold level of *ownership or control* of the shares of the foreign corporation by U.S. persons (citizens or residents). There are two tests:

1. Ownership of more than 50 percent of the voting power or the value of the shares of the foreign corporation by U.S. persons.

2. Where five or fewer U.S. persons own more than 50 percent of the shares or voting power of the corporation.

Ownership by certain relatives or related entities (this is an IRS-defined term) is attributed to the shareholders so that the ownership rules can't be circumvented by dividing ownership within a family, in family trusts, in an estate, or in a family-controlled corporation. All of the shares of a foreign corporation held by related parties are aggregated in determining whether the two tests have been met. The attribution tests are quite complex, and a further discussion is beyond the scope of this book. However, as a general rule, it is not possible to avoid the CFC rules by having shares owned by a relative, trust, partnership, or corporation that is ultimately controlled by a U.S. person or that has U.S. beneficial owners.

If the foreign corporation is deemed to be a CFC, the U.S. shareholders (those who own 10 percent or more of the foreign corporation) must report as current taxable income their proportional share of certain income of the foreign corporation that is classified as "subpart F" income by the IRC. Generally, that will include any investment income of the corporation and it may include other income that is derived from transactions with shareholders or affiliated parties.

Further complications arise if the foreign corporation is deemed to be a *foreign personal holding company* (FPHC). Briefly, that will occur if at least 60 percent of the income of the corporation is from passive investment sources and if more than 50 percent of the corporation is owned (directly or indirectly) by five or fewer U.S. shareholders. Basically, the income of the FPHC is subject to current tax by the shareholders of the company.

If the OS company is characterized as either a CFC or FPHC, U.S. investors are taxed each tax year by the U.S. on their pro rata subpart F income, which consists of passive investment income and certain other types of income even if it is not distributed; there would be no tax deferral. Further, a U.S. investor may have another U.S. tax issue if the income received is designated as being from a *passive foreign investment company* (PFIC).

Tax on the U.S. Grantor

The IRS will tax the grantor of a foreign trust on its worldwide income. The tax is determined on the basis of whether the grantor is a U.S. person and whether there is a U.S. beneficiary.

Currently, there is a difference of professional opinion as to whether a foreign trust should be structured to be classified as a domestic trust, thereby avoiding the foreign trust reporting rules. To qualify, the trust must be subject to the primary supervision of a U.S. court, and one or more of the trustees (or fiduciaries) must be U.S. persons, and those persons must have the authority to control all substantial decisions of the trust.

To meet this test, planners are using multiple trustees—one foreign trustee and two U.S. trustees. Then, when a condition of duress arises, the U.S. trustees resign and the remaining (foreign) trustee changes the situs of the trust to a foreign jurisdiction. This concept is controversial since there may be a reluctance to "pull the trigger" and execute this plan. The IRS deems an automatic duress clause to fail the test to qualify as being a domestic trust.

But there is also a tax issue involved. If there are any appreciated assets in the domestic trust, when the trust becomes a foreign trust it will be subject to a capital gains tax at the time the trust is converted.

Special Tax Concessions by Local Jurisdictions

Some offshore jurisdictions provide special tax laws that make them ideal for special applications. Some that have been identified include Andorra and Cyprus for the EU community, BVI in the Caribbean, Macau on the South China coast, and Nauru in the Pacific. A detailed discussion of each jurisdiction is beyond the scope of this book; however, your offshore consultant should steer you to the site that would best meet your needs.

Excise Tax

The Taxpayers Relief Act of 1997 repealed the excise tax previously imposed upon transfer to foreign entities on or after August 5, 1997.

Alternatively, the IRS was empowered to draft regulations to implement capital gains treatment on such transfers in lieu of the excise tax. Generally, any transfer of appreciated property to a foreign trust for less than adequate consideration is now taxable as a sale or exchange, except as provided by regulations. And when a domestic trust becomes a foreign trust, any unrealized gain in the assets held by the trust is deemed to have been realized and the capital gains tax will apply. However, the capital gain does not apply if the foreign trust is a grantor trust under grantor trust rules.

Taxes on Annuity Proceeds

As a general rule, offshore annuities are taxed in the same manner as onshore annuities. However, it now appears that a fixed-return, deferred annuity issued by a foreign insurance company will be subjected to tax on the accumulations in the contract, as earned. This is because of IRS regulation TD 8754, issued in January 1998, which addresses the tax treatment of "original issue discount instruments." It was the IRS's apparent intent to find a way to stop the growing popularity of the "retirement CDs" that were being issued by banks as annuity contracts. To put a stop to that loophole, the IRS used the original issue discount sections of the tax law to conclude that a fixed-rate, deferred payment annuity contract not issued by a life insurance company subject to sub-chapter L of the IRC would not qualify as an annuity.

The apparent outcome is that foreign single premium life insurance contracts still appear to be tax deferred, even though they are taxed the same as annuity contracts. Variable-rate annuity contracts or fixed contracts that begin payments within a year are also taxed as annuity contracts, even though they are issued by foreign insurance companies.

U.S. Taxes on the IBC Investing in the U.S. Stock Market

As an incentive for offshore companies to invest in the U.S. business economy, offshore investors in the U.S. equity market and some tax-free bonds are not required to pay any capital gains taxes on profits made in the stock market. They do, however, pay a 30 percent tax on dividends. The 30 percent withholding tax is generally withheld at the source—the payor or the stock brokerage firm—and is not distributed offshore.

Tax on Renouncing U.S. Citizenship

A U.S. person has a constitutional right to renounce his or her U.S. citizenship; the problem is that the renouncement in itself does not terminate future tax obligations to the United States.

The determination of whether the expatriation by the U.S. person was clearly intended to avoid taxes is the pivotal issue. To appreciate the current law, it is necessary to review some history of renunciation. In 1996, it was passed into law as an amendment to the Health Insurance Portability and Accountability Act. Before that time, the IRC imposed income taxes on the U.S. source income of former citizens and residents for up to ten years, providing the IRS could demonstrate that the motivation for expatriation was the avoidance of U.S. income taxes.

The IRS was often frustrated with having to prove intent in tax court, and many taxpayers were able to convince the court that they had other reasons for their expatriation. The IRS finally prevailed upon a Congress that thought it would be the popular thing to do— get those rich people who were moving offshore with their money— to amend the tax laws. They eliminated the intent requirement. The test was simply that anyone who has a net worth of at least $500,000 or an average tax liability of more than $100,000 per year for the past five years will be presumed to have expatriated for a tax-avoidance purpose. The IRS is therefore not required to prove intent, and the ten-year rule applies.

Adding insult to injury, as a rider to a separate 1996 immigration bill, there was added a provision that prohibited the return of former U.S. citizens or longtime residents who had expatriated, if they were found to be subject to the presumption of tax avoidance as their motive for expatriation.

In a third 1996 act, some further changes had the effect of closing a perceived loophole with respect to certain kinds of tax-deferred exchanges and to impose tax on the expatriate for any income or gains realized by a CFC from property contributed to the CFC in which the expatriate was a shareholder. (CFCs are quite complex— you should discuss them with your CPA.)

Presently, there is a debate about whether the law prohibiting re-entry of the person renouncing U.S. citizenship is constitutional— but there have been no legal challenges to date. Rumor has it that the U.S. government has not been enforcing the rule to avoid triggering a court challenge.

As a practical matter, if a U.S. person sells all appreciated assets, pays capital gains taxes, and cashes in all tax-deferred income streams (such as a pension), he or she should be able to leave the U.S. without any future tax obligation to the U.S. other than what any nonresident alien might incur. Whether that would alter the rule that prohibits the return of such a person to the U.S. is unclear at this time. Estate and gift taxes can be avoided by removing the property from the U.S. and not owning any U.S. securities.

IRS Requirements for an Offshore Principal Office

Business income derived from a foreign corporation that is not effectively connected with a U.S. trade or business conducted by the foreign corporation is not generally subject to current U.S. income taxes, even if the corporation is owned or controlled by U.S. persons.

With careful management, it would also be possible to have deferred profits from the sale of products in the U.S. by a foreign corporation so long as the corporation does not meet the detailed test for having any "U.S. source income." To the extent that the foreign corporation does have any U.S. source income, it must file a tax return and pay taxes on that income to the U.S. government. Profits from non-U.S. income could be tax deferred to the U.S. owners of the foreign corporation.

In order to defer profits from a foreign corporation, the general rule is that the foreign corporation should not have a business presence in the United States. This would include all or most of the following criteria.

1. Financial reports were provided os.

2. Communications with the shareholders or members was done os.

3. Marketing and solicitation for sales of the IBC's stock was os.

4. New shareholders' or members' subscription for stock was os.

5. General public communication was os.

6. The principal corporate books and records were maintained os.

7. Payments and cash disbursements were made from os.

8. Shareholders' and board of directors' meetings were conducted os.

9. The company's books were audited os.

10. Corporate management is conducted from the os principal office.

Applicable IRS Forms

When the RA's APT is structured as a foreign grantor trust, the trust income, credits, and deductions are attributable to the U.S. grantor. To be in compliance with the tax laws of the U.S. and the grantor's state, certain forms must be filed.[3] These are presented below in numerical order. There are different filing dates for some of them, and unless you have determined whether any one of them needs to be filed, you may not be in full IRS tax compliance. In 1995, I heard that the IRS believed that there were billions of U.S. dollars offshore not in compliance. I don't agree with their high numbers, but don't *you* be their first test case!

Whether you need to file some of these forms depends upon such factors as whether you have a tax-neutral APT structure such as a U.S. trust or a foreign trust, or whether you are reporting on a genuine nongrantor foreign trust.

1. IRS Form SS-4, "Application for Employer Identification Number" for the APT or the IBC. The trustee or company officer must obtain this form upon the creation of the APT or IBC. This form allows you to apply for an employer identification number (EIN).

2. IRS Form 56, "Notice Concerning Fiduciary Relationship," is usually prepared by the trustee to advise the IRS of the creation of a fiduciary relationship. Form 56 requires evidence of the trustee's authority, usually a copy of the trust declaration. It's filed with the first Form 1041 filing, or may be filed earlier, when the fiduciary relationship is created and accepted by the trustee.

3. Treasury Form TD F 90-22.1, "Report of Foreign Bank and Financial Accounts," is generally prepared by that person having certain authority of foreign accounts. By June 30 of each year following the preceding reporting year, this form must be filed by each person who possesses:

- Any financial interest
- Signatory authority
- Other authority over any bank, securities, or other financial account in any foreign country, if *at any time during the reporting year* the account(s), singly or in combination, had a value of more than $10,000

The form is *not* filed with the person's income tax return. It is filed with the Treasury Department at their Michigan location. The instructions carry the correct address. For example, if a U.S. person has an IRA, and that person advises the custodian to place some of the IRA's funds in an offshore bank account, then the form must be filed. The U.S. person who owns the IRA must file, and if the custodian has signatory authority over the offshore account, then the custodian must file as well.

4. IRS Form 709, "United States Gift (and Generation-Skipping Transfer) Tax Return," is filed to report gifting. It must be filed by April 15 for the preceding year in which the gifting was made; this is a disclosure tax return, filed by the settlor even for an "incomplete" gift. A copy of the trust is attached to Form 709.

5. IRS Form 926, "Return by a U.S. Transferor of Property to a Foreign Corporation" is filed by the grantor. This may result in an imposition of an excise tax.[4] The tax is imposed only if one transfers assets that have appreciated in value. This form should be filed on the day of the transfer to the APT, though in reality it is rarely used for corporations.

6. IRS Form 1040, and a state income tax return, are filed on April 15 for the prior year to report APT income on the settlor's individual tax returns. Your special attention is called to the Schedule B attachment to Form 1040, more specifically, Part III. Over the years,

Part III has slowly evolved to include increasingly comprehensive questioning as to offshore financial transactions. Questions probe your degree of control or ownership in foreign accounts. Check the Yes box if the answer to any of the following is appropriate:

- At any time during the tax year (even if for a fleeting second of time),
- You had an "interest" (whatever that means),
- Or, in the disjunctive, you had signatory authority,
- Or you had "authority" (again, whatever that means),
- Over a "financial" account in a foreign country. *Account* is defined to include bank account, security account, or other accounts (whatever that encompasses).
- Where, in what foreign country? You must list them all.

If you had during the prior year a combined foreign account value that never exceeded $10,000 offshore, you may check the No box. Question 12 regards your involvement in foreign trusts:

- If a foreign trust existed at any time during the prior tax year (even for a fleeting moment),
- Were you the grantor of that trust, or,
- Did you transfer any assets to any foreign trust,
- Whether or not you personally were the beneficiary of that trust or had any beneficial interest in that trust?

In addition, the grantor of a grantor trust must report the interest and dividends received by checking the Yes box at the bottom of Schedule B.

7. IRS Form 1041, "U.S. Income Tax Return for Estates and Trusts," is filed by the grantor of a grantor trust.[5]

8. IRS Form 3520, advising the IRS of the "Creation of or Transfers to Certain Foreign Trusts," is now required to be filed with the tax return (including extension of time to file) of the trust grantor who forms a foreign trust, makes contributions to a foreign grantor trust, or receives certain distributions from a foreign trust. U.S. beneficiaries of a foreign trust may be required to report the receipt of

certain distributions or loans from the trust. A separate copy of the form must be sent (at the same time) to the Philadelphia office of the IRS.

9. IRS Form 3520-A, "Annual Information Return of Foreign Trust with a U.S. Owner," must be filed each year by the grantor of a foreign trust that has one or more U.S. beneficiaries during the year. A copy must be filed with the IRS in the Philadelphia office.

10. Customs Form 4790 is for advising with a "Report of International Transportation of Currency or Monetary Instruments" of the importing or exporting of $10,000 or more of currency or other monetary instruments. Filing is done by the shippers or mailers and by the recipients.

The recipient files the form within thirty days after receipt, not with the IRS but with the U.S. Customs Officer in charge at any port of entry or departure. It may also be made to the Commissioner of Customs, Attention: Currency Transportation Reports, Washington, DC 20229.

Shippers or mailers may file by mail if the currency or monetary instruments did not accompany a person while departing or entering the U.S.

Travelers carrying money or instruments must file Form 4790 with the Custom Officer in charge at any customs port when departing or entering the U.S. Curiously, tourists leaving the Bahamas for the U.S. are cleared by U.S. customs in the Bahamas. At that time, they are asked if they are carrying more than $10,000 in currency (note that I didn't specify U.S. currency here) or monetary instruments.

11. IRS Form 5471, an annual "Informational Return of U.S. Persons with Respect to Certain Foreign Corporations," is filed by "certain" U.S. citizens or residents who are officers, directors, or shareholders in certain foreign corporations. Generally, shareholders of a CFC or FPHC are only required to file if they have a 10 percent or greater ownership interest or when they have acquired or disposed of a 5 percent or greater interest in the foreign corporation. Officers or directors of a foreign corporation are generally

Figure 11.1: IRS Form 3520

Form **3520**	**Annual Return To Report Transactions With Foreign Trusts and Receipt of Certain Foreign Gifts**	OMB No. 1545-0159
Department of the Treasury Internal Revenue Service	File in duplicate. Instructions are separate.	**1998**

All information must be in English. Show all amounts in U.S. dollars. File a separate Form 3520 for each foreign trust.

For calendar year 1998, or tax year beginning	2/1 . 19 98 , ending	12/31 . 19 98
Check appropriate box(es): See Instructions.	☑ Initial return ☐ Final return	☐ Amended return
Check box that applies to U.S. person filing return:	☑ Individual ☐ Partnership ☐ Corporation	☐ Trust ☐ Executor

Check all applicable boxes:

☑ (a) You are a U.S. transferor who, directly or indirectly, transferred money or other property during the current tax year to a foreign trust, or (b) You held an outstanding obligation of a related foreign trust (or a person related to the trust) issued during the current tax year, that you treated as a "qualified obligation" (defined on page 2 of the instructions) during the current tax year. See the instructions for Part I.

☑ You are a U.S. owner of all or any portion of a foreign trust at any time during the tax year. See the instructions for Part II.

☐ (a) You are a U.S. person who, during the current tax year, received a distribution from a foreign trust, or (b) A related foreign trust held an outstanding obligation issued by you (or a person related to you) during the current tax year that you treated as a "qualified obligation" (defined on page 2 of the instructions) during the current tax year. See the instructions for Part III.

☐ You are a U.S. person who, during the current tax year, received certain gifts or bequests from a foreign person. See the instructions for Part IV.

Service Center where U.S. person filing this return files its income tax return ▶ Fresno

1a Name of U.S. person(s) filing return William B. Grant and Mary M. Grant			b Identification number 123-45-6789
c Number, street, and room or suite no. (If a P.O. box, see instructions.) 123 Main Street			d Spouse's identification number (see instr.) 234-56-7890
e City or town Granola	f State or province California	g ZIP or postal code 91234	h Country U.S.A.
2a Name of foreign trust (if applicable) Prudence Trust	b Identification number (if any) 123-45-6789		c Number, street, and room or suite no. 123 Main Street
d City or town Granola	e State or province California	f ZIP or postal code 91234	g Country U.S.A.

3 Did the foreign trust appoint a U.S. agent (defined on page 3 of the instructions) who can provide the IRS with all relevant trust information?, ... ☑ Yes ☐ No

If "Yes," complete lines 3a through 3g.

3a Name of U.S. agent William B. Grant	b Identification number (if any) 123-45-6789		c Number, street, and room or suite no. 123 Main Street
d City or town Granola	e State or province California	f ZIP or postal code 91234	g Country U.S.A.
4a Name of U.S. decedent (see instr.)	b Address		c TIN of decedent
d Date of death			e EIN of estate

Part I   Transfers by U.S. Persons to a Foreign Trust During the Current Tax Year (See instructions.)

5a Name of trust creator (if different from line 1a)	b Address	c Identification number (if any)

6a Country code of country where trust was created BD	b Country code of country whose law governs the trust BD	c Date trust was created 2/1/98

7a Will any other person be treated as the owner of the transferred assets after the transfer? . . . . ☐ Yes ☑ No

b Name of other foreign trust owners, if any (a)	Address (b)	Country of residence (c)	Identification number, if any (d)	Relevant code section (e)

Under penalties of perjury, I declare that I have examined this return, including any accompanying reports, schedules, or statements, and to the best of my knowledge and belief, it is true, correct, and complete.

/s/ William B. Grant		4/1/99
Signature	Title	Date
Preparer's signature	Preparer's identification number	Date

For Paperwork Reduction Act Notice, see page 9 of the instructions.   Cat. No. 19594V   Form **3520** (1998)

Figure 11.2: IRS Form 3520-A

Form **3520-A**	**Annual Information Return of Foreign Trust With a U.S. Owner** (Under section 6048(b))	OMB No. 1545-0160
Department of the Treasury Internal Revenue Service	► Certain foreign trusts may have to issue a Foreign Grantor Trust Owner Statement(s) or a Foreign Grantor Trust Beneficiary Statement(s) (pages 3 and 4). See separate instructions.	1998

Note: *All information must be in English. Show all amounts in U.S. dollars.*

For calendar year 1998, or tax year beginning , 19 , and ending , 19

Part I   General Information *(See instructions.)*

1a Name of foreign trust

Prudence Trust

b Identification number

123-45-6789

c Number, street, and room or suite no. (if a P.O. box, see instructions)

c/o William B. Grant
123 Main Street

d City or town	**e** State or province	**f** ZIP or postal code	**g** Country
Granola	California	91234	U.S.A.

2 Did the foreign trust appoint a U.S. agent (defined on page 2 of the instructions) who can provide IRS with all relevant trust information? . . . . ☑ Yes ☐ No

If "Yes," skip lines 2a through 2e and go to line 3.

If "No," you are required to attach a copy of all trust documents as indicated below. If these documents have been attached to a Form 3520-A filed within the previous 3 years, attach only relevant updates.

Have you attached a copy of:

	Yes	No	Attached Previously	Year Attached
a Summary of all written and oral agreements and understandings relating to the trust? . . .	☐	☐	☐	
b The trust instrument?	☐	☐	☐	_____
c Memoranda or letters of wishes?	☐	☐	☐	_____
d Subsequent variances to original trust documents?	☐	☐	☐	_____
e Other trust documents?	☐	☐	☐	

3a Name of U.S. agent

William B. Grant

b Identification number

123-45-6789

c Number, street, and room or suite no. (if a P.O. box, see instructions)

123 Main Street

d City or town	**e** State or province	**f** ZIP or postal code	**g** Country
Granola	California	91234	U.S.A.

4a Name of trustee

Grosvenor Trust Company, Limited

b Identification number, if any

None

c Number, street, and room or suite no. (if a P.O. box, see instructions)

35 Church Street

d City or town	**e** State or province	**f** ZIP or postal code	**g** Country
Hamilton		HM1	Bermuda

5 Did the trust transfer any property to another entity during the tax year? . . . . ☐ Yes ☑ No
If "Yes," attach statement. See instructions.

Under penalties of perjury, I declare that I have examined this return, including any accompanying reports, schedules, or statements, and to the best of my knowledge and belief, it is true, correct, and complete.

Trustee's Signature /s/ William B. Grant   Title Authorized Representative   Date 4/1/99

Preparer's Signature

Preparer's social security number

Date

For Paperwork Reduction Act Notice, see instructions on page 4.   Cat No 19595G   Form **3520-A** (1998)

Figure 11.2: IRS Form 3520-A, continued

Form 3520 (1998)   Page **6**

Part III   *(Continued)*

Schedule C—Calculation of Interest Charge (See instructions.)

54	Enter accumulation distribution from line 43 or 47, as applicable . . . .
55	Enter tax on total accumulation distribution from line 28 of Form 4970 . . . .
56	Enter applicable number of years of foreign trust from line 44 or 53, as applicable (round to nearest half-year). ▶
57	Combined interest rate imposed on the total accumulation distribution. See Table B on page 8 of instructions .
58	Interest charge. Multiply the amount on line 55 by the combined interest rate on line 57 . . . .
59	Tax attributable to accumulated distributions. Add lines 55 and 58. Enter here and as "additional tax" on your income tax return . . . .

Part IV   U.S. Recipients of Gifts or Bequests Received During the Current Tax Year From Foreign Persons (See instructions.)

60   During the current tax year, did you receive more than $100,000 during the tax year that you treated as gifts or bequests from a nonresident alien or a foreign estate? See instructions regarding related donors . . . . .   ☐ Yes   ☐ No

If "Yes," complete columns (a) through (c) with respect to each such gift or bequest in excess of $5,000. If more space is needed, attach schedule.

Date of gift or bequest (a)	Description of property received (b)	FMV of property received (c)

Total   . . . . ▶ | $

61   During the current tax year, did you receive more than $10,557 that you treated as gifts from a foreign corporation or a foreign partnership? See instructions regarding related donors . . . .   ☐ Yes   ☐ No

If "Yes," complete columns (a) through (g) with respect to each such gift. If more space is needed, attach schedule.

Date of gift (a)	Name of donor (b)	Address of donor (c)	Identification number, if any (d)

Check the box that applies to the foreign donor (e)		Description of property received (f)	FMV of property received (g)
Corporation	Partnership		

62   Do you have any reason to believe that the foreign donor, in making any gift or bequest described in lines 60 and 61, was acting as a nominee or intermediary for any other person? If "Yes," see instructions. . . . . . .   ☐ Yes   ☐ No

required to file the form. Any shareholder of a captive insurance company that is a CFC must also file the form. The form must also be filed by the grantor of a foreign trust that is a shareholder of a foreign corporation as described above.

12. IRS Forms 8288/8288-A, disclosing transfers of real property by a foreign APT, must be filed within twenty days of the transfer of the U.S. real property and accompanied by any taxes withheld. U.S. escrow companies or attorneys handling sales of real property transactions may withhold the taxes and forward them to the IRS or be personally held liable to the IRS for the uncollected taxes.

13. IRS Form 8621, "Return by a Shareholder of a Passive Foreign Investment Company or Qualified Electing Fund," may be required from certain U.S. shareholders of a PFIC (mutual fund or unit investment trust). A separate form must be filed for each PFIC in which stock is held. The form is required to be filed with the taxpayer's tax return, and a second copy is to be filed with the Philadelphia office of the IRS. There are no ownership thresholds for not filing the return. All shareholders must file this return if the foreign corporation is a PFIC, which includes an IRC §1291 fund or a qualified electing fund. Ownership of a PFIC may be indirect, or through ownership of other foreign corporations, foreign partnerships, foreign trusts, or foreign estates.

14. Form 8865 has been introduced to report transactions and ownership interests relating to foreign partnerships (or LLCs electing partnership treatment). The form must be filed by any person who controls a foreign partnership at any time during the calendar year, any U.S. person who owns (directly or indirectly) a 10 percent or greater interest in a controlled foreign partnership, a person who contributes more than $100,000 of property to a foreign partnership during the year, and a partner who has a direct or indirect acquisition or disposition of a 10 percent or greater interest in a foreign partnership—even though it is not a controlled foreign partnership. One copy of the form is required to be filed with the partner's income tax return, and a second copy must be filed with the Philadelphia office of the IRS. Indirect ownership of a foreign

partnership would generally include an interest owned by a trust in which the taxpayer is a beneficiary, a grantor trust, an estate in which the taxpayer is a beneficiary, another partnership in which the taxpayer is partner, a foreign corporation in which the taxpayer is a shareholder, or an interest owned by certain relatives.

Classifying Tax Havens Based on Tax Attributes

From a tax viewpoint, an international finance center falls into one of three tax regimens:

1. **Token-tax, no-tax, or zero-tax havens.** This is a true tax haven in that there are no or token taxes assessed. Some examples of zero-tax jurisdictions are Anguilla, Bahamas, Bermuda, the Caymans, Nauru, the Turks and Caicos Islands, and Vanuatu.

2. **Low-tax havens.** The definition of a low tax rate is subjective; however, St. Kitts, the British Virgin Islands, Barbados, the Channel Islands, and Hong Kong are representative of low-tax jurisdictions.

3. **Special exemptions, credits, or privileges.** Tax havens such as Ireland, Madeira, Panama, and the Netherlands Antilles provide special tax concessions to encourage the establishment of certain types of business in their countries.

Endnotes

1 *The Offshore Money Book* uses two excellent publishers as an update service for this book. If you are interested in keeping current on the subject, please E-mail Vern Jacobs, CPA, at osj@rpifs.com and Tom Azzara at taxman@batelnet.bs and request a sample copy of their offshore newsletters. Tell them Arnie referred you.

2 Cash dividends from stock: At the time of drafting this book, the current tax rate on dividends paid on stock to an offshore, NRA person was 30 percent. It is by a withholding tax and is withheld at the U.S. source, either

the paying corporation or by the broker with street stock. The dividend is considered nonexempt U.S. source income. However, the withholding rate may be less for residents of some countries that have tax treaties with the U.S.

3 All of the forms described may be ordered by telephone from the IRS by calling (800) 829-1040 or from the IRS website at www. irs.ustreas.gov/prid/forms_pubs.

This requires the use of the Adobe Acrobat program that was free at the time of drafting this book.

4 IRC §1491 previously imposed an excise tax but it was repealed. Currently, transfers to a foreign entity may be subject to a capital gains tax on any appreciation in the value of the property transferred. As of the time of drafting this, there was no clear indication from the IRS of what changes they would make with respect to this form. There is an exception for a grantor APT.

5 IRC §679 provides that where there is a foreign grantor trust, the grantor of that foreign trust is taxed on all the income of the trust whether or not there is a distribution, if the trust had or could have a U.S. beneficiary.

12

Offshore Communications and Privacy

A country's ability to assert its sovereignty without the interfer-
ence of outside forces (the U.S.A.) is a major deciding factor in
choosing a place to invest and protect personal property.

OSCAR SABIDO,
ATTORNEY, 1995, BELIZE

A SIMPLE THING like a telephone bill often compromises the best-laid plans for offshore privacy. The telephone can not only reach out and touch someone; it can reach back and bite you in the derriere. Your long-distance telephone service provider creates permanent electronic records of every offshore call you make. Upon service of a subpoena, the phone company is compelled to provide your telephone records—in essence, your daily telephone diary. Many privacy aficionados make their sensitive OS calls using a calling (debit) card from public telephones. Only you can decide your comfortable level of privacy.

If you do decide to use the calling card, buy it anonymously, with cash and not as a charge on your U.S. credit card. You will receive a personal identification number (PIN) to use consisting of ten to twelve digits, long enough to ward off hackers. Write it down in your address book in code. Memorize or scramble the 800 number as well, and then shred the calling card. *Never recharge the card again, especially by using a domestic credit card.* It is best to get a new card each time your card has expired.

For frequent callers to the Bahamas, the 242 area code of the Caribbean, you can purchase a local prepaid calling card. As an example, with the Batelco (Bahamas Telephone Company) calling card sold in Nassau, you can call the Bahamas from the United States, Canada, or the United Kingdom using their 800 number in those countries. You can actually get a Batelco dial tone from Nassau in the United States and complete your call through their system with no records on your local telephone bill or in the United States linking the call to you. Buy one at the airport in Nassau.

By the time you are reading this book, it may be possible to engage in full duplex (simultaneous two-way) encrypted voice communications over the World Wide Web. Things are moving so fast in the Internet communications field that you could be talking to your asset manager in the Isle of Man in an encrypted mode over the Web using your cable company's Internet services and not pay telephone toll charges.

Following are some of the more common ways your assets are traced other than the traditional credit report, public records, your checking account, and a real property title search or personal property search at the Secretary of State's office. Who will be searching? Your former (vindictive) spouse, an adversarial former partner or business associate, a plaintiff or potential plaintiff, or, heaven forbid, the IRS.

Passport Review and Travel Agent Records

Frequent visits to high-profile banking destinations without a vacation purpose are red flags, giving snoops a place to start looking for hidden assets. Obviously, multiple visits to some of the following countries clearly will raise suspicion: Switzerland, the Cayman Islands, the Bahamas, Isle of Man, Netherlands Antilles, and other jurisdictions characterized as tax havens. The IRS has labeled over thirty jurisdictions as tax havens.

Telephone Records

By examining your telephone bills for calls made from home, work, hotels you frequent (use a calling card, it's cheaper), and your cellular phone, as well as your fax bills, telex records, and saved or deleted E-mail messages or documents on your computer hard drive, one can identify undisclosed business associates and professionals and ascertain agendas. Remember that deleting a file on your computer doesn't remove it, but simply disables the file on the hard drive. A utility file can resurrect it. More can be obtained in a lab. An examination of the telephone directories in any geographic region where you live, work, or have a presence may be revealing. With the new CD technology inexpensively providing millions of names and phone numbers, such telephone number and name searches are becoming routine. For example, after I had appeared in an episode of PBS's "Frontline" that investigated former corrupt banking practices in the Caribbean, a prospective client located me by using his national CD business phone directory. He was quite proud of his feat! He also proved my point.

Frequent Flyer Programs

Miles aren't just miles. A review of your various airline frequent flyer mileage statements reveals scuba diving trips to Virgin Gorda. Isn't that in the British Virgin Islands, where they "hide" money? Also, an emotional plaintiff who can't afford to travel might be most upset by those jaunts of yours to perceived vacation destinations. Miles are now given when you shop, at your brokerage firm, and when you refinance your house. Miles tell a story.

Wastebaskets and Garbage Cans

Get a crosscut shredder and use it! If it's not crosscut, it's not shredded. With enough time, effort, and money, one can easily glue quarter-inch strips back together again. It may be a very boring jigsaw puzzle, but it can be accomplished. A private investigator friend of mine told me that they even have software to do it now! Don't let a cheap shredder lull you into a false sense of security. You can buy a lightweight crosscut shredder for around $279 to $700, depending on the number of sheets you want to shred on each pass through the machine (four to ten, with or without staples or paper clips). The peace of mind it affords even makes the sound of the shredding therapeutic. (I affectionately named mine "Janet Reno.") Don't forget to shred any carbon paper, charge slips, typewriter ribbons, telephone messages, phone bills, airline frequent flyer statements, and printer ribbons from typewriters, printers, or the new low-cost fax machines. I still use a fax that utilizes an ink cartridge, just for privacy reasons.

If you can only afford a quarter-inch shredder, place the shreds in your kitchen garbage trash compactor at least daily and cover them with something moist like coffee grounds or orange peels to distort them, and then compact or add to your garden compost pile. That should prevent computerized reconstruction.

Some people print out sensitive materials only on one special colored paper and never leave the office unless all of the pages of that color are properly disposed of. They don't go into files but just sit on the desktop. Take them with you at lunchtime for further privacy. It's curious how in a computerized age we tend to use more, not less, paper. Note: When you place your garbage can curbside for collection it is no longer protected by the U.S. Constitution against eavesdropping. Anyone is free to take your trash and snoop.

Computer Files

Save sensitive materials on an encrypted segment of your hard drive on your computer only. Use a different password or PIN for each account you have and store it in the encrypted mode on your computer. Provide the pass phrase for decryption in a double-sealed envelope to your offshore attorney to be opened only upon your death or long-term disability. It is protected there under attorney-client privilege. Work only in the secured mode. Don't make clear text backups on floppies or on an unsecured backup tape. Turn off your computer when not in use. Stop using paper records, except as a backup master located offshore. Communicate on the Internet by encrypted E-mail using PGP—anything else is an open postcard. You'll be surprised how much cleaner your desk will be, too!

Business Associates

The people with whom you do business may have offshore involvement. Keep a list of OS associates in a separate file or book, for your eyes only.

Your intentional or inadvertent disclosure of offshore activities to the wrong people may lead to unique problems. A disgruntled worker or spouse may be tempted to blackmail you or alert the IRS or other taxing agencies on the anonymous 800 telephone lines if they want to be vindictive. In fact, the IRS even claims that they offer rewards for reporting tax fraud, but statistics show that few people collect very much.

Companies and private investigators may specialize in this type of asset search. There should be no difficulty in finding your assets onshore, but it's not often easy to search offshore because of stricter privacy. Unauthorized disclosure of banking and financial information offshore is a crime in many jurisdictions.

Encryption

Attacks against encryption techniques are succeeding at a frightening rate. This effort is being accomplished by governments, private enterprises, and hackers, and through industrial espionage. In the U.S., computer secrecy experts warn that encryption "locks" proposed by the U.S. government are far too susceptible to attack. Government intelligence and industrial spying pose more of a threat than do hackers.

Illicit decryption has become economically feasible for industry. In 1996, it was reported that a code-breaking computer system could be devised for as little as $30,000. Secrecy experts claim that this computer could break an encryption key of forty bits in under twenty seconds. The current U.S. standard is a 56-bit key, which the experts claim could be broken in three hours. A cost estimate for illicit decryption is around $38 per key. With faster computers, the 56-bit key could be broken in as little as six minutes. For security, computer experts now suggest a 90-bit system.

Currently, self-teaching software and powerful computers are making decryption easier. The software is for sale to anyone. Using combinations of fuzzy logic and artificial intelligence, computers are able to work in any language looking for the trends normally used in written language and the style of writing in an E-mail message. By continually iterating, a 1,024 message can be decrypted in hours for around $750,000 a page. Are you worth it?

13

The Captive Insurance Company

AMERICAN ENTREPRENEURS have always sought to improve their company's bottom line, or face the consequences. A major expense of running a business may be mandated or defensive insurance costs, as well as basic insurance needs. In a business, costs are always under scrutiny. Whether insurance is dictated by law or carried at levels constituting good business practices, it still costs money. What is particularly frustrating to a businessperson is the ratio of the substantial dollars expended for insurance premiums as compared to the dollars returned for claims and litigation defense. The comfort of being insured doesn't necessarily compensate for the cost of the insurance. Consequently, the concept of becoming self-insured can look more and more attractive, to some extent, in low-risk but high-premium industries, mostly because of some tax benefits that exist. The strategy of *captive insurance* may be quite attractive to obtain insurance where it is not otherwise available or affordable, and self-insurance helps avoid the need to go "bare."

In the U.S., creating an onshore company for self-insurance can be so costly and time consuming because of overregulation that it is, for all practical considerations, not feasible. Voilà—the concept of the offshore insurance company, or technically the *captive insurance company* (or the *captive*), is born. Approximately 40 percent of the U.S. insurance market is offshore. Any U.S. full-time trial attorney has a horror story about not being able to collect on a judgment from an OS captive. I believe this is the exception rather than the rule. (Scammers do sell inexpensive and non–IRS-compliant captives for a "buck" that are grossly undercapitalized and unable to pay out on claims.)

The captive may be structured in various formats, depending on the purpose and the needs:

1. The *captive of associated companies* is formed for a group—for example, an association of affiliated hospitals. This is the basic parent captive insurance company, and usually is a wholly owned subsidiary of the company forming the captive (for example, where a Fortune 500 company wishes to create an offshore captive to insure the risks of its own parent).

2. The *group captive* might also be formed for member companies in a certain industry banding together. A group or association (trade or professional), having a common interest, may create a captive to respond to the special needs of the smaller to medium-size companies or professional associations.

3. Where a captive is underutilized or where it is being done for profit, it can go into business in the "rent-a-captive" field and provided coverage to nonrelated others.

4. A variation of Item 3, the *cell captive*, is emerging in some jurisdictions. A cell creates an autonomous insurance company within the framework of an insurance company. Each cell is a separate profit and loss entity within the master insurance company; therefore, its losses are self-contained.

The Cayman Islands insurance laws define three types of insurance businesses:

1. One that insures a person against liability for loss due to a risk.

2. One that, upon the occurrence of a defined event, pays money to the insured or beneficiary.

3. One that carries out the function of re-insurance (called the *re*) among other insurers. (Re-insurance companies share the risk of primary insurance companies for a fee.) Expect to see Brazil become a major source of re-insurance coverage in 2000.

Initially, the captive partially protects itself against catastrophic exposure by re-insuring some of the risks with other companies, the re, through underwriters or buying insurance from wholesalers. As reserves accumulate in the captive, the necessary level of re-insurance diminishes and the reserves increase hyperbolically.

Captive coverage is not limited to companies. A captive could also insure other entities such as groups of "related" persons, hospitals, professional practices, partnerships, LLCs, foundations, officers, directors, and so on. Several tax havens favor and court such business, such as Bermuda, the Caymans, British Virgin Islands, Turks and Caicos Islands, and Guernsey, to name a few. Bermuda is considered the leading international insurance domicile, but the Caymans, BVI, and TCI remain quite popular in this specialty as well. Combine a favorable government environment such as we now see in BVI with a level of regulation to assure the ability of the insurer to respond with qualified professionals, and this industry attracts the world's insurance business. The Canadian province of New Brunswick announced it was developing regulations on classes of businesses and fees in order to compete in the world's captive marketplace.

Why would you form a captive insurance company offshore?

1. Coverage for risks not readily insurable by your regular insurance underwriters. Examples include environmental hazardous waste, sexual harassment, earthquake, and director and officer liability.

2. Cost efficiency. If the loss history of the parent is considerably better than the industry, there may be a premium savings by self-insuring. By reducing the many intermediary parties in the insurance industry, savings can be achieved. Costs savings can also be achieved by going directly into the re-insurance market for risk sharing.

3. Cash flow. There is control of the cash flow offshore from the premium payments while waiting for a future claim. Risks can be managed internally, resulting in cost savings.

4. Taxation. There may be certain tax-deferral and investment buildup benefits of the offshore captive from the reserves. Here lies a tremendous advantage. The captive has the ability to accumulate earnings and designate them as reserves against claims. Under current U.S. tax law, these earnings are free of U.S. income taxes up to certain limits.

Some jurisdictions offer captives "off the shelf." Although these might be tempting at first blush, do explore the features of such a product and inquire as to which is the best jurisdiction for you in terms of setup costs, maintenance costs, and capital reserve requirements.

Let's explore the following scenario. Widget, Inc., is one of the most conservative, low-risk companies operating in a field that traditionally has high insurance premiums because of a general perception affecting them or a history of high claims by other companies in the field. An audit shows that for every dollar they pay in premiums, they get back only 25 cents of benefits. Widget has an exceptional year and is flush with cash. As a closely held company, it doesn't have to account to outside shareholders, so the officers initially decide to form an offshore captive insurance company and become self-insured, in a small way.

What type of licensing should they apply for initially? Using the Caymans again as an example, there are three classifications of insurers. The three categories are *local*, *exempt*, and *external*. In addition, there are three types of licenses granted; casualty, life, and all-inclusive.

After meeting with professionals in Georgetown (not to be confused with George Town, Bahamas) and introducing themselves to the necessary insurance company administrators, actuaries, and government officials as part of the process for qualification, they create the Paradigm Insurco, a Cayman Islands captive insurance company. Most jurisdictions restrict the use of company names such that any word suggesting the business of insurance or assurance is limited only to those companies licensed as such by the jurisdiction. Some restricted words are *indemnity, guaranty, insurance, re-insurance*, and *underwriting*.

The surplus cash of Widget (a domestic, or onshore, corporation) capitalizes Paradigm, and they then start to reduce their onshore insurance coverage and premiums. The officers and directors do some international financial planning here, as well, acquiring stock interest in Paradigm. Widget can be further capitalized by individuals using cash or their highly appreciated stock, without the exchange for their product being treated as a sale. Later, Widget may sell the stock without paying any capital gains taxes in the U.S.

Obviously, this process is not without some concern—what if Widget is hit with a killer lawsuit and a runaway judgment? But, from a philosophical point of view, business and life itself are risks. Fortunately, after several years of continuing low claims, Paradigm is now a fully funded captive insurer with more than adequate reserves. Little by little, more and more of Widget's insurance is handled by Paradigm. At first, Paradigm shared the risk with other insurance companies, called re-insuring. By this time, Paradigm may be able to share less of the risk with other[1] insurance companies and re-insure or co-insure the risk through them. In general, they ultimately would be Class A, which permits a local or OS insurer to carry on business on the Islands. More likely, they would start as a Class B restricted licensee, permitting Paradigm, as an exempt insurer, to operate OS but not locally. A Class B unrestricted license allows Paradigm to carry out its insurance business on the Islands but not for domestic (local) business—it is their next level before going to Class A status.

As this scenario unfolds, Paradigm amasses surplus funds after claims are paid in a tax-free, favorable jurisdiction. The offshore assets of Paradigm are put to work and earn tax-free dividends, interest, and capital gains, all professionally managed os by an asset manager. It can operate as an insurance company anywhere in the world.

Some time in the future, Paradigm may retain one or more officers of Widget as consultants and pay them for their services. Unfortunately, they may have to travel to Georgetown for many meetings.

I have seen this work very well. A former environmental engineering consultant teamed up with his friend, who was already an insurance broker, and formed a captive in the Caymans (joining around 400 other insurance companies). The broker "cherry-picked" from his better, low-risk, low-claims companies. They offered these companies lower premiums and made tons of money. All were satisfied.

Is a captive insurance company right for your company? Perhaps not now, but keep it in mind.

Costs, Formation Fees, and Capitalization

Capitalization of the captive is the major startup cost. The minimum share capitalization of the captive wishing to write property and casualty business is lower than to write life insurance as well. Formation costs in the more prestigious jurisdictions vary from $50,000 to $100,000. Capitalization for a typical jurisdiction such as the British Virgin Islands depends upon the type of captive formed. For a general insurance company, there is a $100,000 minimum solvency margin requirement. For a life insurance company, the minimum solvency margin is higher—$200,000. If you want your captive to write life and general coverage, the solvency margin increases even further to $300,000. Don't overlook the monthly operating fees of around $2,000 to $3,000. It is not economically feasible for a small business.

Typical Statutory Requirements

1. Maintain certain financial ratios and margins

2. Annual audits

3. Acceptable loss reserve practices

4. Restrictions on certain types of assets that may be invested in by the captive

5. Annual statutory filings

6. Audited financial statements

Global Insurance Resource on the Web

InsureWeb is an insurance resource available through the Web. InsureWeb is a computer on the Internet where registered brokers—agents, brokers, and re-insurance brokers—can offer risks to carriers—registered insurers, wholesalers, MGAs, and re-insurers.

InsureWeb serves the worldwide community and therefore can serve any geographical area. In addition, a search feature allows any carrier to accept business from a designated group of brokers.

The site can be reached at

http://insureweb.com

Endnote

1 This is a pivotal point. IRC §162 prohibits a current deduction for premiums paid to a wholly owned (captive) insurer. If the captive provides insurance to other companies or is not wholly owned, a deduction may be allowed.

14

Applying What You Have Learned

*Success in your venture is the journey and
not the destination.*

ANONYMOUS

A Case Study: Putting the Pieces Together

LET'S TAKE A journey to an international financial center and apply
the materials you have mastered so far to a case study. I have selected
the British Virgin Islands as a proposed site for your APT and have
given BVI my subjective rating on a scale of 1 to 10 in each of the
following areas. In another exercise, for an IBC, a different final
numerical score for the proposed site could result.

1. **Geographic considerations.** Only about three miles from
   the U.S. Virgin Islands (St. John). Why don't you take a
   ferry ride from St. Thomas for a day? The British Virgin
   Islands are a mere 60 miles south of Puerto Rico. A short
   hop on American Eagle gets you to Beef Island, the site of
   their airport. **Rating: Easy to get there, so let's say 9**

2. **Political and fiscal independence.** As a British overseas
   territory, the military defense of BVI is provided by the
   United Kingdom, which also handles its external affairs.
   Banking is monitored and regulated by the Bank of
   England. Status of the BVI is similar to the IFC of Jersey.
   Rating: 8

3. **Language.** English is the official language. **Rating: For Americans, 10**

4. **Currency.** The official currency is the U.S. dollar. There are minimal exchange costs for financial transactions. **Rating: 10**

5. **Economy and economic freedom.** *Economy*: Tourism is number one. The financial industry infrastructure is quite good since, based on the numbers, it is the premier site for exempt companies. It has one of the highest per capita incomes in the Caribbean.

   Economic freedom: In 1999, the Heritage Foundation and the *Wall Street Journal* compiled an annual Index of Economic Freedom of twenty-seven Latin American and Caribbean countries on a regional and worldwide ranking. The Bahamas was ranked first regionally and eleventh on a worldwide basis, compared with, for example, Panama fourth and twenty-eighth, respectively, Trinidad and Tobago 6/41, Barbados 7/41, Belize 13/54, and Costa Rica 13/65. BVI wasn't listed, but I would put it at a notch down from the Bahamas. **Rating: 7**

6. **Political stability.** A conservative population provides for a very stable community. **Rating: 9**

7. **International relations.** Strongly linked to the United Kingdom, BVI is a British overseas territory, not an independent country. Not part of the EC. But will suffer from gradual erosion in banking privacy because of new concerns about tax evasion by the U.K. and the requirements for banking transparency. **Rating: 6**

8. **Political stability.** Quite stable. **Rating: 9**

9. **Transportation and communications.** Regularly scheduled air transportation to San Juan and Antigua (another tax haven). Good communications. **Rating: 8**

10. **Time zone.** In Greenwich Mean Time +4 zone. Good for the Eastern Seaboard; poorer for the West Coast, with a four-hour differential. **Rating: 8**

11. **Banking secrecy.** Will erode with time due to U.K. pressures for compliance with EU directives. **Rating: 9, but will go down to zero in time**

12. **Double tax treaties.** MLAT with the United States. (It is getting rare that quality jurisdictions do not have such treaties with the United States.) **Rating: 9**

13. **Statute of Elizabeth/rule against perpetuities.** Ignored in this case study. **Rating: NA**

14. **Proposed changes in U.S. and U.K. tax haven laws.** Ignored in this case study. Too much is in flux with the U.K. pressures upon their overseas territories. **Rating: NA**

My total rating score is 102/120, which I consider to be a very good score. Using these rating parameters, a rating of 110 is excellent, and 120 impossible to achieve. If the problems in Item 14 would be remedied, the score would be much higher.

Why don't you try this analysis on another jurisdiction—perhaps the Bahamas or the Cook Islands? You can expand the parameters to as many different elements as you wish. *You* determine what is important for you.

A Test for the Reader

If you would like to determine whether you now have a modicum of understanding of the information in this book, I have postulated some questions to challenge you.

Questions

1. Can you name at least seven uses for the APT?

2. Why wouldn't you name the following as beneficiaries of your APT or foreign grantor trust?

   a. Your U.S. estate
   b. Your U.S. creditors

c. Creditors of your U.S. estate

3. Why would an individual trustee of an APT be preferred over a bank trustee?

4. What is the difference between the Caricom model of the IBC and an exempt company under the Channel Islands model?

Answers

1. Asset protection; tax planning; estate planning; substitution for a will, trust, or living trust; privacy and confidentiality; holding entity; circumventing exchange controls and restrictions on hold title to real or personal property; tax deferral and other tax benefits.

2. (a) You shouldn't return the offshore assets to the U.S. and subject them to possible real estate taxes unless necessary; (b) You should not alert your U.S. creditors to the existence of an OS APT; (c) You should pay them with domestic money.

3. I have seen a lack of permanence with bank personnel due to transfers and job relocation. Large institutions other than private investment banks don't provide much in personal services. Better continuity may be achieved with an individual trustee or a small trust company.

4. See Chapters 6 and 10.

Avoiding Offshore Scams: Greed-0-Nomics 101

Since you're going OS, don't let down your traditional safeguards. There are less-than-savory members of the financial community (in other words, con artists) and scams all over the world. It is not a uniquely U.S. problem, and the U.S. doesn't have a monopoly on pyramid and Ponzi schemes. Know the people with whom you are working. Don't be dazzled by figures: numbers do lie, and promoters' claims may run to hyperbole. Do a spot audit on some of the figures provided to see if they check out and *you* can verify them. If they won't provide the detailed figures, walk away. If you don't understand how it works, don't get involved.

What is best? A referral by an OS professional can often be treated as a personal guarantee by that individual. The referrer's personal reputation in a small community is at stake; even worse, his or her work permit could be subject to revocation by a regulatory body. Here is my basic scam alert list: before you write that check, refresh yourself by rereading it.

1. **Windfall test.** If it's so good, why are they sharing it with you? If it is a get-rich scheme, have you ever really seen one work? "Guaranteed" and "safe" high returns of 50 to 300 percent are inherently suspect. Don't get seduced, or you will be reduced in your wealth and never see the money again.

2. **Guarantees alert.** The higher the return, the higher the risk. You can't get one without the other. Who is providing the guarantee, and how strong is that person?

3. **Safety test.** How credible is the person making the claim of safety for your funds? Who is he or she? What is the company?

4. **Issuer test.** Who is the original source of the offering? Check it out with state and federal regulators. If the offering is required to be registered with your state and isn't, that in itself is a scam alert to you. Why wasn't it registered? Get real references and check them out. Be cautious of shills being used as references.

5. **Hype marketing.** Do your own independent research before investing in the offering.

The Nigerian Scam

The latest variation of the old Nigerian scam solicits nonprofit organizations and churches. The Nigerian scam feeds on greed and
naivete with a get-rich-quick scheme. It offers millions of dollars for
doing very little. You have a better chance of winning your state's lot-
tery, and at least some of that is going to a good cause.

Trying to catch up on my workload one Sunday at the office, the
fax machine rang, startling me. As I read the message in amazement,
I realized they're still trying the same scam, whiskers and all. I have
seen several variations of this fax and have added excerpts from similar requests in brackets ([ ]). Note that this is presented exactly as
it was received, egregious errors and all.

From: Panasonic FAX SYSTEM PHONE NO.:

Sep. 03 1999

10:18PM P1
52 Kinsway Road,
Ikoyi, Lagos,
Nigeria.

ATTN: ARNOLD L. CORNEZ

Telephax:
234-1-5850501
234-1-5850503

Dear Sir,

STRICTLY CONFIDENTIAL
[REQUEST FOR URGENT BUSINESS TRANSACTION
TRANSFER OF $35M AMERICAN DOLLARS]

I am DR. LIPMAN DABUP, Assistant Director of Finance and
Supplies [I am the Financial Controller] at Nigeria National
Petroleum Corporation. Your esteemed address was give to me
by a business associate, who assure me in confidence to try your
ability and reliability to handle this pending Transaction.

[The money in question which want to remit into your account is not related to arms (dealings) or drugs. It is money we got from gratification on contracts we awarded to some foreign firms towards technical assistance analysis, supervision of the operation and behaviour of the components of the N.N.P.C. Also supply, erection and optimisation for the computerised remote control network.]

The business is, there is a floating fund of US$25m (TWENTY-FIVE MILLION U.S. DOLLARS ONLY). The fund is the interest element of the extra gains made by Nigeria from Oil Sales during the Gulf War. The actual Proceeds has since been turned over to Government. This fund being the interest element, has remained unaccounted for in the Account of the Nigerian National Petroleum Corporation.

As a result of changes in Nigeria, we the men in charge at the Nigerian National Petroleum Corporation (NNPC), the Federal Ministry of Finance and the Central Bank of Nigeria (CBN) have decided to wire this money to any trustworthy company or organisation who will at last share this money with us.
You are to have 30%, 5% for Local and International expenses incurred by both parties and 65% for us (the officials). You are therefore required to send to us as quickly as possible through Fax your Account number, Name, Address, Telephone, Telex and Fax Number of your bank.

[This money is now ready for wire transfer by the authorities of the Central Bank of Nigeria. Into an account that will be provided. We have finalised all arrangements for this project but our problem lies that we do not have a foreign account as such an account is against the civil service law of conduct Beurue in Nigeria. We have taken recognition of the foreign and ambassadorial nature of the contract and have made a perfect home work for a hitch free transfer of this fund into an account you will provide.]

I would like to inform you that we have made every necessary arrangement to finish this transaction as soon as we receive your documents. This business must remain secret, because individuals involved are Senior Government Officials and any information leakage may harm them.

[We will invest part of our own share of funds in your Company by expanding its industrial scope. Finally, we will want this project to carried out on the following terms.

(1) That you will provide an account where there is a free banking policy and where toll will not be taxed much on this money.

(2) That you must maintain absolute sincerity and confidentiality.

(3) That our share of the funds be remitted into your account will be given to us.]

Please reply urgently stating your private telephone and fax number for faster communication.
Best Regard,
/s/
DR. LIMAN DAPUP
[Yours Faithfully,
/s/
Mallam Jakubu Gowon]

Send the details in paragraph 4 by fax only.

NB. Do not discuss with your bank yet.

Here is another form of a solicitation letter seen on the Internet. It originated in the Congo, so it rightfully should be called the *Congo scam*. Again, it is presented exactly as received.

The President,

URGENT INVESTMENT PROPOSAL
I am Masala Mobutu Seseko the son of the former President of the Republic of Congo who died recently after the treachery of the Kabila insurgence.

I have in my possesion the Personal Identifiction Number
(codes) and Password to a Security Vualt here Europe where
there are two boxes containing the sum US$15million each beign
part of my father's estate which we were able to salvage during
the subsequent passage out of my country.

The Kabila government is still seeking to freeze and confiscate
any assets traceable to my Late Father or any member of his
family, I am therefore looking for a partner who i can entrust
with the codes and password to help me remove the boxes since
no names were used to open the vault. You will in addition bank
and invest (with my approval of the projects) as a FRONT for
me, until the situation becomes more favourable.

If you are interested in a working partnership please call me
immediatly to discuss in more details the Logistics and
modalities.

I do not need to remind you the need for the utmost secrecy and
confidentiality, if this transaction is to succeed.

Yours Faithfully

Masala.

For further information check out this site:

www.scambusters.org/scambusters11.html

There *is* a Central Bank of Nigeria, but they disclaim any relationship with NNPC. In an effort to protect their goodwill, the Central
Bank of Nigeria periodically advertises in U.S. newspapers an alert to
such a scam. There is no NNPC that I have been able to confirm.

The prestigious "60 Minutes" did an excellent exposé on Nigeria, portraying it as a very corrupt country with a political environment where bribery and payoffs rule. I saw the scam for the first
time over thirteen years ago.

In January 1996, I received a call for assistance from a desper-
ate person in Marin County, California. One minute into the call, it
became clear he had lost tens of thousands of dollars and was quite

embarrassed about being conned by the Nigerians despite the fact that alerts have been all over the media and frequently showcased in OFFSHORE on the Internet. A Texas associate of mine told me that his clients ignored his warnings and took a chance with a $17,000 advance for attorneys' fees and government charges to Nigeria. The money was lost, of course. The scam only works where it can pander to your greed—what I call "greed-o-nomics."

In the second fax, there is usually a request for an advance for governmental fees in the range of $10,000. Response to the second fax is followed by a further request for attorney fees, for duty, for taxes, customs, and on and on. Another $10,000 to $25,000 goes to Nigeria. Then comes the need for you to travel to Nigeria with more money. By this time you have so much money and time invested in the "deal" that you might even go and visit Nigeria. Don't go—cut your losses! Save yourself money and time, avoid the aggravation, and make a donation to your favorite charity instead and at least get a tax write-off.

The Prime Bank Note, Prime Bank Guaranty, and Roll Program Scam

One of the major advantages of being a coeditor of the *Offshore Journal* an Internet newsletter, is that it places me at a focal point of developments. Starting in 1985, I received numerous inquiries and requests for information on "roll programs."

Requests for information on this scam continue. These programs essentially purport to secretly and privately buy prime bank guaranties at discount from major world banks in need of short-term money and rapidly resell them for a profit, each sale being called a *tranche*. With multiple purchases and sales throughout the year, it is claimed vast fortunes can be made.

The following roll program claims are the actual (read: uncorrected) language used in various promotional materials:

- "A risk-free means of investing."
- "High returns that investmentwise sound too good to be true, yet are realistic."
- "Arbitrage, utilizing unpublicized liquid and freely-transferable obligations, major international banks

(J. P. Morgan, Barclays, Credit Suisse, Paribas,
Deutsche Bank, etc.) as with securities."
- "Offered to quickly raise tens to hundreds of millions
  without notice; features of issuers of structure, much
  higher returns vs. publicly-available like investments,
  1–10 year maturity selection and liquidity provide for
  continuous demand on resale."
- "Instruments, programs relatively unknown; due to
  fears of disintermediation by large depositors in
  lower-yielding obligations, existence vehemently
  denied by banks."
- "U.S. and foreign government referencing for
  verification, sanction available."
- "$1,000,000 to $10,000,000 minimums."

Don't ask me what it means! I'm still struggling with my fear of
being "disintermediated." Would you give the roll program promoter
who wrote the above promotional materials $1,000,000? Of course
not. But many others did, resulting in substantial losses and frauds.
Annualized returns of as high as 1,600 percent were promised in the
literature and believed by gullible investors.

The infamous roll program is known by many other sophisticated and seductive names that also use obscure vocabulary. For
example, ponder the following terms: the prime bank note by one of
the 100 largest world banks; the prime bank guaranty; the self-
liquidating loan; tranches; the irrevocable and transferable letter of
credit. Once promoted by smooth, very persuasive marketers, it has
gone from slick advertising in the sacrosanct *Wall Street Journal* to
word-of-mouth solicitations to finally being driven underground
because it very likely violates federal and state security laws. If you
have any doubts, check with the SEC. For further reading, I suggest
you obtain several publications from the International Chamber of
Commerce.

It continues to sell because of investors' fantasies that they'll get
a much higher "insider rate" of return on their money and because
they allow a lapse of their normal investment safeguards, failing to
recognize the practical impossibility of what is being offered. Structured as a catch-22 situation by the scammers, it never works and

gullible investors forfeit their up-front fees because all the precedent conditions can't possibly be met.

There is a legitimate private market where banks do collateral security trading. This is a public market where Moody's or Standard and Poor's rated medium-term promissory notes are privately traded in the banking system. This legitimate program was likely the source for eventually structuring the fraudulent prime bank guaranty scam program.

An OFFSHORE subscriber reported reading an advertisement in a Florida newspaper by a person looking for this type of investment. Judging by the nature of the "ad," the subscriber and I speculate that it was a sting by either a federal agency or the state because it was clearly marketing an unregistered security, a crime.

Others claim that the roll programs and also the so-called *self-liquidating loans* are 99.9 percent scams. That doesn't leave much room for other possibilities. Again, I have never heard of anyone successfully closing one of these. One reader reported that he had personally spoken to officers of the Securities and Exchange Commission, and they have a complete package of documents disclosing roll program scams all across the U.S. With all the litigation past and pending, you can obtain public court records and other information on all the deals that didn't materialize or didn't succeed, and nothing from anyone who can document that they did succeed. Those who lose are reluctant to admit to their naivete.

In early 1999, I received the following E-mail message:

> I reviewed your site on the web and wanted to drop you a line about a specific "bank trading fraud" which was perpetrated against hundreds of individuals in the U.S., Canada, Australia and New Zealand. Currently there is an ongoing criminal investigation and an SEC action pending in the U.S. Federal Court in CA. The action is against Rudolph Linschoten aka Dr. Van Lin and Marshall Ronald using the name Sabre Asset Management. The scam was textbook Prime Bank Trading Schemes. The pitch was 100% return every 90 banking days and over 6 million U.S. was collected starting in 1996. At this time no one has received a dime of even their principal back and most lost their life savings. And disgustingly enough Rudolph Linschoten continues

to operate the same business he used to lure individuals into this fraud at offshore seminars through his company Investors International and make millions of dollars from unknowing individuals which he then uses this money to pay the attorney fees to fight those who are trying to recover the money he defrauded from them! And these individuals have moved all of their money and assets offshore to keep the people they defrauded from recovering their money! SEC has a litigation release on their site but that's the only place I found that has any information available to warn anyone about these individuals and their fraud! Hope you decide to list this one on your site so that it will help get the word out and protect others from losing any more money!

An attorney friend of mine confirmed this, so I feel comfortable including it here as a warning to you.

The Self-Liquidating Loan Scam

The "liquidating loan" ads have disappeared in business magazines and other publications promoting these programs, but now show up on the Net. They have gone underground, but seem to reappear on occasion. The promoters claim you can easily get a $500,000 or $50,000,000 loan without any credit check. They can't document that they've obtained one for themselves, but they claim to be the experts.

Obviously, anyone or any entity lending money wants to make a profit and minimize risk. "Everything must have a make sense characteristic to it. If it's too good to be true, boy, it probably isn't true, unless you're naive," writes an OFFSHORE subscriber.

Scam variations may also include the marketing of worthless books or reports. "Once again, people in their greed snatch up these books, making the promoter more money," continues the subscriber. "Now, I do a lot of research on investment and moneymaking ideas. My background being banking, a loan officer, mortgage officer, investment broker, etc., I have spent a considerable amount of time, like everyday, reading international newspapers, magazines, etc., looking for investment ideas that are real and sound. Through my research, I have composed a list of over 500 of the best (top) CTAS (commodity trading advisors) in the world. This kind of investment is about as close as you can get to 'major' returns without using the roll program, which I said I don't think exists."

Readers comment further of commodities and futures trading, "that this is a legitimate legal business, which is registered with the FTC (Futures Trading Commission), the government, the SEC, requiring a business operating license, audited financials, something real that you can put your finger on and say, yes, this is real . . . no smoke, no mirrors, no Houdinis playing disappearing tricks with your last $10 million dollars (if you or I ever had that much!), none of that questionable stuff. The futures and commodities business is very risky, but that shouldn't scare away the roll program investors, since they already are in an even riskier *ghost investment* vehicle."

Another subscriber reports, "I have also personally spoken with the Comptroller of the Currency, and have been given the same information. I have also spoken to a top Letters of Credit officer, manager of the department at Sea-First Bank, formerly owned by BofA, and have received the same negative reply. He is German, and has traveled the world, and has never seen any of these work. As far as I am concerned, the roll programs do not exist. If they do, they are rarely successful, otherwise, the only way they exist is as a scam."

Some will always argue that the roll program is a secret method used only by the very elite banking community—most people and professionals aren't familiar with it, and that's why so many people get ripped off and lose millions. These people believe they know something secret, possess insider information that not even the commercial bankers who do letters of credit every day worldwide and the top people at the U.S. Comptroller of Currency office have access to. They become so caught up in the scam and mesmerized with the euphoria over the possibility of making millions that they lose all ability (if they ever had it) to use good judgment, logic, reason, and especially to exercise due diligence before getting involved. Our subscriber summarizes quite well with this statement: "The promoters, white collar criminals, who market these scams know that the victims are greedy, and they are masters at manipulation of this personal weakness of the victim."

Pitfalls of Bribery

Unfortunately, in many jurisdictions, the typical business model frequently "greases the palm" with what is commonly known as bribery. In the FSU, the traditional Eastern European business model uses bribery as everyday business practice. Following this model can lead Americans into serious problems with the U.S. Justice Department for violating the Foreign Corrupt Practices Act. From its inception in 1977, more than seventeen companies have been prosecuted by U.S. authorities for bribery, leading to fines and imprisonment. You can also be prosecuted with an additional civil action.

Farewell to the Reluctant American

If you still are asking, "How do I get back *my* money from offshore?" I have apparently failed you. If you were seeking asset protection, your assets are not yours any longer! That is how you achieve asset protection. After studying this book, you will understand your offshore consultant better when he or she explains this concept to you.

With the correct language in the trust deed, the grantor of a trust could reserve the power in the trust to reacquire an asset by substituting other property of equal value. But a little bit of knowledge is a dangerous thing. After reading this book, if you think you have what it takes to play games offshore and outsmart the IRS, good luck to you. I don't even want to know you. The U.S. Internal Revenue Service has many smart people and unlimited resources, and they will wear you out, timewise and cashwise, using computer databases to trace your transactions. Tax evasion is a serious subject, and it is a crime. The IRS may assess a taxpayer a substantial penalty for tax fraud.

Any time some promoter wants to sell you on a new strategy or concept for asset protection or tax avoidance using such pitches as "aggressively utilized by prominent families such as the Kennedys, Mellons, Rockefellers, Fords, and Hunts," or perhaps a variation of "formerly, only the rich could use these strategies," run, don't walk, to the nearest exit. You'll thank me later.

Tax-neutral structures don't invite an IRS audit, but can provide asset protection. Don't expect your structure to do everything. It can't!

Offshore tax deferral or avoidance is always encouraged. It is achieved by using arrangements such as deferred annuities, offshore insurance policies, or participation in offshore insurance companies or banks, all of which are legal in the U.S.

Asset protection is not just for the wealthy. Early asset protection measures are imperative as part and parcel of your long-term total estate planning. You are committing fraud against your contingent creditors if you implement AP structures after being sued or with knowledge of a bona fide claim against you. U.S. judges will not let you manipulate the legal system to play offshore games to your advantage to conceal assets from your legitimate claimants or judgment creditors. The judges will many times ignore the law and legal precedents and proceed on the equities to punish you. And in most cases you can't afford to appeal their decisions. However, where there is early bona fide intent to implement estate planning, and that encompasses OS strategies as well, it should fare better in a fraudulent conveyance attack within the U.S. legal system (see Chapter 7, page 90).

Competent local professionals familiar with the OS financial and tax arena are difficult to find. You need someone who sees the big picture. This is not the place for unjustifiable loyalty to your domestic professionals, as much as you like them, even if they have been your best friends of many years. Practice global, geographic, and professional diversity.

Practice privacy. Go digital and save a tree. Better yet, go PGP and then thank Phil Zimmerman, its creator, with a donation to his legal fund. Although the U.S. government dropped its case against him (claiming he was instrumental in exporting PGP internationally over the Internet, a federal crime) in January 1996, he is now trying to determine the extent of their inquiry into his personal life by litigation.

After studying *The Offshore Money Book*, you will be better prepared to attend seminars on the subjects of asset protection and utilizing offshore structures for wealth conservation. You'll be surprised how much incorrect, noncompliant tax advice and outright illegal material and information are being propagated. So beware—some seminars are merely infomercials. And before you take the big plunge, why don't you visit the offshore people with whom you will entrust your money? Be careful out there!

Lest you get the wrong notion after reading this book, for the record, I love my country, the U.S. of A. During my lifetime, I have visited over twenty-five countries and still believe that ours is the best on earth, even though the so-called American Dream is fading somewhat. Nevertheless, our American civilization is definitely *not* crumbling, just being redefined under a new model.

But I don't like the runaway growth of government; I don't like the gradual intrusion of government into my private life; I don't like the blur of distinction between the two major political parties in our country, the Republicrats and the Democricans; I don't like it when the interest on our national debt eats up most of my federal income taxes; I don't like an income tax system that is incomprehensible and unfair, one that only a CPA can interpret; I don't like confiscatory taxes and social engineering redistributing our hard-earned wealth; I don't like corporate America's lack of social responsibility; I don't like overregulation by government controlling our business and personal lives; I don't like the moral lapses in Washington, D.C.; and I really don't like our present litigious society driven by a surplus of very creative attorneys. But this still is a great country with the highest standard of living in the world! This is my personal commentary as the author, hopefully not construed by you as being too negative.

See you on Paradise Island, or in Basseterre or, even better, the Côte d'Azur—but only for a "visit."

Au revoir.

Arnie

E-mail: offshore@bahamas.net.bs

www.offshore-net.com

P.S. Keep on surfing the Net! Let me know of any interesting offshore sites.

15

Tax Havens of the World

THIS CHAPTER INCLUDES a discussion of some of the attributes of tax havens of the world that will give you a sense of what is important in the evaluation and selection process. Following this discussion is comparative information on a mélange of selected IFCs. It is not a precise shopping guide but a report, a narration of what I have seen, felt, and observed.

This chapter is not intended to be a substitute for the many fine books that compare and characterize the tax havens of the world. It is a presentation of my impressions of several havens, my candid comments. From it, I trust you can develop your own yardsticks for evaluating and selecting the havens in which you feel most comfortable.

Depending on how you define a tax haven, there probably are more than fifty tax havens in the world. Because of the limitations of this book—so much to write but so little space—only some are discussed. But total exclusion from this list does provide a message; I would probably not use them.

Selected Tax Havens of the World

The following list includes my subjective ranking (on a scale of 1 to 10) and is presented in alphabetical order. No haven was given a score of 10, because no haven can be all things to all people; there is no such thing as a perfect jurisdiction.

Please note:

APT = Asset protection trust or statutory trust, dependent upon the haven's trust act or ordinance

BWI = British West Indies.

IBC = Exempt company or international business company, as appropriate, depending upon the exempt company act or ordinance of the tax haven

NR = Not ranked

NWI = Netherlands West Indies

WI = West Indies

+ = Favorable

− = Unfavorable

− − − = Really avoid

Alaska

NR   A newcomer (Alaska Trust Act, April 1, 1997) in the field of asset protection, Alaska permits self-settled APTs, nicknamed the "tundra trust." In reality, this is an asset protection experiment, and we won't know whether the experiment will work until the first test case. I don't want my client to be that test case! Alaska is attempting to divert AP business from other states and countries. How long must we wait to evaluate the efficacy of their new trust laws? The tundra trust is structured with the grantor as trustee and with no current beneficiary, attempting to provide full creditor protection. Alaska has no rule against perpetuities (dynasty trusts and spendthrift trusts can apparently be located there) and no trust income tax. There is a four-year statute of limitations on fraudulent conveyances; private noncharitable trusts may then be perpetual. Some trustees and investments may be located anywhere, even out of

Alaska. Some of the features of the new Alaska trust statute are reported to be substantially identical to section 456.080.3 of the Missouri statutes of 1989. To read it, just go to one of these sites:

www.actec.org
www.io.com/~karisch/alaska.htm
www.hompesch.com/news.htm
www.actec.org/public/?Template=WhatsNewPublic
www.actec.org/public/?Template=ShowPublicLinks

Alderney

NR   This tax haven in the Channel Islands is northeast of Guernsey. New Companies Law Ordinance of 1998 regulates foreign companies operating in Alderney providing a Register of External Companies, a public record.

Andorra

NR   Andorra is a low-tax jurisdiction with a population of 63,000. It has excellent banking secrecy laws and no taxes on income, capital gains, capital transfer, inheritance, or sales. There is no national currency, though the Spanish peseta and the French franc circulate. There is no foreign exchange control, and numbered banking accounts are available. Foreign persons are permitted to hold secret bank accounts, and accounts are held in all major world currencies. No tax is levied on earned interest and dividends on bank accounts.

Anguilla

6   Anguilla is a British overseas territory in the British West Indies. It's a low-profile haven with banks monitored by the Bank of England. APT legislation is in place. Anguilla passed a new ordinance in December 1998 to increase its attractiveness as an IBC site, and it has one of the most high-tech company registrar offices in the world. Anguilla's ACORN system (Anguilla Commercial Online Registration Network) permits electronic incorporation 365 days a year, twenty-four hours a day, anywhere one has electronic access, worldwide. Most documents may be filed electronically. Anguilla has been very aggressive in maintaining very low filing fees to induce IBCs to transfer there.

Antigua and Barbuda

4   Antigua has a high profile with the U.S. because of Antigua's successful 1998 defense of an attempt by the U.S. to recover money on deposit there, as well as its tightening of banking privacy, which may encourage money laundering. Antigua has the highest per capita income in the eastern Caribbean. There are no exchange controls, no information exchange agreements with any other country (has not executed the MLAT with the U.S.), and no income taxes. It is an English common-law jurisdiction. There were reports in 1998 of Russian gangster influence in Antigua (see reports of the failure of the European Union Bank in the press and on the Internet). The jurisdiction's inability to get a handle on the 1999 Caribbean Bank of Commerce problem lowers its ranking.

For IBCs, Antigua offers offshore corporate law and strict confidentiality. Its banking system survived U.S. government litigation for the recovery of money-laundering funds held there; the court found that the U.S. courts had no jurisdiction over the money or Swiss American Bank in Antigua since all the banking activities relating to the funds occurred in Antigua.

In 1999, the U.S. Treasury Department warned U.S. banks to be especially careful of transactions with financial institutions in Antigua and Barbuda, purportedly because of concerns that Antigua is softening its money-laundering safeguards. Essentially, U.S. banks are now required to carefully scrutinize all financial transactions between the U.S. and Antigua. If you send a wire transfer to an Antigua bank, expect the sending bank and U.S. government agencies to take a close look at the transfer.

Aruba

5   The Netherlands Antilles and Aruba are autonomous parts of the kingdom of the Netherlands. The Netherlands Antilles include the islands of Bonaire, Curaçao, Saba, St. Eustatius (also known as Statia),

and Saint Maarten (Dutch side). Aruba has a Dutch legal system and is known for eleven lavish casinos (suspected of money laundering for Colombia and Panama and of corrupt local politics). Banking privacy has been eroded by laws entitled *Melding Obgebruikelijke Transacties*, requiring banks to report any "unusual transactions." The Freezone is also under investigation involving money transactions.

Austria

8   Austria is a highly developed, stable democracy with a modern economy and excellent banking privacy (+). It is a principal gateway to transacting business in the former Soviet Union.

Bahamas

8   This is a very mature tax haven—an independent country since 1973, the third oldest democracy in the world. In 1999, tourism provided for more than 50 percent of its gross national product. The 1999 Index of Economic Freedom of Latin American and Caribbean countries ranked the Bahamas first in the region and eleventh worldwide. More than 400 banks and trust companies are registered there (+). The Bahamas is in the same time zone as the U.S. Eastern zone (+), and it has enacted APT legislation and the International Business Companies Act (patterned after the successful BVI act) (+). The jurisdiction does not recognize foreign judgments. It is the fourth largest in international banking, and has new, stronger criminal legislation with respect to money laundering.

There is no requirement to retain books in this jurisdiction, and there is total privacy at company register. The Bahamas is second in popularity for IBC formation to the Caymans, and more than 90,000 IBCs are registered there. There is a two-year statute of limitations for fraudulent transfers to an APT; rule against perpetuities is based on a "wait-and-see test" (−). Certain tax attributes are very favorable, such as no personal or corporate income taxes, no capital gains taxes, no withholding taxes of any kind, no gift or death taxes, no inheritance taxes or death duties, no probate fees, no sales taxes, and no employment taxes. Guarantees against future taxes are provided by the government for periods up to 50 years. Exempt trusts can receive a guarantee up to 100 years. A very close relationship with the U.S. is essential for the Bahamas financially and to provide political stability for the country (−). More recent changes include the amended Trust Act, which provides the option of having a trust executed under Bahamian law regardless of existing foreign judgments. The Domicile of Trust permits individuals who reside in countries that do not recognize the concept of trusts to establish trusts in the Bahamas, and the Fraudulent Dispositions Act discourages the use of an APT for fraudulent disposition of properties located in the Bahamas or any other jurisdiction.

Bahrain

NR   A tax haven.

Barbados

6   for tax-haven attributes, 7 for business development. This is a low-profile haven with continuing political and economic stability and no recognition of foreign judgments. Population is 270,000; it is around twice the size of Washington, D.C., with a labor force of 140,000 highly skilled workers. The literacy rate is 97 percent, the citizens speak English, and the British common-law legal model is in use, as is the Barbados dollar (equivalent to U.S. 50 cents). Barbados has been an independent country since 1966. It has no restrictions on foreign ownership of business enterprises, and has excellent infrastructure, banking (44 banks), and financial services, sufficient legal and accounting professionals, and courier services by Federal Express, DHL, and UPS. Barbados has enacted APT legislation and is an attractive jurisdiction for IBCs. It has a double-tax treaty with the U.S. and other countries, is a good site for formation of FSCs, and is a low-tax jurisdiction with a maximum tax rate of 2.5 percent.

Belgium

NR   Prior reputation for being the insurance fraud capital of the world.

Belize

3.5   This Central American country (the former British Honduras) is not yet in the same league as the Bahamas, Bermuda, Costa Rica, and the British Virgin Islands. It is a developing country and has a long way to go to reach the higher level of performance and professionalism provided elsewhere. However, it has enacted APT legislation. It is at a lower tier in the OS world's listings of tax havens, not yet an international financial center. You should want and need more than a tax haven. Belize's banking system survived an attack by the U.S. SEC attempting to recover funds.

As a retirement location in Central America, some dislike it and others think it's great. Belize brings in the retirees' money and creates economic gains for the locals. There really are only two Central American retirement locations on my OS list—Costa Rica and Belize. Between the two, I still prefer Costa Rica. It has been reported that close to 30,000 Americans have retired in Costa Rica, which is a brief flight from Los Angeles, Houston, or Miami.

Belize is a relative newcomer to the world international financial scene and has much to learn, including how to create the correct political and regulatory climate to attract flight capital and offshore consultants' business. Belize's regulators appear to be ineffective. The Internet is awash with offers for $200 Belize trusts, and they are being sold in a multilevel marketing scheme. Noncompliant claims of U.S. tax-free income abound. You can't get an efficacious and worthwhile trust deed for $200! You don't want a trustee who drives a taxicab by day and writes trusts at night. I'm concerned for those who may be deceived with a false sense of accomplishment and protection but in reality are left holding a weak, nonpersonalized trust—a boilerplate document. And what about those $850 second-year trustee fees that they don't mention? There is no recognition of foreign judgments (+), and no statutory recognition of creditor "classes" (+). Belize has enacted APT legislation (+) and encourages redomiciling of foreign IBCs in its jurisdiction, waiving first-year fees. More than 11,000 IBCs are registered allowing bearer shares and no disclosure of shareholders.

Bermuda

8   This British overseas territory is only a brief flight from New
York. Bermuda has a very high cost of living (–), good employment
opportunities for expatriates, and good infrastructure (+). It is the
least expensive location for an OS mutual fund (+). Bermuda has no
income tax, withholding tax, capital gains tax, capital transfer tax,
estate duties, or inheritance tax (+). However, Bermuda does recognize U.S. judgments (–), and has no binding effect upon choice of
law (–). Bermuda has enacted APT legislation (+), and permits a 100-
year vesting period (+), where required; there are no provisions for
the settlor being his own trust protector (–). The statute of limitations is six years and allows claims arising within two years of trust
settlement (– –). There is provisional abrogation of the Statute of
Elizabeth (+). Bermuda amended its IBC companies act in 1998, making it a good site for IBCs (+). Certain tax attributes make Bermuda
particularly attractive—guarantees against future taxes are provided
by the government for periods up to 50 years. Exempt trusts can
receive a guarantee up to 100 years. Insurance business is closely
linked with London and New York in what is referred to as the
"world's central insurance triangle." In fact, Bermuda is considered
the OS insurance capital of the world (+). It has an excellent supporting infrastructure and serves as the offshore arm of the American insurance industry because of eagerness to take on re-insurance
and risk sharing, less regulation, more privacy, and rapid response
to customers' needs. Bermuda is the home of OS subsidiaries of many
U.S. insurance companies. Disputes are settled by binding arbitra-
tion. There is no guaranty fund for failed companies (–). Bermuda
has 1,400 captive insurance companies.

British Overseas Territories (in general)

Flash: Watch the slowly spreading banking and fiscal transparency in
these territories mandated by pressures from the U.K. In 1999, the
U.S. (through the U.K.) was successful in forcing the four British territories in the Caribbean and Atlantic region (Bermuda, Caymans,
British Virgin Islands, and Turks and Caicos) to cooperate with U.S.
authorities in the investigation of alleged money-laundering and tax-

evasion offenses. In 1999, the Isle of Man declared a moratorium on the formation of new nonresident companies pending the anticipated imposition of EU standards on the overseas territories.

British Virgin Islands

8   This British overseas territory is in a good location for an OS mutual fund (+). Banks are monitored by the Bank of England, providing bank stability. One must make a personal appearance to open bank accounts. Special tax laws exist (such as no taxes), and more than 220,000 IBCs are registered. BVI is a strong IBC jurisdiction (++)—there is total privacy at company register (+), and bearer shares are permitted. Trust laws are weak (–), and APT legislation has not been enacted (–). BVI is the premier haven for IBC formation, with more IBCs than any other jurisdiction.

Canary Islands

6   It has implemented new company laws—nonresident companies pay only a 1 percent annual tax, and no local members are permitted—for OS business only.

Campione

NR   Landlocked Italian domain in the Swiss canton of Ticino. No personal income taxes.

Cayman Islands

8   This British overseas territory is one of the most successful and largest tax havens. It is an English common-law jurisdiction and the fifth largest offshore IFC in the world, with over 590 banks and trust companies (monitored by the Bank of England), more than $500 billion (U.S.) on deposit, and 28,000 exempt companies. It's a good locale for an OS mutual fund (+). There are no personal or corporate income taxes, and no capital gains, inheritance, or gift taxes. The statute of limitations is long. Incorporation costs are higher than in the Bahamas and BVI (–). Foreign judgments are not recognized,

but an MLAT with the U.S. is in place (–). The Cayman Islands serves as a situs for mutual funds and insurance companies, including the "rent-a-captive" cell type of insurance company. Caymans mutual funds are particularly popular with the Latin American markets. The IBC Act of 1990 requires meetings to be local (–). The government registers directors (only one director required), bearer shares are permitted, and there are no corporate name restrictions. Foreign language registrations are accepted, even in Chinese, providing there is an authenticated translation by a Cayman Islands–approved translator. There is no privacy at company register. The Caymans enacted new APT legislation in 1998 (+), with laws that are considered models for other banking jurisdictions. A unique feature of Cayman's APT law is that there need not be a full nexus for the trust—the trustee and trust assets may be situated in another jurisdiction. Only a creditor in existence at the time of creation of the APT has standing to sue (future creditors are without standing). The six-year statute of limitations (–) on the ability of a creditor to attack transfers of assets to an APT is a major negative factor. It appears that a U.S. bankruptcy trustee would not have standing to enforce a derivative creditor right, and only the actual creditor could file an action in the Caymans against the trustee (+).

The Caymans is considered susceptible to U.S. influence (–). A long (150 years) perpetuities period (+) and positive tax attributes make the Caymans particularly attractive. There are no personal or corporate income taxes, no capital gains taxes, no withholding taxes of any kind, no gift or inheritance taxes or death duties, no probate fees, no sales taxes, and no employment taxes. Guarantees against future taxes are provided by the government for periods up to 20 years from registration; exempt trusts can receive a guarantee up to 100 years. An IBC may be redomiciled in another jurisdiction but continue to operate as a Caymanian company. The Cayman Islands Stock Exchange was introduced in January 1997.

The Channel Islands

8   The Channel Islands has low tax rates, as well as some reluctance to implement APT legislation. Where the trust deed contains

the necessary powers, a trustee has the power to change the proper law of a Jersey trust (as distinct from Guernsey) to the laws of another jurisdiction; trusts have transferability. The converse is also true in that Jersey will accept orphan trusts. The Channel Islands is exempt from many EU regulations.

Cook Islands

5   The Cook Islands recognizes the concept of community property (+), but is considered susceptible to U.S. influence through New Zealand (−). Standard of proof for fraud is the U.S. criminal burden of proof "beyond a reasonable doubt" (+). A Pacific Rim leader, Cook Islands has a somewhat overly aggressive trust protectionist statute that some characterize as hostile to creditors. Foreign judgments are not recognized (+); APT legislation has been enacted (+) and a special APT called the international trust exists. The Cook Islands has the shortest statute of limitations on fraud—two years from the date the claim arose (+) or one year from the date of transfer of the asset to the trust to the APT (+). It also has the strongest anticlaimant laws (+) (there need not be a full nexus for the trust—the trustee and trust assets may be situated in another jurisdiction). Only a creditor in existence at the time of creation of the APT has standing to sue (future creditors are without standing). The six-year statute of limitations (−) on the ability of a creditor to attach transfers of assets to an APT is a major negative factor. The Cook Islands is sometimes used as a final flight jurisdiction because of these characteristics: for example, it provides retroactive protection of "immigrant" (recandled or moved) trusts, permits a 100-year perpetuity period, and permits a quasi-charitable trust.

The "Orange Grove" case decision will most likely have lasting impact upon statutes of limitations in the U.S. as well as other jurisdictions. The opinion in the case will be used to justify treating Cook Islands APTs as shams. The trial judge in the Cook Islands was concerned that the jurisdiction's laws cannot really be intended to cut off the claims of creditors so quickly, because doing that would ignore fairness and would make the Cook Islands a renegade jurisdiction in the eyes of the rest of the world. But, contrary to what the judge held, the Cook Islands legislature passed amended laws that said to the world that it really did intend to cut off creditors' claims very quickly, and that its financial industry and banks were making money creating APTs. The danger arises that U.S. judges may feel comfortable ignoring the Cook Islands APT laws because of this legislative position. A 1999 report stated that it was being used as a money-laundering center by "apparently American" middlemen to hide Russian mafia funds. Vanuatu and Samoa were the other countries named.

Costa Rica

7   Costa Rica is a stable Central America democracy, the best retirement country in Central America (+). But the inflation rate is very high, affecting the exchange rate for the U.S. dollar (−). It is a middle-income developing country with a strong democratic tradition, classified as a low-risk investment jurisdiction based on political, financial, and economic factors (+). Costa Rica is considered susceptible to U.S. influence (−); an information exchange agreement with the IRS has eroded banking privacy (−). A deposit insurance program, self-insured and funded by five government-owned banks, is pending.

Cuba

NR   Cuba is a future tax haven and excellent investment opportunity presently for all but Americans. The Cuban government is meeting with successful offshore service providers to implement its tax-haven status.

Cyprus

5   Cyprus is a developed Mediterranean island nation divided de facto into two areas. The government of the Republic of Cyprus is the internationally recognized authority on the island, but in practice its control extends only to the Greek Cypriot southern part of the island. The northern area operates under an autonomous Turkish Cypriot administrative zone supported by Turkish troops. In

1983, this section declared itself the "Turkish Republic of Northern Cyprus," which is recognized only by Turkey. Foreign judgments are not recognized (+); APT legislation has been enacted, but Cyprus is still considered a raw, untested jurisdiction. The Greek zone has attracted several foreign banks. Cyprus is currently reported to be on the UN red list because of money-laundering practices.

Delaware

NR   Delaware passed laws that permit you to establish a trust to protect your assets from your creditors and name yourself as beneficiary, but the state is still not tested by the legal system. Until that test occurs, it is not a good site for asset protection.

Denmark

8   Denmark seeks to become a tax haven by providing an attractive tax system and holding company structures. Denmark plans to introduce a system that offers significant tax breaks to holding companies. The following measures have received a first reading in the Danish parliament: Withholding taxes on company dividends transferred out of Denmark to an overseas parent company would be abolished where the overseas parent holds at least a 25 percent of share capital of the Danish company. Dividends received by a Danish company from foreign nonfinancial subsidiaries would be tax free if the parent company holds at least a 25 percent of the share capital of the dividend-paying company for a continuous period of at least one year.

Dominica

5   Dominica is the northernmost Windward Island in the West Indies. Another example of an obscure tax haven, Dominica is a developing island nation located between Guadeloupe and St. Lucia, off the beaten track, with a low profile and a friendly business-oriented government. Dominica wants your tax haven business. Still relatively underdeveloped as an offshore financial center, its government is always interested in discussing business ventures providing mutual

benefits. It has an IBC Act of 1996, a trust act called the International Exempt Trust Act of 1997, the Insurance Act of 1997, and the Exempt Insurance Act of 1997. (There is no mutual fund act.)

Dublin, Ireland

NR   Excellent where dual-tax treaties are effective.

France

NR   At the time this book was written, France was weakening banking privacy by seeking to impose bank disclosure requirements in response to civil officials, without disclosing any cause for the inquiry, for money transfers to other countries in amounts over U.S.$20,000 (–). France is also seeking a means to clamp down on tax evasion. The laws of trusts are not recognized as a legal concept in this jurisdiction (–). France is not considered a tax shelter.

Gibraltar

8   As the U.K. forces Gibraltar to make its financial dealings transparent, it will slowly capitulate. This British overseas territory, highly stable since 1713, does not recognize foreign judgments. Gibraltar offers full exemption from income taxes and estate duties (+). A register of IBC members must be kept in Gibraltar (–), and no changes of shareholders or beneficial ownership are allowed without consent of local authorities (–). Shareholders and directors of IBCs are of public record, requiring nominees (–). Gibraltar has enacted favorable APT legislation (+), and APTs are not registered by each transfer into the trust (–). There is a two-year statute of limitation on fraud (+), and an objective test for fraudulent intent is used instead of the badges of fraud test (+).

Grenada

3   Grenada is a developing island nation and a tax haven. Americans are very popular here, but the jurisdiction is ranked low (–). I

seriously downgraded this haven in March of 1999 because of the way it mismanaged a banking scandal involving its jurisdiction.

Guernsey

8   Guernsey is one of the better-equipped IFCs (+), but is not a common-law jurisdiction (−). Guernsey is located off the Normandy Cherbourg peninsula between the French and British shores. This premier Channel Islands jurisdiction manages more than U.S.$100 billion for the offshore community. Although Guernsey trades with the EC, it is outside of the "EC directive" intended to harmonize the old financial directives of the EU, and thus can be unique. It is part of the British Isles, but not the U.K. It was given the right to domestic self-government. Politically stable because there are no political parties, it has a low-tax regimen. There are no inheritance taxes, death duties, capital transfer taxes, or VATs. With an abundance of professionals and a well-regulated financial environment, it attracts IFC business from the global community. Its more than seventy-three banks from seventeen different countries and more than thirty-five captive insurance companies are certainly a testimonial to its position as an IFC. It has a new product, the protected cell company—it is a legal "person," and each cell is segregated from the other cells. Ranking of this haven will be reduced since Guernsey is complying with the U.K.'s demands that it essentially close its offshore financial service centers and become fully fiscally transparent within the European Union.

Hong Kong

NR   The jury is still out until the control by mainland China stabilizes. In 1999, increasing Chinese influence on Hong Kong laws led me to believe that Hong Kong will diminish in importance as a tax haven.

Ireland

7   Ireland has established (in 1987) an international financial services center (IFSC) in Dublin. It is a full EC member and a good locale for management of an OS mutual fund (+), though it is a costly jurisdiction for formation of an OS mutual fund (–). There is a double-tax agreement with the U.S., and the local government believes that their IBCs are being misused. Called Irish nonresident companies, newer companies (IBCs) must disclose the beneficial owners (–); this requires using a second entity, either a trustee owner or a second IBC that issues bearer shares. The tax rate is not more than 10 percent; Ireland is one of the most tax efficient countries in the EU for non-resident companies. Irish nonresident companies are extremely flexible and may engage in any lawful business in any country and in any currency without restriction. Nonresident companies pay no tax to the Irish Inspector of Taxes; nominee directors and shareholders are allowable; there is no annual exempt fee or government duty; companies give the protection of limited liability in the execution of business. The Republic of Ireland is the only full member of the EU offering these facilities. In mid-1999, Dublin was reported to be the most rapidly growing international financial center. The growth rate exceeded those of Bermuda, Jersey, and the Caymans.

Isle of Man

8   The Isle of Man maintains a very high standard for regulations. It is under pressure from the U.K. for more open banking and company disclosures. It is not an APT jurisdiction and it has high establishment and annual costs (–). It has excellent regulatory monitoring (+) and is a safe haven, with 20 percent income and corporate taxes and no capital gains or inheritance taxes. It has high incorporation costs for an IBC (–). It has not enacted APT legislation (–), has not overridden the Statute of Elizabeth (–), and has newly enacted LLC laws that do not require directors, shares, or audit, and are tax free.

In 1999, under severe pressure from the U.K., the Isle of Man government proposed "an immediate moratorium" on the creation of the special class of nonresident companies, which has been criticized by the U.K. It was suggested that they served as "attractive vehicles for evasion of taxes in other jurisdictions." The Isle of Man also announced that it would immediately regulate corporate service providers and amend its double-taxation treaty with the U.K. This is only the start, and the U.K. will continue to put more and more pressure upon the jurisdiction for total fiscal transparency.

Jamaica

NR   Jamaica is a developing nation in economic disarray. The banking system is in shambles, and unemployment and the crime rate are high.

Jersey

8   Jersey is considered the "offshore Europe" or "offshore U.K." by many. It is an excellent IFC with new limited liability partnership laws in 1998, no exchange control restrictions (+), low income tax of 20 percent since 1939, and excellent regulation of banking and financial services industries (+). It is not a common-law jurisdiction (–). Unfortunately, Jersey is expected to become less attractive as a tax haven as it succumbs to U.K. pressure to become fiscally transparent.

Labuan

5   This newcomer in the South Pacific is the international OS financial center (IOFC) of Malaysia. It is a common-law jurisdiction in which English is widely used. Labuan is principally a haven for Islamic financial services and products, and has more than 800 trading and service companies, 55 banks, 20 trust companies, and 10 insurance companies. There are no exchange controls when dealing with residents, and taxes are low.

Liberia

NR   A tax haven.

Liechtenstein

7   Liechtenstein's legal system consists of local civil and penal codes. It accepts compulsory ICJ jurisdiction, with reservations. No double-tax treaties are in place, and the only tax agreements are with Switzerland and Austria. Liechtenstein provides an excellent form of a codified (as opposed to common-law) trust, one of the best and most flexible trusts, called the "family foundation," as well as the private foundation structure called the *Stiftung*. It is used as a model in other jurisdictions, such as Panama. Several companies provide trust services in St. Vincent and the Grenadines.

Luxembourg

7   Luxembourg has more than 190 banks, and is the leader among offshore mutual funds, with more than 3,700. The legal system is based on civil law. It accepts compulsory ICJ jurisdiction. Languages include German, French, English, and Letzeburgesch. In general, it is an outrageously costly locale for an OS mutual fund (–).

Madeira

7   This gateway to Europe has special tax concessions for preferred businesses and a promising free-trade zone. Shelf companies are available, including Madeira's special SGPS holding companies.

Malaysia

6   IBCs are available.

Malta

NR   A tax haven.

Northern Mariana Islands

NR   Located in the Pacific Ocean, Northern Mariana is reported to have one of the most complicated tax systems in the world.

Marshall Islands

6   An independent country, the Marshall Islands has enacted APT legislation (Trust Act of 1994). Trusts must be registered with the registrar (–) and must have two local trustees (–).

Mauritius

7   Sited in the Indian Ocean, Mauritius is a developing nation with a stable government and a growing economy. It is a gateway (using holding companies) to India, the Middle East, and South Africa. It

has double-tax treaties with member countries in the Indian Ocean Rim Association, and is utilized as a situs for mutual funds. A low-tax jurisdiction, its maximum rate is 35 percent. Mauritius has enacted APT legislation. Offshore services include captive insurance, aircraft registration, mutual fund registration, and leasing. There is a very favorable India-Mauritius double-tax avoidance scheme or agreement. Offshore banking, insurance, and fund management may be carried out by offshore companies (Mauritian Offshore Business Activities Act of 1992). Languages spoken include English, French, and Creole.

Melchizedek, Dominion of

o   This fictional nation is based on the phantom Taongi Atoll on the Island of Karitane, somewhere in the Central Pacific, and on Ruthenia, Malpelo, and Clipperton. Geologists report that you need a submarine to get to Karitane since it is around 1,000 feet under the water's surface. The Dominion of Melchizedek is a fraudulent scheme and a nonexistent tax haven! There is no such nation, though it is claimed to have applied to the UN for recognition (too many years ago) but at present may be only "recognized" by several very minor, third-world, radical African countries. The last time I inquired, there was only a fax machine and an E-mail address, and only somewhere that claimed to be the "Ecclesiastical Dominion of Melchizedek." I met with its "leader" (Tzemach David Netzer Korem, the reputed founder of the Dominion of Melchizedek, who sits on their board of elders) in San Francisco for dinner several years ago. He lost interest in me when I didn't want to "buy" something. They are in the business of selling regular and diplomatic passports, banking licenses, IBCs, and trusts. I would think that a banking license from this operation would be worthless in the conventional world banking community. They gave me a laugh when they added some new government departments, including a "Bureau of Investigations" and an "Olympic team." Must be for underwater swimming and watered stock. The U.S. Comptroller of the Currency has stated that the Dominion of Melchizedek is a nonrecognized sovereignty. Banking licenses from there are not recognized!

Montserrat

o (–)   This British overseas territory is currently more famous for its volcano eruptions than its status as a tax haven.

Nauru

2 (– –)   Nauru is third-tier tax haven, a small island nation in the Central Pacific (south of the equator) hungry for filing fees for IBCs and granting of Class B bank charters. It is jokingly said that "Every Russian and his dog has a bank in Nauru." Nauru doesn't make public information about the number of offshore companies registered or banking licenses chartered (low-cost private banking licenses). These banking licenses have questionable value and very limited recognition in the world banking community, thus little efficacy. They are touted as having significant tax-deferral benefits, but may not survive in an attack by the IRS.

I seriously downgraded this haven in March of 1999 because of the way it mismanaged a banking scandal involving its jurisdiction, and because of the reported unscrupulous use by foreigners for fraud or money-laundering purposes. A 1999 report stated that Nauru was being used as a money-laundering center by "apparently American" middlemen to hide Russian mafia funds. It further indicated that Nauru's offshore banking center and tax haven, regarded by Pacific Islands business executives as being the most secretive of six operating in the region, brought this country considerable revenue. Banking business is good for the Nauruians—they are among the world's wealthiest people, with an estimated gross national product of approximately $16,500 per person and a very low cost of living. Nauru was formerly a source of phosphates, but its mines are tapped out; they need foreign source income and have turned into an international financial center.

The Netherlands

NR   Holding companies are exempt from paying value-added taxes.

Netherlands Antilles

8   (Excludes Aruba.) The Netherlands Antilles is an autonomous part of the kingdom of the Netherlands. The Netherlands Antilles include the islands of Bonaire, Curaçao, Saba, St. Eustatius (also known as Statia), and Saint Maarten (Dutch side). This is a good locale for an os mutual fund. It is opening a new free-trade zone, the Hato FTZ, providing special tax breaks. It is a good source for second passports for retired people (+) and is excellent for holding companies (+).

Nevada

7   Nevada is the only state in the U.S. that does not prohibit corporate bearer shares (+). It has no income tax information exchange agreement with the IRS (+), but also has the highest IRS corporate audit rate of all the states (–). Following are some of the characteristics that make Nevada a U.S. tax haven for Americans holding offshore assets that have returned, and for foreigners. Wyoming is also popular with the Germans for similar characteristics. The principal attributes of the Nevada corporations are:

1. No corporate income taxes

2. No taxes on corporate shares

3. No franchise taxes

4. No personal income taxes

5. No information sharing agreement with the IRS

6. Nominal annual fees

7. Minimal reporting and disclosure requirements

8. Names of stockholders are not of public record, indirectly permitting bearer shares

9. Officers and directors may be non–U.S. persons

10. A director need not be a shareholder

Nevis

6 Nevis has enacted APT legislation and affords protection to "immigrant" trusts that resettle there (+). Incentives are provided with total company tax exemption and freedom of exchange controls—this jurisdiction seeks the world's tax-haven business. With fast company formations (in one hour), expeditious statutory requirements, and competitive pricing, Nevis is attracting the offshore community—but it does not permit commercial insurance companies to operate from its jurisdiction. Nevis has probably the best offshore LLC laws of all the havens. Also see St. Kitts.

New Brunswick, Canada

NR Developing regulations to compete in the captive insurance market.

New Zealand

7 A tax haven for foreigners.

(Cybernation of) New Utopia

0 New Utopia amounts to a bizarre plan to drag dozens of oil platforms over a reef situated 115 miles west of the Cayman Islands to create a new floating nation. The project was to be financed by the issuance of new currency. The U.S. SEC didn't find the project very amusing and sought a restraining order. In April 1999, a federal judge in Tulsa, Oklahoma, granted the SECs request for an emergency restraining order against Lazarus R. Long, who calls himself Prince Lazarus, and his New Utopia company. The order froze all money raised by Long through the allegedly fraudulent scheme, estimated at around $100,000. Long called the SEC's case a "witch hunt," but said he has complied with the SEC's request to stop selling the bonds and will return the investors' money. Later, he said, he wants people to be able to continue "donating" money to the New Utopia government.

Niue

4 Niue, an example of an obscure South Pacific tax haven, is located just east of the international date line. It is a British commonwealth. Although a self-governing territory, it ultimately comes under the jurisdiction of New Zealand. New Zealand has put pressure on Niue to clean up its act and reduce incidents of money laundering by tightening its laws. Niue permits *oral* trusts; written trusts must be registered with the registrar (–). Niue has tried to assure corporate form security by copying the typical IBC style of legislation as used in many Caribbean jurisdictions (+). Its trust laws are still not clear (–). Any one of three languages may be used in drafting the IBC documents: English, Chinese, or Cyrillic. (Take a Cyrillic document to your U.S. lawyer to have it explained to you!) It would still be cheaper to create a company in the Bahamas. The fees in Niue would be about the same as in BVI. Niue has enacted APT legislation.

Palau

NR A tax haven.

Panama

6 Ranked 45 out of 174 countries in 1998 as far as achievements in human development, Panama has the Stiftung type of private foundation. It has fully recovered from the U.S. "invasion" to capture General Manuel Noriega. It has zero inflation rate, a lower cost of living than Costa Rica, no tax on foreign source income, special tax benefits, and strict banking privacy laws, but consequently suffers from a reputation for bank money laundering for drug money. Some special opportunities and structures include stock companies, open ship registration (providing the so-called "flags of convenience"), the colon free zone, the Panama Canal, trusts, factoring, and the private interest foundation (PIF). The PIF as an entity is the latest structure established by the Panamanian legislative branch. The PIF is a legal entity and consists of the following essential parties: a founder, who establishes the foundation and funds it with assets, referred to as the patrimony; and a foundation council to administer the PIF's assets, complying with the charter and objectives of the PIF.

For IBCs, Panama features low incorporation fees (thus it has many more registered corporations than most other offshore centers). It is more complex for an IBC than other jurisdictions in some respects. There is no required minimal capitalization; bearer shares are permitted; a minimum of three directors are required (may be any nationality); natural persons are required as officers; and a president, secretary, treasurer, and a registered Panamanian agent domiciled in Panama are required. The IBC can have perpetual life or be a company that is limited in duration. Panama has enacted Liechtenstein-type trust laws (+).

St. Kitts (St. Christopher) and Nevis

7   A low-profile, twin-island federation located in the northern part of the Lesser Antilles in the eastern Caribbean. This stable parliamentary democracy with an English common-law legal system features a state-of-the-art telecommunications system, including Internet access. Foreign judgments are not recognized. St. Kitts is a source of second (economic) passports, as well as exempt companies, companies limited by guaranty or shares, and partnerships. Companies may be structured as being exempt from local taxes. No personal income taxes exist, but generous investment and trade incentives do. MLAT with the U.S. has not been executed (+). There are no gift, sales, turnover, or estate taxes, but nonexempt companies are subject to up to 38 percent income tax on profits. Currency is the East Caribbean dollar (ECD), pegged at a rate of 1 equals U.S.$2.70.

St. Lucia

NR   St. Lucia is a developing island nation with over 160 lawyers and more than 30 law firms; it recently established an offshore or international financial sector. New acts are being passed: IBC Act, Registered Agents and Trustees Act, International Trust Act, International Insurance and Re-insurance Companies Act, and the

Mutual Fund Act. In the future, China will attempt to exert influence on this Caribbean country by such acts as a gift of $4 million to build a local sports stadium. (This was how China rewarded St. Kitts for breaking diplomatic ties with Taiwan.) Look for the Chinese to invest heavily into the local financial community. This may become China's second-largest Caribbean operating base, one of its financial centers.

St. Thomas

NR St. Thomas is a jurisdiction used for FSCS and special exempt companies for offshore corporations. Primarily used by non-American companies.

St. Vincent and the Grenadines

5 A developing island nation, St. Vincent is a tax haven providing miscellaneous offshore products, including low-cost insurance companies. Its asset protection legislation appears to be very good, and infrastructure is slowly developing. St. Vincent is in the process of rewriting and refining its insurance laws. It has somewhat tarnished its reputation by licensing undercapitalized insurance companies, allowing self-insurance scams, and a poor qualification process. St. Vincent offers low-cost Class A banks of questionable value (–) and has executed MLAT with the U.S. (–). On the favorable side, for asset protection purposes, it does not recognize U.S. judgments (+).

São Tomé and Principe

NR This new free-trade zone on a tiny island off the west coast of Africa is intended to serve market and industry needs for Gulf oil companies and to function as a free-trade haven.

Sark

NR I think that every household on this island is an exempt international company manager.

The Seychelles

4   Seychelles is an island nation in the Indian Ocean off the east coast of Africa. It has no treaties with the U.S. (+). It is high profile for money laundering, attracting "suspect" money for eventual bank laundering. The Seychelles has a company act (+) and requires only one shareholder and one director. There is no requirement to keep a public record of officers and directors (names and addresses) (+) or to conduct an annual meeting (+). APT legislation has been enacted, and an international trade zone (SITZ) exists.

Sri Lanka

NR   A tax haven.

Switzerland

9   Although Switzerland is an IFC, the law of trusts is not recognized as a legal concept in this jurisdiction—civil jurisdiction is used instead. It is the premier tax haven in the world, managing more than U.S.$400 billion (estimated to be approximately one-third of the world's offshore funds).

Tonga

NR   Tonga's offshore banking license information is not public record; it is highly secretive and consequently encourages money laundering.

Turks and Caicos Islands

6   Named after the Turkish pirates who buried their treasure there. Although its ranking is on the rise, it still has far to go as a first-tier jurisdiction. TCI is in the Eastern standard time zone. It is a British overseas territory with an English common-law system, and it is very popular with Canadians. There is no direct tax on income, companies, capital gains, profits, and there are no gift taxes or death taxes.

The infrastructure is still not fully developed. Financial services are regulated by the Financial Services Commission. There are no exchange controls. There is daily FedEx and DHL service. TCI is emerging as a captive insurance jurisdiction. It has enacted new (1998) APT legislation, has a three-year statute of limitations from date of transfer, and uses the bookkeeping test for solvency of settlor (+). It is an excellent IBC jurisdiction (+ +).

United Arab Emirates

NR   A tax haven.

U.S. Virgin Islands

NR   Used as an FSC holding company situs for U.S. companies to achieve tax breaks.

Vanuatu

4   Formerly called the Anglo-French Condominium of the New Hebrides, this nation of eighty-three islands in the South Pacific is one of the fastest-growing industrial environs in the Pacific Rim. It is catering to an explosive growth in this region for tax havens. It offers the ability to create private banking (of questionable value) at a relatively low cost, either for one's own business or personal needs or for providing merchant banking services. One of the principal reasons for locating here is economics: the country is still small and seeking entrepreneurs, so the establishment costs are cheaper and the regulatory agencies are more cooperative. Limiting pressures can be successfully exerted by Australia and New Zealand.

There are no domestic income taxes or exchange controls. Service providers have complained of the slowness of the local bureaucracy in getting things done there (–). A 1999 report stated that it was being used as a money-laundering center by "apparently American" middlemen to hide Russian mafia funds. The Cook Islands and Samoa were the other countries named.

Western Samoa

2   This emerging offshore financial center offers attractive products such as the hybrid company and companies limited by guaranty and by shares. Its IBC act follows that of BVI. Its company act for companies limited by guaranty follows the British law model.

Note: By coupling or combining tax havens in series (sometimes referred to as *layering*), further tax-treaty or tax-deferral benefits may be achieved; plus, better asset protection is afforded through greater privacy by utilizing geographic diversity. This is a complex topic best left to an international tax specialist.

Glossary

abusive trusts. A sham combination of onshore and offshore trusts intended primarily for tax evasion (marketed with illegal income or estate tax claims) and the subject of constant scrutiny and attack by the IRS. Such trusts are usually offered on the Internet or by seminars by trust promoters, are a mass-market product, and are clearly illegal. The promised unrealistic tax advantages should be their tip-off. The five general types are called: the *business trust* (also the UBO or BO), the *equipment* or *service trust*, the *family residence trust*, the *charitable trust* (don't confuse this with the legitimate *charitable remainder trust*), and the *final trust*.

accommodation address. A mail fowarding site, also called a *mail drop*. For privacy, offshore mail to U.S. persons containing foreign stamps and return addresses are not desirable. Instead, one should arrange for a U.S. addressee to accept the mailings and forward them according to standing instructions. See Appendix C for such a mail forwarder.

actuary. A trained statistician who (in the context of this book) performs a calculation based on mortality, date of birth, and health of an annuitant, as well as other tables, to determine the parameters of an annuity. The actuary is usually aided in this task by computer programs complying with IRS guidelines.

adverse trustee. An archaic term denoting one who has a substantial, beneficial interest in the trust assets as well as the income or benefits derived from the trust, or a trustee related to the creator by birth, marriage, or an employer-employee relationship. The term is generally found in the context of the so-called business trust or dual-trust program, and is to be avoided as not being a U.S. tax-compliant structure.

advocate. A term used in some British common-law jurisdictions (Isle of Man, Channel Islands, and Scotland) for either a barrister or solicitor.

A.G. A German public company called an AktienGesellschaft. The A.G. is supervised by its board, called an *aufsichstrat.*

agent. An individual or organization appointed by a principal to act on his or her behalf with the power to bind the principal. This places the risk of financial exposure upon the principal, along with placing the right to bind that principal in some other party's hands. The power of the agent varies in jurisdictions, and the status should be verified. Certain jurisdictions prohibit the assignment of the agent's powers by the agent to another. The Small Business Job Protection Act of 1996 created a new form of foreign trust agent. Since a foreign trust is now required to provide reports to the IRS about the income and assets of the foreign trust, the foreign trust is required to appoint someone (usually the grantor) to serve as an agent to whom the IRS can send legal notices.

all crimes anti-laundering legislation. U.K. laws whereby tax evasion is considered a money-laundering crime.

alternate director. Where permitted by law, a director may appoint an alternate to vote for the company on behalf of the absent director.

American Depositary Receipt (ADR). Used by giant multinational companies to trade their stock on the New York Stock Exchange. It avoids the need to convert their accounting systems to be compliant with SEC regulations.

annual meeting. An assembly of shareholders, officers, and directors in which resolutions are considered and the financial health of the company is considered. Not all tax havens require annual meetings.

annuitant. The beneficiary or beneficiaries (in a last-to-die arrangement) of an annuity who receives a stream of payments pursuant to the terms of the annuity contract. The U.S. does not consider an annuity an insurance contract.

annuity. A tax-sheltering vehicle providing a stream of payments; an unsecured contract between the annuity company (or a private individual) and the annuitant(s) that grows tax deferred and is used to provide for one's later years, yielding a life income at predetermined intervals.

anstalt. A Liechtenstein entity. The rights of the anstalt remain in the founder until shares are issued. The intent is to avoid taxes by not having taxable distributions until the founder elects to do so. The shares, when issued, are transferred by the founder. The shares are generally bearer documents. Where not bearer interests, the ownership of the shares is recorded in the deed of transfer. The anstalt is neither a corporation nor a trust under Liechtenstein law.

anti-deferral rules. With respect to the IRC, deferral of taxes is achieved by using OS deferring structures such as banks, insurance companies, or brokerage companies. To avoid failing the "economic benefit test," non–U.S. persons need to own (or benefit from) the OS entity, and it must be engaged in active business and trade outside of the U.S.

AP. See *asset protection.*

APT. See *asset protection trust.*

articles of association. Similar to an expanded version of the articles of incorporation as used in the U.S. The bylaws of the corporation are stated within the articles of association, establishing the rules and regulations for the management of the corporation, IBC, or exempt company.

asset. Real or personal property having value. Without value, it is merely a property holding with potential.

asset manager. A person appointed by a written contract between the IBC (or the exempt company) or the APT and that person to direct the investment program. It can be a fully discretionary account, or limitations may be imposed by the contract under the terms of the APT or by the officers of the IBC. Fees to the asset manager may be based on performance achieved, trading commissions, or a percentage of the valuation of the estate under his or her management.

asset protection (AP). Taking a proactive position with one's assets (real and personal property) and legally placing them beyond the immediate reach of potential or future claimants, creditors, and/or adversaries. This goal is achieved by making the asset unattractive (by the placement of debt or encumbrances) and legally unreachable by such claimants.

asset protection trust (APT or FAPT). A special form of irrevocable trust, usually created (settled) offshore for the principal purpose of preserving and protecting part of one's wealth offshore against creditors. Title to the asset is transferred to a trustee. Usually tax neutral, its ultimate function is to provide for the beneficiaries of the APT.

asset stripping. Reducing the equity in real property or placing debt on personal property to make it a less attractive asset and thus reduce risk of litigation; more simply, acts that discourage litigation.

authorized capital. With respect to a corporation or company (IBC), the sum value of the aggregate of par value of all shares that the company is authorized to issue. See also *flight capital.*

badges of fraud. Conduct that raises a strong presumption that it was undertaken with the intent to delay, hinder, or defraud a creditor.

Bank of Credit & Commerce International (BCCI). An international bank established by Pakistanis in Dubai some thirty years ago that failed spectacularly after phenomenal growth, all based on Middle Eastern oil money. The *Wall Street Journal* called it the "most infamous rogue bank of the 1980s." With its principal office in Luxembourg, it had subsidiaries worldwide. It was symbolic of a major U.S. and global banking scandal in the early 1990s involving fraud and the laundering of offshore and illicit monies and an anti-Israeli agenda by some Arab countries. It resulted in significant banking failures, financial losses of $18 billion, criminal prosecutions, and major changes in the world's banking system. The bank collapsed in 1991. In 1996, a Federal Reserve judge fined Saudi financier Ghaith R. Pharon $37 million and barred him from U.S. banking activities.

Bank of International Settlements (BIS). Structured like America's Federal Reserve Bank, controlled by the Basel Committee of the Group of 10 (G-10) nations' central banks, it sets standards for capital adequacy among the member central banks. It is considered the central bank for European (EU) central bankers and conducts monthly meetings. Frequent agenda items are the major emerging markets.

BCSB. Basel Committee on Banking Supervision.

beneficial interest or ownership. Not a direct interest, but rather through a nominee holding legal title on behalf of the beneficial owner's equitable interest. Provides privacy, confidentiality, and convenience, and avoids use of one's own name for transactions.

beneficiary. The person(s), company, trust, or estate named by the grantor, settlor, or creator to receive the benefits of a trust in due course upon conditions the grantor establishes by way of a trust deed. The fully discretionary trust is an exception. The beneficiary could be a charity, foundation, and/or person(s), characterized by "classes" in terms of their order of entitlement or hierarchy.

black money. Dirty or tainted money carrying with it the problems of prior criminal activity, tax evasion, money laundering, terrorism, or drug trafficking. More governments are imposing know-your-customer requirements upon fiduciaries, bankers, trustees, and offshore service providers to limit the laundering of black money.

BO. Business organization. Also referred to as a UBO (unincorporated business organization).

board of trustees. A board acting as a trustee of a trust or as advisors to the trustee, depending upon the language of the trust indenture. See also *committee of advisors*.

bourse, bolsa, and **borsa.** A stock exchange.

British Commonwealth. Countries recognizing Queen Elizabeth II as their head of state. The countries are presented in descending order based on their date of independence: United Kingdom, Dominion of Canada, Australia, New Zealand, Jamaica, Barbados, the Bahamas, Grenada, Papua New Guinea, Solomon Islands, Tuvalu, Saint Lucia, Saint Vincent and the Grenadines, Belize, Antigua and Barbuda, Saint Kitts (Christopher) and Nevis.

British public company. See *public limited company*.

British West Indies (BWI). In the Caribbean, including the U.K. overseas territories of Anguilla, the British Virgin Islands, the Cayman Islands, Montserrat, and the Turks and Caicos Islands.

business trust. A trust created for the primary purpose of operating or engaging in a business. It is a person under the IRC. It must have a business purpose and actually function as a business.

BWI. British West Indies.

bylaws. A corporation's governing document spelling out the rules and regulations controlling the company. For its counterpart for offshore companies, see *articles of association*.

Canadian Deposit Insurance Corporation (CDIC). The Canadian equivalent to the U.S. FDIC.

capital. See *authorized capital* or *flight capital*.

Caricom. Caribbean Common Market, the Caribbean Community. Consists of fifteen member countries of the Caribbean Community. Members include: Antigua and Barbuda, Bahamas, Barbados, Belize, Dominica, Grenada, Guyana, Jamaica, Montserrat, St. Kitts and

Nevis, St. Lucia, St. Vincent, Suriname, and Trinidad and Tobago. They have set as a goal that there will be a single market, allowing for the free movement of labor. Conspicuous by their absence are the Cayman Islands and the British Virgin Islands, two major players in international banking, insurance, mutual funds, and finance. Very loyal to the U.K. and the EU. In the "banana war" in early 1999, they took the side of the EU, against the U.S., threatening to scuttle the special law enforcement treaties with the U.S. that allow the U.S. to pursue those trafficking in drugs on the high seas who attempt to elude by entering the territorial waters of the Caricom country.

cash repatriation. A strategy used by multinational companies to get earnings from offshore subsidiaries to their parent companies at the lowest tax cost possible.

cash reporting. It is necessary to report to the Treasury Department as you are exiting the U.S. for a foreign country (even for a vacation) and carrying more than $10,000 in cash or negotiable instruments (such as travelers checks or money orders) per person. Failure to do so can result in high forfeitures.

central bank. The central bank for the United States is the Federal Reserve System. Internationally, a central bank is a bank under the administration of the government intended to carry out the fiscal policy of the country.

certified public accountant (CPA). The offshore counterpart is the *chartered accountant.*

CFC. See *controlled foreign corporation.*

CID. The Criminal Investigation Division of the Internal Revenue Service. Has approximately 3,000 employees, as well as the power to secure search warrants, use the grand jury, and execute raids. Seeks to assist in the collection of approximately $195 billion of U.S. taxes that remain unpaid on an annual basis. Its primary mission is to investigate criminal violations of the Internal Revenue Code. Possesses sophisticated financial computers and expertise; approximately 25 percent of its talents and resources are used by other government agencies as part of criminal investigations.

commercial annuity. An annuity issued by an insurance company (as compared to the *private annuity*, issued by a noncommercial entity or person).

committee of advisors. Provides nonbinding advice to the trustee and trust protector. Friendly toward settlor, but must maintain independence. If the relationship with the settlor is too close, the committee can be construed as an alter ego of the settlor.

committee of trust protectors. An alternative to using merely one trust protector. Friendly toward settlor, but must remain independent. See *trust protector.*

common law. The early English system of case law of the British Empire, as opposed to strictly construed statutory law. Based on observance of precedent as guidance.

common law trust. May be marketed as a scam trust program. See *abusive trusts.*

company. A restricted corporation—for example, an IBC or exempt company. Consider whether there is owner liability, or liability is limited by shares, by guaranty, or by both, as in the hybrid company.

company act or ordinance. Legislation enacted by a tax haven to provide for the incorporation, registration, and operation of international business companies (IBCs). More commonly found in the Caribbean tax havens. For a typical example, read the Bahamas' International Business Company Act of 1989.

Comptroller of the Currency. Attempts to monitor illegal banking operations in the U.S. In late 1998, advised the banking community that the Caribbean Bank of Commerce was operating illegally in the U.S. using a banking license from the Dominion of Melchizedek, a nonexistent entity.

conditional SWIFT. A wire transfer technique that uses the SWIFT system to transfer funds conditionally between banks, subject to the performance (meeting a condition precedent) of a third party.

consol. An obligation that has no maturity date and pays perpetual interest payments. Sometimes referred to as a *perpetual bond* or an *annuity bond.*

constitutional trust. A scam trust program. See *abusive trusts.*

constructive trust. Created by implication where a party holds the assets of another on behalf of the beneficiaries. Courts may construe that the circumstances create a constructive trust.

contingent beneficial interest. An interest given to a beneficiary that is not fully vested by being discretionary, with powers resting in the trustee or some other designated party. In theory, since they are inchoate interests, not truly gifting, they are unvested, not subject to an attachment by the beneficiary's creditor, and not reportable as an IRS Form 709 gifting.

controlled foreign corporation (CFC). A creature of U.S. tax law, but of concern to responsible offshore service providers. An offshore company that, because of ownership or voting control by U.S. persons, is treated by the IRS as a U.S. tax reporting entity. IRC §951 and §957 collectively define the CFC as one in which five or fewer U.S. persons own 50 percent or more of the total voting stock on any one day in the tax reporting year.

CPA. Certified public accountant.

creator. A person who creates a trust, also called a *settlor* (an offshore term) or *grantor* (an IRS term). Usage depends upon the country, citizenship or residency, and application.

CTR. Currency transaction reports, imposed upon U.S. banks and other financial institutions.

current account. An offshore personal savings or checking account not paying interest. Usually a short-term holding account awaiting some other event.

custodian. A bank, financial institution, or other entity that has the responsibility to manage or administer the custody or other safekeeping of assets for other persons or institutions. A fee is generally charged for these services.

custodian trustee. A trustee that holds the trust assets in his or her name.

debenture. Debt that is not backed by any security or collateral, but rather by a debtor's integrity and net worth, as in *bank debenture trading program.*

declaration of trust. A document creating a trust; a trust deed.

DIA. Defense Intelligence Agency.

discretionary trust. A grantor trust in which the trustee has complete discretion as to distributing income and/or principal to beneficiaries. There are no limits upon the trustee, or it would cease to be a discretionary trust. A letter of wishes could provide some guidance to the trustee without having any legally binding effects. Provides flexibility to the trustee and the utmost privacy, but considered by some to be too loose. For tighter trustee control, use a trustee's memorandum placed in the trustee's file.

donor. A transferor. One who transfers title to an asset by gifting.

Dora, Project. An IRS project to track outbound wire transfers and match them to tax returns and help identify unreported income, such as that of U.S. Internet gamblers.

Drug Enforcement Agency (DEA). Maintains vast intelligence indices to search for money laundering where drug trafficking is suspected.

dual criminality test. The *rule of dual criminality* is defined as acts committed within another jurisdiction that are not considered criminal or or not offend any law of that jurisdiction. For example, requests for assistance on tax matters (possible tax or fiscal crimes) from another country (under MLAT or otherwise) could be rejected under the dual criminality test. In the Cayman Islands, specifically excluded under MLAT are any matters that relate directly or indirectly to the regulation (including the imposition, calculation, and collection) of taxes. However, in their defense, the Caymans provide serious support to the world's financial community for other acts con-sidered fiscal crimes, such as narcotics trafficking, fraud, and money laundering.

EC. The European Commission of the European Union (EU), a fifteen nation trading group. The twenty commissioners of the EC are appointed by their respective EU member country and are a most powerful body. The principal economic block of the world's financial community, they direct EU policies and day-to-day activities. In a 1999 scandal, all twenty members of the EC resigned.

ECB. The European Central Bank, the counterpart of the U.S. Federal Reserve.

Economic Recovery Act of 1981. See the *Foreign Investor in Real Property Tax Act of 1980 (FIRPTA)*. Quite important with respect to foreign persons owning U.S. real estate.

ECU. European currency unit.

EEC. European Economic Community, the predecessor to the EU.

equity trust. May be marketed as part of a scam trust program under many names. See *abusive trusts.*

ESOT. An *employee stock ownership trust*, sometimes called an employee stock ownership plan or ESOP. The ESOP Association, based in Washington, D.C., has material on the subject. Find it on the Internet at www.nceo.org.

estate. Interests in real and/or personal property that comprise your net worth, both while living and after your death. (Many improperly think of an estate as being merely the property of the deceased.)

EU. European Union, represented by the European Commission (EC).

European Central Bank (ECB). An independent organization that does not report to any government agency.

exchange controls. Government-imposed restrictions upon the free convertibility and transfer of currency to another country. Encourages flight capital and created a currency black market.

exempt company. Also an IBC; a corporation (also referred to as a company) registered in a tax haven that has very limited abilities to engage in business within that country. It is usually given tax-exempt status and has very limited reporting requirements to the haven.

ex parte. An application for an injunction filed and heard without notice to the other side to protect assets.

expatriate. To retain citizenship but sever other ties with your mother country and become a resident and domicile of a foreign country.

express trust. An expressly created trust (see *constructive trust*) evidenced with a sufficient written document a referred to as a trust deed.

family estate trust. May be marketed as a scam trust program. See *abusive trusts*.

family holding trust. A trust that is created specifically to hold the family's assets consisting of real and/or personal property. May be marketed as a scam trust program. See *abusive trusts*.

family limited partnership (FLP). A limited partnership created for family estate planning and some asset protection. It is family controlled by the general partners. A highly appreciated asset is transferred into the FLP to achieve a capital gains tax reduction. Usually, the parents are the general partners, holding a 1 to 2 percent interest. The other family members are the limited partners, holding the balance of the interest in the partnership. Commonly referred to as a *flip*.

family protective trust. A U.K. term. See also *asset protection trust* (APT), *grantor trust,* and *nongrantor trust*.

FAPT. Foreign asset protection trust. See also *asset protection trust* (APT or FAPT).

Federal Reserve System. The U.S. central bank, it is a quasi-governmental agency comprised of twelve regional federal banks.

fiduciary. A person or entity put in a position of trust by acceptance of the role or by factual circumstances.

FinCEN and FinCEN central database. Officially, the U.S. Treasury Department's Office of Financial Crimes Enforcement Network. Housed in Washington, D.C., and Detroit, Michigan, are the sup port buildings for their headquarters. FinCEN is the U.S. government's central financial crime computer center and organization. So-called suspicious activity reports (now called SARs) from banks are compiled there. The database is shared with many government agencies (including state agencies). Known agencies using the database include DEA, FBI, IRS, U.S. Customs, and U.S. Postal Inspectors.

FIRPTA. Foreign Investor in Real Property Tax Act of 1980.

fiscal offenses. The U.K. equivalent of tax evasion.

flight capital. Money that flows legally or illegally offshore and likely never returns. The recipient country is one likely to have political stability, banking privacy, and low or no taxes. Flight is exacerbated by a lack of confidence as government grows without bounds, the cost of government grows out of control, and the federal deficit grows; it is further precipitated by increasing concerns over invasion of personal privacy, rampant litigation, and the threats of further confiscatory direct and indirect taxes.

FLP. Family limited partnership.

foreign. May be used in a geographic, legal, or tax sense. When used geographically, it is that which is situated outside of the U.S. or is characteristic of a country other than the U.S.

Foreign Investor in Real Property Tax Act of 1980 (FIRPTA). Under FIRPTA and the Economic Recovery Act of 1981, unless an exemption is granted by the IRS, upon the sale of real property owned by offshore (foreign) persons, the agency, attorney, or escrow officer handling the transaction is required to withhold 10 percent of the gross sales proceeds at the closing of the sale transaction.

Unless withheld and submitted to the IRS, the party handling the sale transaction is personally liable for the taxes.

foreign person. Any person, other than a U.S. citizen, who resides outside the U.S. or is subject to the jurisdiction and laws of a country other than the U.S. and referred to as a nonresident alien.

foreign personal holding company (FPHC). Different than a controlled foreign corporation. Discuss with your CPA.

foreign personal holding company (FPHC). An offshore foreign personal holding company subject to special IRS rules.

FPT. Family protective trust. See also *asset protection trust (APT or FAPT).*

fraudulent conveyance. A transfer of an asset that violates the fraudulent conveyance statutes of the affected jurisdictions.

global. A term unique under U.S. parlance that means worldwide.

GmbH. A form of a limited liability company, *Gesellschaft mit beschrankter Haftung,* used in Austria, Germany, and Switzerland. Considered a private company under German and Swiss law. Limits liability of the owner/members to articles of association and the stated, agreed-upon capital contribution and any further requirements imposed by the articles.

grantor. An IRS concept—a person who creates (funds or settles) a trust or transfers real property to another entity. In a U.S. grantor trust, the grantor is the person responsible for U.S. income taxes on the trust income. The grantor may have a reversionary interest in a trust, and may have the right to substitute assets and change beneficiaries. Grantor trusts are used to avoid probate or for U.S. asset protection purposes and may also be used as a spendthrift trust.

grantor trust. A trust created by a grantor and taxed to that grantor (settlor). A creature of U.S. tax law only, not a term used elsewhere. A pass-through entity in which the grantor is taxed on the income of the offshore trust. Used only for asset protection.

harmful tax competition. An effort by the EC countries to reduce corporate tax breaks that distort free competition.

high net worth (HNW) person. An individual with more than $500,000 in liquid assets to manage. (This is a subjective number based on evaluation criteria.)

holding company. A holding company derives its net flow through assets and worth from the stock equity that it holds in its subsidiary companies, including from licensing agreements, royalties, and dividends from equity holdings.

homestead exemption. State or federal bankruptcy laws that protect one's residence from confiscation by a judgment creditor or loss in a personal bankruptcy.

hybrid annuity. An annuity in which part of the annuitant's payment is pegged to a fixed-rate and part to a variable-rate program.

hybrid company. Available in a limited number of jurisdictions, a company that is limited by guaranty and has share capital. Also referred to by some as a *contract hybrid*, it provides no special tax benefits for U.S. persons. The basic elements are:

1. Shareholders' liability to the company is limited by guaranty.

2. Persons contributing capital are called *members* and receive pro-rata interests based on their respective capital contributions. The unique term *entry subscription* is applied to the funds put into the company by the members.

IBC. A corporation. See *international business company* or *exempt company*.

IBRD. International Bank for Reconstruction and Development. (Also known as the World Bank.)

IFC. International financial (or banking) center.

illicit enrichment. Accumulation of wealth by government officials that cannot be supported on the basis of their salary and other income. Generally used as an indicator of corruption in Latin America.

immediate annuity. An annuity contract that commences payments in the next time period from the purchase date. Usually paid for with a lump sum.

imminent risk of dying. An insured or private annuitant having a 50 percent medical probability of dying within one year of the date of execution of an insurance or annuity contract.

inbound. Coming into the U.S.; onshore; such as funds being paid to a U.S. person from an offshore entity.

incomplete gift. Where the settlor has reserved the right to add or delete beneficiaries to the trust, it is construed as an incomplete gift. See *contingent beneficial interest.* Also applies where the settlor has retained other powers over the trust assets.

independent trustee. A trustee who is independent of the settlor. *Independence* is generally defined as not being related to the settlor by blood, marriage, adoption, or an employer-employee relationship.

Inland Revenue. The tax-collecting unit in the U.K., the Commissioners of the Inland Revenue. The U.K. counterpart to the IRS and Revenue Canada.

intangible assets. Personal property owned by you that is not tangible. Includes such items as stocks, bonds, bank account balances, and money market funds.

interbank rate of exchange. The bank-to-bank rate, as between banks in the open market.

interest in possession. Under U.K. trust law, where the settlor reserves the right to receive the trust income, raising Inland Revenue tax ramifications.

INTERFIPOL. International Fiscal Police. The tax crime counterpart to INTERPOL.

international business company (IBC). A corporation, in reality an exempt company, formed (incorporated) under a typical company act of a tax haven but *not* authorized to do business within that country of incorporation; intended to be used for global operations. Owned by member(s)/shareholder(s). Has the usual corporate attributes.

International Chamber of Commerce (ICC). Headquarted in France, an international body governing international financial transactions.

International Deposit Insurance Corporation (IDIC). In 1998 and 1999 claimed to be an insurance company insuring bank accounts, when in fact it was not licensed to conduct the business of insurance anywhere. Later changed its name to International Deposit Indemnity Corporation.

international financial and banking center (IFC). A jurisdiction or country identified as being a tax haven. Usually has a favorable policy by the local government to attract foreign funds. Note the difference between an IFC and an offshore financial center. The IFC tries to attract business to its jurisdiction, while an OFC just seeks fees and other revenue.

International Trade and Investment Companies (ITIC). The only companies authorized by the Chinese government to borrow funds from foreign sources for investment in China or for lending purposes. More than 250 exist; the most familiar, due to financial failure, is the Chinese central government's own CITIC (China International Trust and Investment Corporation).

international trust. A Cook Islands term for a special type of an asset protection trust. Governed by the laws of the Cook Islands.

INTERPOL. International Criminal Police Organization. The network of multinational law enforcement authorities established to exchange information regarding money laundering and other criminal activities. More than 125 member nations.

IOFC. International offshore and financial center.

IRC. The U.S. Internal Revenue Code, or the tax code, or tax laws.

IRS. The U.S. Internal Revenue Service, an agency of the Treasury Department. Its charter is to administer the Internal Revenue Code. With a budget of more than $7.8 billion per year, it is the fourth largest "company" in the U.S.

joint annuitant. The survivor who continues receiving a stream of payments upon the death of the other annuitant.

jurisdiction. Used in this book as a generic name for a sovereign country in which their own laws apply. Synonymous with *tax haven* or *international financial center.*

Kuiu Thlingit Nation. A purported Native American Indian tribe that is used as a backdrop by scam artists to concoct phony bank licenses.

laundering (money laundering). The act of converting dirty money to clean money by multiple cleansing transactions, including flowing through legitimate banks and businesses. To support an accusation of money laundering, there must be a direct nexus between specified unlawful activities and the movement of money. Commonly charged in criminal matters in the U.S. where money has been moved without the payment of due taxes. Know-your-customer requirements are gradually being imposed upon the banking system, intended to stem the flow of dirty money into legitimate banking channels.

layered trusts. Trusts placed in series, where the beneficiary of the first trust is the second trust, and so forth; used for privacy. Where used with abusive trusts to avoid U.S. taxation, it is usually tax evasion.

layering. May be achieved with numerous combinations of entities. For example, 100 percent of the shares of an IBC being owned by the first trust, which has as its sole beneficiary a second trust. May be perceived as an abusive trust.

LC. Another abbreviation for *limited liability company* (LLC).

letter (memorandum) of wishes. Written advisory request to a trustee, usually from the settlor. The letter has no binding legal power over the trustee. There may be multiple letters. They must be carefully drafted to avoid creating problems with the settlor or true settlor, in the case of a nongrantor trust, becoming a co-trustee. The trustee cannot be a pawn of the settlor, which would give credibility to a suspicion that there never was a complete renouncement of the assets. Sometimes referred to as a *side letter*.

limited company. Not an international business company. May be a resident of the tax haven and is set up under a special company act with a simpler body of administrative laws.

limited liability. The liability of guarantors and the shareholders as to calls or litigation is limited by their guaranty.

limited liability company (LLC and LC). Consists of member owners and a manager, at a minimum. Similar to a corporation that may elect to be taxed as a partnership or as a corporation. More specifically, it combines the more favorable characteristics of a corporation and a partnership. The LLC structure permits the complete pass-through of tax advantages and operational flexibility found in a partnership, operating in a corporate-style structure, with limited liability as provided by the state's laws.

living trust. Revocable trust, for reduction of probate costs and to expedite sale of assets upon death of grantor. Provides no asset protection.

LLC. Limited liability company.

limited liability limited partnership (LLLP). Intended to protect the general partners from liability. Previously, the general partner was a corporation to protect the principals from personal liability. Under the LLLP, an individual could be a general partner and have limited personal liability.

limited liability partnership (LLP). A form of the LLC favored by and used for professional associations, such as accountants and attorneys.

Loro-Nostro account. An account or correspondent account established between two banks paying at the Interbank rate.

Ltd. Limited.

mark. Abbreviation for German currency, the deutsche mark.

Mavera injunction. A court injunction preventing a trustee from transferring trust assets pending the outcome of a lawsuit.

Melchizedek, Dominion of. This is a fictitious tax haven and scam operation.

member. An equity owner of a limited liability company (LLC), limited liability partnership (LLP), limited liability limited partnership (LLLP), or a shareholder in an IBC. The counterpart of a shareholder in a corporation or a partner in a partnership.

memorandum. The memorandum of association of an IBC, equivalent to articles of incorporation.

migration clause, automatic. Language contained in an APT to cause the trust to automatically migrate or flee to another jurisdiction upon a condition of duress. Alternatively, the trustee may be granted such powers and cause the trust to migrate—this would not be automatic migration. The migration language affects the status of an APT and determines whether it is a domestic or foreign trust under the IRC. Automatic migration provisions may not pass the court test and the control test. Failure to pass either test makes a domestic APT become a foreign trust.

MLAT. Mutual Legal Assistance Treaty.

money laundering. See *laundering.*

Mutual Legal Assistance Treaty (MLAT). An agreement among the U.S. and many Caribbean countries for the exchange of financial and banking information for the enforcement of criminal laws.

nongrantor trust. Usually, an APT created by a nonresident alien on behalf of the U.S. beneficiaries.

nonresident alien (NRA). Not a U.S. person as defined under the Internal Revenue Code (IRC); an entity or person that is neither a U.S. citizen nor a permanent resident in the U.S.

OECD. Organization for Economic Cooperation and Development.

OFEX. Options and Futures Exchange.

offshore (OS). Offshore is an international term meaning not only out of your country (jurisdiction), but out of the tax reach of your country of residence or citizenship; synonymous with *foreign, transnational, global, international, transworld,* and *multinational,* though *foreign* is used more in reference to the IRS.

offshore banking. Banking operations and activities involving two or more countries.

offshore center or offshore financial center. See *international financial and banking center* (IFC). A more sophisticated tax haven.

Offshore Group of Banking Supervisors (OGBS). Supervisors of banks in many tax havens under their jurisdiction. Members include Aruba, Bahamas, Bahrain, Barbados, Bermuda, Cayman, Cyprus, Gibraltar, Guernsey, Hong Kong, Jersey, Liechtenstein, Lebanon, Malta, Mauritius, Netherlands Antilles, Panama, Singapore, and Vanuatu.

offshore trust. See *asset protection trust.*

operating company. An operating company derives its net worth from the equity that it obtains from sale of its own products and services on a day-to-day basis.

OS. Offshore.

outbound. Assets flowing offshore from the U.S., as opposed to *inbound.*

ownership. Ownership constitutes the holding or possession of limited liability company legal claim or title to an offshore asset.

paradis fiscal. French phrase for a tax haven.

person. Any individual, branch, partnership, associated group, association, estate, trust, corporation, company, or other organization, agency, or financial institution under the IRC.

personal foreign investment company (PFIC). An offshore personal foreign investment company subject to special IRC rules.

personalized portfolio bonds (PPB). Being improperly marketed offshore to Americans who work offshore but create difficulty because of onerous IRS reporting requirements and nonqualifying aspects where the American files a tax return.

portfolio manager. See *asset manager*. Distinguished from an *asset allocation manager.*

preferential transfer. A disposition of an asset that is unfair to some of the creditors or claimants of the transferor. Commonly arising in bankruptcy matters or in claims of fraud by creditors where asset protection measures were taken to hinder, frustrate, or delay collection efforts.

pre-filing notice. Mailed by the IRS to taxpayers believed to be participating in fraudulent trust programs. The notice requests that the receiver seek professional counsel before filing his or her next tax return.

Prime Bank Trading Program, Guarantees, or Debentures. A deceptive scheme to defraud people of money.

private banking. Os banking services for high net worth persons. Also called *private investment banking.*

private interest foundation (PIF). A form of foundation created under Panamanian laws.

probate. The legal process for the distribution of the estate (assets, real and personal property) of a decedent. One may avoid or minimize the costs and delays of the probate process with the use of the living trust.

Proceeds of Crime Section. A Canadian task force established to detect and support prosecution of money laundering that merges the

Royal Canadian Mounted Police with local police forces, customs, and the Crown Prosecutor's office.

protector. See *trust protector*. Occasionally used for foundations, as in a foundation protector.

PT. An acronym for either *perpetual tourist* or *perpetual traveler*, denoting persons seeking to become "stateless" and therefore free of tax burdens (at least so they claim). The designation of PT carries with it some negative connotations in that it is usually associated with tax protest or antiestablishment groups seeking to evade taxes.

public limited company (PLC). A U.K. *public* limited company, as opposed to the U.K. *private* limited company.

pure equity trust. A special type of irrevocable trust marketed by promoters. The trust assets are obtained by an "exchange" of a certificate of beneficial interest in return for the assets, as opposed to traditional means, such as by gifting. Provides no tax benefits.

pure trust. A contractual trust, as opposed to a statutory trust, created under common law. It has a minimum of three parties—the creator or settlor (never grantor), the trustee, and the beneficiary—and each is a separate entity. A pure trust is claimed to be a lawful, irrevocable, separate legal entity; it provides no tax benefits.

purpose trust. An offshore trust providing a mission or charter and leaving to the discretionary offshore trustee the power as to distributions.

RA. Reluctant American. Caution: means *resident alien* in other literature, but not in this book.

recandle. To move and reactivate a trust in another tax haven.

redomiciliation. The transferring of a trust or an IBC to another willing jurisdiction for adoption.

register. The register of international business companies and exempt companies maintained by the registrar of a tax haven.

registrar. The registrar of companies, a government body controlling the formation and renewal of companies created under a jurisdiction's company act, as well as LLCs and LPs (also trusts, where provided for under the local trust act).

re-insurance company. An insurance company that takes on layers of risk of the primary insurer for a fee. This enables the primary insurer to share the risk of loss with the "re."

RICO. Racketeer Influenced and Corrupt Organizations Act. A professional service provider or trust promoter who assists in money-laundering schemes or scams may be drawn into the web of criminal prosecution under RICO.

rifugio fiscal. Italian term for a tax haven.

rule against perpetuities. A legal limit on the lifetime of a trust or the remote vesting of assets in the beneficiaries of a trust. May be void *ab initio* (from the beginning), a fixed term, or determined on a wait-and-see basis. Under basic common law, there was a prohibition against trust assets being held more than twenty-one years after the death of the last trust beneficiary who was living at the time the trust was created. This has been abrogated or modified in most offshore jurisdictions.

SA. société anonyme.

SAR. Suspicious activity reports issued by U.S. banks.

securities. Shares and debt obligations of every kind, including options, warrants, and rights to acquire shares and debt obligations.

self-settled trust. English common-law nomenclature for what is called under the IRC a *grantor trust.* This trust is usually revocable, and the grantor is also the beneficiary.

settle. To create or establish an offshore trust. Done by the settlor (offshore term) or the grantor (U.S. and IRS term).

settlor. The entity that creates or settles an offshore trust and usually funds and transfers assets to the trust.

shares. Evidence of an equity position in a company. Depending upon the laws of the issuer's country, shares may registered, bearer, voting and nonvoting, unnumbered, common, preferred, or redeemable. Different classes of stock may be issued as well as no-par value shares. Limitations of the shares are in the memorandum or in the articles of association of the IBC.

side letter. Letter of wishes.

SIPC. The Securities Industry Protection Corporation. Provides up to $500,000 insurance protection for your U.S. stock brokerage account.

situs (site). The domicile or controlling jurisdiction of a trust. It is the principal jurisdiction in a conflict-of-laws situation. It may be changed to another jurisdiction. The orphan trust is rekindled in another jurisdiction. Movement may be automatic by language contained in the trust deed.

société anonyme (SA). A limited liability corporation established under French law. Requires a minimum of seven shareholders. In Spanish-speaking countries, it is known as the *sociedad anonima.* An important characteristic of both is that the liability of the shareholder is limited *up to* the amount of one's respective capital contribution.

Sparbuch. An Austrian numbered savings account, now unavailable due to pressures from the EU.

special custodian. An appointee of the trustee in an APT.

special investment advisor. An appointee of the trustee in an APT.

spendthrift trust. A trust intended to protect the beneficiary from his or her actions, shielding the assets from being wasted by the beneficiary and protecting the assets from the creditors or claimants of the beneficiary.

statute of limitations. In the context of a trust, the deadline after which a party claiming to be injured by the settlor of an APT should no longer file an action to recover damages.

statutory. That which is fixed by statutes or codes (as opposed to the common-law body of cases, generating what is referred to as "case law").

steureroase. German phrase for a tax haven.

Stiftung. A Liechtenstein form of private foundation. Created by civil statute, it is a model for foundation structures worldwide. Although written for civil-law jurisdictions, it has been adapted well for the English common-law jurisdictions.

sub-part F income. Under IRC §957, any U.S. persons who own 10 percent or more of a controlled foreign corporation (CFC) report their proportional share of certain corporate income on their income tax returns. Taxes are due even where the CFC fails to distribute the income to the shareholder. There are exceptions for eligible CFCs for the income of banks, security dealers, and financing. Sub-part F income includes any investment income or gains and some operating income derived from transactions with U.S. shareholders of related companies.

SWIFT. Society for Worldwide Interbank Financial Telecommunications. A global wire transfer system.

Swiss Postfinance. Operates more than 3,000 "ordinary post offices" within Switzerland that also process financial transactions, similar to a bank.

tax-avoidance transaction. A lawful method of avoiding taxes, as contrasted with tax evasion, which is a felony in the United States. Tax experts almost universally agree that this term is impossible to define.

tax haven. An international banking and financial center providing privacy, asset protection, and the expectation of some tax benefits.

tax regimen. The local tax treatment of income, foreign source income, nonresidents, and special tax concessions, which, when combined, form complex issues. The local tax rate is not the exclusive factor. One must consider the ramifications of dual-tax treaties between or among the countries involved ("treaty shopping") in the total analysis.

TCI. The Turks and Caicos Islands.

trading program. The bank debenture trading program. To be avoided, a scam.

tranche. Part of a bond series issued for sale in a foreign country. In the U.S., for example, " . . . underwriters will sell an extra tranche of shares held in reserve. . . ."

transmogrifying. The conversion of nonexempt assets to exempt assets. Generally done as part of prebankruptcy planning.

true settlor. Used in a trust where the true grantor is not the trust settlor, and his or her identity is kept private by the trustee. Compare with the *grantor trust.* This is a non-U.S. concept.

trust. An entity created for the purpose of protecting and conserving assets for the benefit of a third party, the beneficiary. It is also a contract affecting three parties—the settlor, the trustee, and the beneficiary. A trust protector is optional, but recommended. In the trust, the settlor transfers asset ownership to the trustee on behalf of the beneficiaries. The trust must be revocable (also called *restrictive*) or irrevocable (called *flexible*). With a discretionary trust, the trustee is granted very broad powers as to distribution of the principal, interest, and income to the beneficiaries.

trust deed. An asset protection trust document or instrument.

trustee. A person independent of the settlor who has fiduciary responsibility to the beneficiaries to manage the assets of the trust as a reasonable, prudent businessperson would do in the same circumstances, and who administers the trust deed according to the written wishes of the settlor. The trustee defers to the trust protector when required in the best interest of the trust. The trustee reporting requirements, defined at the onset, should include how often, to whom, and how to respond to instructions or inquiries; global investment strategies; fees (flat and/or percentage of the valuation of the trust estate); anticipated future increases in fees; hourly rates for consulting services; seminars and client educational materials; and so on. The trustee may have full discretionary powers of distributions to selected beneficiaries. Ideally, the trust protector can compel the trustee to resign, even without cause.

trust indenture. A trust instrument, such as a trust deed, creating an offshore trust.

trust protector. A person appointed by the settlor to oversee the trust on behalf of the beneficiaries for additional security and the peace of mind of the settlor. In many jurisdictions, local trust laws define the concept of the trust protector. Note that the trust protector's role is not necessarily clear in all jurisdictions, and trust acts are being amended to remedy this problem.

trust settlement document. Trust deed.

typo-piracy. The practice of establishing a domain name virtually indistinguishable from another domain, for the purpose of attracting visitors who incorrectly enter the name of the website they wish to visit. This practice is sometimes illegal.

UBO. Unincorporated business organization. Avoid using this structure.

Uniform Partnership Act (UPA). One of the generic bodies of laws adopted by some states or used as a baseline for other states as a recommended model of laws.

UO. Unincorporated organization (same as UBO). Avoid using this structure.

upstreaming. The process of retaining earnings offshore through the billing process or transfer pricing strategies. Prenegotiated transfer pricing agreements with the IRS are to be encouraged here.

URL. Universal resource locator on the World Wide Web. A combination of letters, numbers, and punctuation that comprise an address for a website.

U.S.C. U.S. Code (of statutes).

U.S. person. A term unique to the IRC. Any person or legal entity, including a foreign citizen, who resides in the United States or is subject to the jurisdiction of the U.S. tax system (regardless of where the person is situated worldwide).

variable annuity. An annuity in which the cash value is vested in stocks or mutual funds. The ultimate payback is a function of how well your program performs during the intervening period before the maturity of the annuity. Self-selection of specific securities is not currently allowed under IRS regulations.

vetting. The process used by the offshore (or onshore) consultant for qualifying the prospective client to determine whether he or she is a good candidate for offshore asset protection; as in to "vet" the prospective client. Consultants are seeking a smoking gun—perhaps undisclosed money laundering, a spousal dispute, hiding assets, tax evasion, concealment of money, or current or prospective litigation.

viatical settlement contract. The purchase of the death benefits under a life insurance policy from the terminally ill owner of the policy. It is a means for the dying person to enjoy the death benefits while living. The contract is considered a debt instrument.

World Association of International Financial Centres. Newly established in Vancouver, Canada, with a charter of protecting the offshore financial industry.

World Bank. Formed to be the bank lender and technical advisor to the developing countries, utilizing funds and technical resources from the member nations (the depositors). Headquartered in Washington, D.C. Also known as the International Bank for Reconstruction and Development (IBRD).

Publications

DISCLAIMER: I HAVE no financial or other interest in the following publications, except where noted. Note that when compiled, these websites were valid, but sites do change and close.

Asset Protection

The Jacobs Report on Asset Protection Strategies
Vernon K. Jacobs, CPA, editor.
 P.O. Box 8137
 Prairie Village, KS 66208
 Phone: (913) 362-9667
 E-mail: osj@rpifs.com

Mark Nestmann, editor
Asset Protection International, publishers
 Toronto, Canada
 E-mail: assetpro@nestmann.com
 Website: www.nestmann.com
 Phone: (416) 352-5086

(Author's note: I provide consulting advice to this publication.)

Special Reports
www.jim-bennett.com

Bank Directory

For a listing of almost every bank with an Internet presence, visit
www.qualisteam.com/eng/conf.html

For further international banking information, try
www.killen.com/kwr/ibs.htm

To ask a question about international banking, E-mail
b@nker.com

Books

I have bought and read virtually all the books on asset protection
and offshore, keeping the bookstores "green." My library includes
such classics as a rare first edition of Robert Kinsman's *Guide to Tax
Havens*, written in 1978, in which he said "Contrary to popular
belief, foreign tax havens still make sense for many people." Those
pearls of wisdom have not changed to date! This is my minimal reading list for you. This list excludes those books whose principal purpose is to characterize tax havens' attributes in detail and to educate
the reluctant American and Canadian. I have also excluded those
written to glamorize the author, feed his ego, and market his talents.

Unfortunately, since this is a very dynamic subject, most books
are partially obsolete when published. This bibliography intentionally excludes those books that mass-market banking licenses from
minor tax havens that one has difficulty locating on a map (Dominion of Melchizedek, Vanuatu, Niue, and so on) and have reputations for chicanery. The following are available from the publisher
or author, if your favorite bookstore can't get them for you. For
updates on this list, go to www.offshore-net.com and click on
"bookstore."

Bulletproof Offshore Asset Protection by Jim Bennett. Strictly for the newbie, a fast one-hour read. Lacks depth on the topic.

The Computer Privacy Handbook by Andre Bacard. The standard handbook for the industry.

Due Diligence for the Financial Professional by L. Burke Files, Thomas R. Nesbitt, and Joseph Agiato. Assists you in practicing due diligence *before* getting involved.

Hide Your Assets and Disappear by Edmund J. Pankau. For future expatriates. On the *New York Times* bestseller nonfiction booklist for March 1999.

International Tax Summaries by Coopers & Lybrand. Covers different kinds of taxes in about 110 different countries. Published by John Wiley & Sons.

International Trust Laws and Analysis by Walter H. Diamond. All you could ever need to evaluate, establish, and maintain offshore trusts in any jurisdiction. For the professional.

The Offshore Advantage by Terry L. Neal. A must-read if you are interested in Nevis.

Tax Havens of the World by Diamond and Diamond. Three-volume set, exploring thirty characteristics in detail for sixty-five tax havens. Published by Matthew Bender & Company.

Tax Havens of the World by Thomas P. Azzara. Covers over twenty tax havens; very heavily into taxes and the IRC for those needing more of this type of in-depth information. Buy the latest (seventh) edition.

Tax Haven Roadmap by Richard Czerlau. 1998 revised edition, published in Canada.

Guatemala Living and Retirement Newsletter

lifestyles@centramerica.com

Hotels, Travel Alerts, and General Travel

Hideaway Report. If you love to travel and stay first class, or just to vicariously enjoy the good life, subscribe to Andrew Harper's *Hideaway Report,* "a connoisseur's worldwide guide to peaceful and unspoiled places"—so they claim, and with appropriate justification. Write them at:

P.O. Box 300
Whitefish, MT 59937

Caribbean Travel & Life. Available at your newsstand or by subscription. A must-read for frequent travelers to the Caribbean.

Travel alerts by the U.S. State Department. Available 7 days a week, 24 hours a day.

Phone: (202) 647-5225
Fax: (202) 647-3000
Website: http://travel.state.gov

Language Translators

Babelfish is a free, five-language translation service that translates words, phrases, and websites. The ten alternatives are translations from:

- English to French or French to English
- English to Spanish or Spanish to English
- English to German or German to English
- English to Italian or Italian to English
- English to Portuguese or Portuguese to English

The translation is far from being precise, but it does give you a significant understanding and sense of the foreign text. Go to

www.babelfish.altavista.com

Accent Translation Software

www.accentsoft.com

Legal Information Sites

Hague Academy of International Law

www.hagueacademy.nl

American Society of Comparative Law

www.comparativelaw.org

Offshore News

Internet Offshore Entrepreneur and *Offshore Light*. Their website is an offshore information news, events, and reference site.

Website: www.goldhaven.com
E-mail: info@goldhaven.com

Offshore Finance Canada. Published six times a year in Canada. Canada's leading magazine on international business, finance, and investment. Highly recommended for staying abreast of the offshore financial community.

Phone: (514) 939-2800
Fax: (514) 939-2881
E-mail: island@aei.ca
Website: www.offshorefinancecanada.com

Offshore Finance U.S.A. Published six times a year in the U.S. (I am on the editorial advisory board of this publication.)

Phone: (514) 939-2800
Fax: (514) 939-2881
E-mail: island@aei.ca
Website: www.offshorefinanceusa.com

Offshore News from the Bahamas. Free monthly by entertaining and knowledgeable writer and consultant Roy Bouchier. To request a subscription:

P.O. Box N-1201
Nassau, Bahamas
Phone: (242) 356-2036
Fax: (242) 356-2037

E-mail: itiltd@itiltd.com
Website: www.itiltd.com

Free International Asset Protection/Privacy Catalogue

Mark Nestmann, author
E-mail: pbs@top.monad.net
Website: www.nestmann.com

Scope International Limited. An overly prolific source of materials on going offshore. Some strategies are too tax aggressive for U.S. persons, and some materials are quite dated. Check the publication date before buying. Read with caution.

230 Peppard Road
Emmer Green, Reading, Berkshire RG4 8UA
Great Britian

The Sovereign Society. Extensive offshore reading materials, newsletter, and books. Prestigious board of directors including the authors of *The Sovereign Society* and bestseller author John A. Pugsley. For the expatriate and others.

P.O. Box 2697
London W1A 3TR U.K.
Phone: 44 171 447 4055
Fax: 44 171 447 4041

Offshore Investing

The Lorne House Report from the Isle of Man. Excellent free monthly newsletter on worldwide investing.

E-mail: general@lorne-house.com

Privacy

Computer Professionals for Social Responsibility

www.cpsr.org

ISPI Clips is a free E-mail service from the Institute for the Study of Privacy Issues (ISPI). (I am on the editorial advisory board of this publication.) To receive ISPI Clips on a regular basis (one to six clips most days), send the following message, without the quotes: "Please enter [your name] into the ISPI Clips list: [your E-mail address]" to:

ispiclips@ama-gi.com

The Institute for the Study of Privacy Issues is a small, contributor-funded organization based in Victoria, British Columbia. ISPI operates on a not-for-profit basis, accepts no government funding, and takes a global perspective. They gratefully accept all contributions. For a contribution form with postal instructions, please send the following message: "ISPI Contribution Form" to

ispi4privacy@ama-gi.com
Phone: (250) 383-1877

The Financial Privacy Report, Mike Ketcher, editor. One year (twelve issues), $144.

P.O. Box 1277
Burnsville, MN 55337
Phone: (612) 895-8757

Scam and Fraud Alerts

Abusive trusts, constitutional trusts, and so on:

www.nafep.com/new.html
www.rpifs.com/taxhelp/otpuretrust.htm

Offshore Alert, "The Pen Is Mightier Than the Fraud." By fax and the Web, $595.00/year, monthly: *Offshore Business News & Research, Inc.* An investigative newsletter covering offshore financial services in the Bermuda-Caribbean region.

123 S. E. 3rd Avenue, Box 173
Miami, FL 33131
Phone: (305) 372-6267
Fax: (305) 372-8724

E-mail: info@offshorebusiness.com
Website: www.offshorebusiness.com

Prime bank note, roll program, bank debenture scam

www.goldhaven.com/scams3.htm
www.iccwbo.org/business_world/1998/icc_instruments.htm

The Adkisson Advisor

http://www.quatloos.com

Nigerian offers for hidden wealth participation

http://home.rica.net/alphae/419coal

Taxes

Offshore Tax Strategies by J. Richard Duke, Esq. and Vernon K. Jacobs, CPA

www.rpifs.com/taxhelp

International tax analysts mailing list. To subscribe, send E-mail to majordomo@lists.tax.org with the message "subscribe international" (without the quotes).

Tax and international links by Vernon K. Jacobs, CPA

E-mail: osj@rpifs.com
Website: www.rpifs.com/vkjcpa

Telecommunications

Telefónica de Argentina's on-line guide, white and yellow pages.

www.paginas-doradas.com.ar

World Trade

Latin Trade. Available at your newstand or by subscription. A must-read for those doing business with Latin America or frequent travelers to that region of the world.

Asset Protection and Offshore Service Providers and Organizations

THE FOLLOWING OFFSHORE service providers are of very high quality, or the individuals maintaining the sites are those I personally know or know to have quality reputations. I may have had a past or may have a current business or personal relationship with them, direct or indirect. This is a courtesy top-quality list provided to you without warranty.

Service Providers

Accounting

www.kpmg.com

The Adkisson Analysis. One of the best informational websites. Also see their asset protection information.

www.falc.com

American Citizens Abroad (ACA) website. Has many useful resources and news items. ACA is a nonprofit association "dedicated to serving and defending the interests of individual U.S. citizens worldwide." It's headquartered in Geneva, Switzerland. Their website includes an assortment of news items, an extensive collection of links to related websites, and information on tax issues, citizenship, and medical insurance for Americans abroad.

www.aca.ch

Armored Car Services

For the wealthy expatriate with "friends" looking for him.

www.ogara.com

Asset Protection Clinic

http://aprotect.com/assprot.htm

Asset Protection Guide Online

http://asset-protection.com/apguide.html

Asset Protection Index

www.rpifs.com/oapn

Basel Trust Corporation, Channel Islands

St. Helier, Jersey
Phone: 44-153-460-1900
Website: 101735.751@compuserve.com

Donlevy-Rosen & Rosen

Excellent asset protection informational website.

www.protectyou.com

Dual Citizenship FAQ

www.webcom.com/richw/dualcit

Duke Law Firm Expert

Expert international tax advice.

E-mail: richard@assetlaw.com
Website: www.assetlaw.com

Engel Reiman & Lockwood p.c.

Very professional and informative website.

www.asset-protection.net

Embassy & Consultant Worldwide Directory for All Nations

Here's an outstanding resource for anyone looking for any embassy in the world, indexed by host country and by guest country—including consulates and offices in multiple cities of the host country. It is the product of Roger Gallo, developer of the www.escapeartist.com website.

www.embassyworld.com

Embassy Web–International Websites

www.embpage.org

Escape Artist

www.escapeartist.com

EuroBanc Limited

St. Kitts Class A private and merchant bank, mutual fund management, insurance company formation, trust services, credit cards.

info@eurobancltd.com or www.eurobancltd.com

Graham Thompson & Co.

Gilbert A. Ward, Attorney at Law
Shirley St. & Victoria Ave.
P.O. Box N-272
Nassau, New Providence, Bahamas

Phone: (242) 322-4130
Fax: (242) 328-0386

International Secondment

Popular KPMG booklets provide practical tax and human resource information regarding transfers to and from twenty-nine countries.

www.tax.kpmg.net/int'l_executive_services/iespyis.htm

International Trade & Investments Limited, Nassau

Roy Bouchier can open doors of opportunity for you in the Bahamas.

E-mail: itiltd@itiltd.com
Website: www.itiltd.com

Vernon Jacobs, CPA, Research Press, Inc.

E-mail: osi@rpifs.com
Website: www.rpifs.com/vkjcpa

David S. Lesperance, Barrister and Solicitor

A well-respected Ontario, Canada authority on renunciation of U.S. citizenship, worldwide second passports, and expatriation.

relocate@netaccess.on.ca

Limited Liability Company Resources

www.llc-usa.com

Market Advisors, Inc. Journal

Phone: (402) 476-3604

Money-Laundering Alert

www.moneylaundering.com

Money-Laundering Compliance Website Index

freespace.virgin.net/silkscreen

Nestmann: Offshore Asset Protection

www.nestmann.com

Offshore E-mail Letter

www.offshore-net.com

The Offshore Institute

Office of the President
St. Helier, Jersey
British Isles
Phone: 44-153-400-0900
Fax: 44-153-460-7876

Jersey:
baseltrustjersey@compuserve.com

Isle of Man:
meridian@mcb.net

Orlando Mail Drop

P.O. Box 608039
Orlando, FL
pcalby@ix.netcom.com

The Overseas Oversight Group U.S.A, LLC

Providing APT formation and trust protector services. Currently utilizing St. Vincent for their trusts and the Isle of Man for their trust protector services.

E-mail: oversight1@aol.com
Website: www.oversightgroup.com

The Offshore Pilot

Request a sample of their newsletter:
 E-mail: marketing@trustserv.com
 Website: www.trustserv.com

The Puffin Newsletter

Newsletter from the Isle of Man, published by Skye Fiduciary Services Limited (now Skyefid).

 E-mail: mail@skyefid.co.im
 Website: www.skyefid.co.im

The Trusts and Trustees Website

 http://www.trusts-and-trustees.com

Turks and Caicos Islands

McLean McNally, international attorneys

 mclean@caribsurf.com

Universal Corporate Services, Nassau

ucs@bahamas.net.bs

U.S. Department of State Travel Advisories

 E-mail: dostravel@listserv.uic.edu
 Website: http://travel.state.gov

Web Searches on Offshore: Who's Who

www.offshore-whoswho.com

Internet Resources

Disclaimer. The following list of Internet websites and E-mail addresses for various tax havens is provided without any warranty, only to assist you in your international financial research. This listing provides only those E-mail addresses or websites known by me. Those marked with an asterisk do not meet my subjective standards as a commentator and are provided merely as a curiosity to the reader. Websites were correct when compiled, but are dynamic and move, close, or change frequently.

Andorra

www.servissim.com

Anguilla Business Services

www.aibs.com.ai

Antigua

Antigua Overseas Bank
aob@candw.ag

Swiss American Bank
Phone: (268) 480-2240

E-mail: hcm@law.com
Website: www.hcmlaw.com

E-mail: imt@cms-sa
Website: www.cms-sa.com

robertsck@candw.ag

Aruba

auafincen@mail.setarnet.aw

centrust@setarnet.aw

Asset Protection International–Mark Nestmann

www.nestmann.com

Asset Protection News

The newsletter is available online at

www.protectyou.com

Asset Protection and Offshore E-mail Forum

Available for those who are interested in asset protection and/or an assortment of offshore topics. Participation is open to the public. For more information about the forum see the instructions at

www.rpifs.com/apfhelp.htm

Bahamas

www.bahamas.com

www.interknowledge.com/bahamas/investment

itiltd@itiltd.com

Corporate formation, low fees
www.ucservices.com
(817) 354-4888

Banks

www.escapeartist.com/offshore3/banks.htm

www.saninvest.com

Barbados

clientinfo@firsthorizon.com

E-mail: altabank@caribsurf.com
Website: www.altabank.com

merchant@caribsurf.com

Barbados Investment and Development Corporation
E-mail: barinvest@interlog.com or bidc@interport.net
Website: www.bidc.com

lawcott@caribsurf.com

E-mail: nab@cascap.com

Barbuda

E-mail: hcm@law.com
Website: www.hcmlaw.com

Belize

www.travelbelize.org

E-mail: bblbcsl@btl.net
Website: www.bhiofs.com

Corporate formation, low fees
www.ucservices.com
Phone: (800) 551-2141 or (817) 595-4777

Belize First magazine

Bermuda

Bermuda statistical information on-line featuring data relating to the government, employment, population, and climate, presented in an easy-to-read format.

www.bermudacommerce.com/statistics.html

www.bermudacommerce.com

E-mail: stdlife@ibl.bm
Website: www.standardlife.ca

Bermuda Stock Exchange (BSX)
E-mail: jmacphee@bsx.com

Website: www.bsx.com

Insurance Services
wrsl@ibl.bm (William R. Storie & Co., Ltd.)

British Virgin Islands

www.bvi.org

danpenco@caribsurf.com

cowlth@caribsurf.com

ilsbvi@intlawsys.com

E-mail: admin@owomfg.com
Website: www.owomfg.com

Central Intelligence Agency (CIA)

www.odci.gov/cia

Cook Islands

Asiaciti in the Cook Islands is available as an institutional co-trustee of an APT.

E-mail: asiaciti@intnet.mu
Website: www.asiaciti.com

Costa Rica

arcrsacc@sol.racsa.co.cr

www.cinde.or.cr

www.costaricainfo.com

www.cocori.com/healthtourcr

Credit Card Program by Infiniti Global Axxess.

E-mail: sales@axxess-international.com
Website: www.axxess-international.com

Cuba

International Trade & Investments, Ltd., Bahamas
E-mail: itiltd@itiltd.com
Website: www.itiltd.com

Curaçao

Phone: (31)10-436944

Currency Exchange

www.wiso.gwdg.de/ifbg/currency.html

Currency Rates–Bloomberg On-line

www.bloomberg.com/st/markets/fxc.html

Currency Converter & Financial Forecasts

www.oanda.com

Cyprus

aekassapis@zenon.logos.cy.net

E-mail: consult@cosmoserve.com
Website: www.cosmoserve.com

bonalbo@ibm.net

Cyprus Tourism Organization
www.cyprustourism.org

Defense Intelligence Agency (DIA)

http://140.47.5.4

Dominica

E-mail: ims@tod.dm

E-mail: investments@cwdom.dm

Website: www.goingoffshore.com

E-mail: imt@cms-sa.com
Website: www.cms-sa.com

cms@cms-sa.com

Legal Services
burtong@tod.dm

E-mail: lawrencea@cwdom.dm
Website: www.delphis.dm/alicklawrence.htm

serrantass@tod.dm

Dominica National Development Corporation
ndc@cwdom.dm

Electronic Cash System

stud2.tuwien.ac.at:80/~e9018967/mo.html

Estonia

www.divec.com

info@divec.com

www.privacy-consultants.com

Expatriates

www.hiway.co.uk/expats

www.escapeartist.com

Foreign Exchange Rate Converter

For the eleven currencies that are taking part in the introduction of
the Euro. The CHF, GBP, JPY, and the USD are preprogrammed into
the calculator. The exchange rates to the Euro can be edited and
saved. In addition, the Euro calculator contains the graphic images

of the Euro coins and banknotes. Installation is available in four languages: German, English, French, and Italian. Go to

www.jml.ch/extras/elibrary/calc-ind.html

www.latimes.com

Click on "Business" for their foreign exchange rates.

General

E-mail: falc@falc.com
Website: www.falc.com

www.goldhaven.com/ioi/Title1.htm

Grenada

dencamp@caribsurf.com

lewis&renwick@caribsurf.com

www.microtec.net/~alebel/ecocitz.htm

E-mail: imt@cms-sa.com
Website: www.cms-sa.com

Hong Kong

E-mail: aall@asiaonline.net
Website: www.aallandzyleman.com

E-mail: asiaciti@asiaciti.com.hk
Website: www.asiaciti.com

Internal Revenue Service

Includes Actions on Decisions (AOD), Service Center Advice (The Office of Chief Counsel provides legal advice to IRS service centers and related IRS functions with respect to their tax administration responsibilities), Chief Counsel (CC) Notices, ADP and IDRS Infor-

mation (the public version), IRS Written Determinations, Internal
Revenue Manual (IRM) Online, and more:

www.irs.ustreas.gov

For tax protestor laws:

www.cilp.org/~maule/taxprot.htm

Ireland

corpacc@iol.ie

E-mail: info@offshore-services.ie
Website: www.iol.ie/offshore

Isle of Man

E-mail: general@lorne-house.com
Website: www.lorne-house.com

E-mail: ilscorp@intlawsys.com
Website: www.intlawsys.com

ilscopr@intlawsys.com

oversight1@aol.com

charles.cain@skyefid.co.im
Website: www.skefid.co.im/skye

E-mail: int-serv-dev@gov.im
Website: www.gov.im/int-serv-dev

Jersey

E-mail: ems@contractorworld.com or
alan@contractorworld.com

Kyrgyzstan, City of Bishek

www.bishkek.kg

Liechtenstein (and Swiss) Banks

www.swconsult.ch/chbanks/index.html

www.swissbanknet.ch

E-mail: fiducia@ekvwa.lol.li
Website: www.lol.li/fiduciana

Liszt

http://www.liszt.com

Luxembourg

www.kbl.lu

Luxlegal, Law of Luxembourg, is a mailing list about law, especially business law and tax law, in Luxembourg. To subscribe, go to:

http://luxlegal.listbot.com

Madeira, Portugal

mmcl@mail.telepac.pt

Mauritius

E-mail: mobaa@bow.intnet.mu
Website: www.mobaa.net

E-mail: asiaciti@intnet.mu
Website: www.asiaciti.com

100100.3112@compuserve.com

Melchizedek, Dominion of*

www.melchizedek.com

Monaco

E-mail: vonernst@aol.com

www.kbl.lu

Nevis

E-mail: info@eurobancltd.com
Phone: (800) 541-1441

E-mail: nevamtru@caribsurf.com
Website: www.offshoreagents.com

E-mail: nevfin@caribsurf.com
Website: www.nevisweb.kn/nevcomm.html
Phone: (869) 469-1469
Fax: (869) 469-0039

E-mail: imt@cms-sa.com
Website: www.cms-sa.com

www.life-international.com

Niue*

mossfon@sin.net.nu

Privatization

private@aol.com

Romania

E-mail: marketing@mail.bcr.ro
Website: www.bcr.ro

Samoa

E-mail: asiaciti@intnet.mu
Website: www.asiaciti.com

Seychelles

E-mail: ical@seychelles.net
Website: www.seychelles.net/ical

insurance@seychelles.net

E-mail: siba@seychelles.net
Website: www.siba.net

St. Kitts and Nevis

E-mail: info@eurobancltd.com
Phone: (800) 541-1441
(242) 356-2095

E-mail: skanfsd@caribsurf.com
Website: www.fsd.gov.kn

St. Vincent and the Grenadines

gmstewart@caribsurf.com

E-mail: imt@cms-sa.com
Website: www.cms-sa.com

E-mail: infor@intmng.com
Website: www.intmng.com

remlaw@caribsurf.com

oversight1@aolcom

Switzerland

www.swconsult.ch/chbanks/index.html

www.swissbanknet.ch

Turks and Caicos Islands

misick@tciway.tc

E-mail: mslaw@tciway.tc
Website: www.mslaw.tc

templetr@tciway.tc

World Trade

www.tradecompass.com

www.worldtradezone.com

www.census.gov/foreign-trade

www.owens.com

www.exporthotline.com

www.tradeaccess.com

www.aib-world.org

INDEX

303